D0278710

Business Development in Asia and Africa

The Role of Government in Adjusting Economies

General Editor: **Professor Richard Batley,** International Development Department, School of Public Policy, University of Birmingham

Over the last two decades there has been a strong emphasis on reducing the role of government and on reforming traditional public sector bureaucracies. The new conventional view has become that, where possible, services should not be provided directly by government but be contracted out or privatized. Where this is not possible, the predominant view has been that the public sector itself should change by setting up semi-autonomous agencies and by making public management more performance- and customer-oriented.

This series investigates the application of such reforms in Africa, Asia and Latin America. Underlying the enquiry is the question whether reforms which were initially conceived in countries such as Britain and New Zealand are appropriate in other contexts. How much sense do they make where levels of public management capacity, market development, resources, political inclusiveness, legal effectiveness, political and public economic stability are quite different?

To investigate these issues, the series covers four service sectors selected to be representative of types of public sector activity – health care, urban water supply, agricultural marketing services and business development services.

Titles include:

Paul Jackson
BUSINESS DEVELOPMENT IN ASIA AND AFRICA
The Role of Government Agencies

Anne Mills, Sara Bennett and Steven Russell
THE CHALLENGE OF HEALTH SECTOR REFORM
What Must Governments Do?

The Role of Government in Adjusting Economies
Series Standing Order ISBN 0–333–94618–9
(*outside North America only*)

You can receive future titles in this series as they are published by placing a standing order. Please contact your bookseller or, in case of difficulty, write to us at the address below with your name and address, the title of the series and the ISBN quoted above.

Customer Services Department, Macmillan Distribution Ltd, Houndmills, Basingstoke, Hampshire RG21 6XS, England

Business Development in Asia and Africa

The Role of Government Agencies

Paul Jackson
Lecturer
School of Public Policy
University of Birmingham

First published 2002 by
PALGRAVE
Houndmills, Basingstoke, Hampshire RG21 6XS and
175 Fifth Avenue, New York, N.Y. 10010
Companies and representatives throughout the world

PALGRAVE is the new global academic imprint of
St. Martin's Press LLC Scholarly and Reference Division and
Palgrave Publishers Ltd (formerly Macmillan Press Ltd).

ISBN 0–333–73621–4

This book is printed on paper suitable for recycling and made from fully managed and sustained forest sources.

Cataloguing-in-publication data

A catalogue record for this book is available from the British Library.

A catalogue record for this book is available from the Library of Congress.

10   9   8   7   6   5   4   3   2   1
11   10   09   08   07   06   05   04   03   02

Printed and bound in Great Britain by
Antony Rowe Ltd, Chippenham, Wiltshire

Contents

Preface

This book originated within a research programme funded by the Economic and Social Committee on Research (ESCOR) of the Department for International Development (DFID) in London. The facts presented and views expressed are those of the author and do not necessarily reflect the views of DFID.

The research programme involved five UK research groups: the International Development Department (IDD) of the School of Public Policy, University of Birmingham; the Health Economics and Financing Programme, Health Policy Unit, London School of Hygiene and Tropical Medicine; the Overseas Development Group of the School of Development Studies, University of East Anglia; the Water Engineering and Development Centre of Loughborough University of Technology; and the Department of City and Regional Planning, the University of Wales. Overall co-ordination was provided by Richard Batley of IDD, University of Birmingham.

The research on the business support sector was jointly developed and planned by Paul Jackson and Richard Slater. After an initial literature review, country case studies were planned with the lead being taken by Paul Jackson in Ghana and Zimbabwe, and by Richard Slater in India and Sri Lanka. Collaboration and support was also provided by Ram Khanna, T.K. Bhaumik, R. Basu, George Larbi, Sunil Chandrasiri and Asoka Gunawardena. This book has been written by Paul Jackson and the opinions therein do not necessarily reflect the views of all of the collaborators.

I am most grateful to all of the individuals who supported the country studies, and also to Peter Kilduff of Leeds University, Paul Temple of London Business School and Richard Boulter of DFID who formed a steering committee for the research. I would also like to thank the contribution to my thinking of my colleagues in IDD, particularly Richard Batley, George Larbi, Richard Slater and Philip Amis.

The IDD is a wholly self-financing institution, and undertakes several related activities, including teaching, research and consultancy in the UK and overseas.

PAUL JACKSON

List of Abbreviations

CABS	Central African Building Society
CIDA	Canadian International Development Agency
DNV	Det Norske Veritas
ESAP	Economic Structural Adjustment Programme
DFID	Department for International Development
ODA	Overseas Development Administration
IDA	International Development Agency
LFL	Lanka Fabrics Ltd
MIGA	Multilateral Investment Guarantee Agency
NIE	New Institutional Economics
UNIDO	United Nations Industrial Development Organisation
ZIPAM	Zimbabwe Institute of Public Administration and Management

---

To my **Mam** and **Dad**, for always encouraging me,
for my wife **Anne** for her patience, and to my
two little monsters **Sam** and **Andrew** who
allowed me the time to finish this book

1
The Policy Environment for Industry

Introduction

Stabilisation and structural adjustment policies have dominated policy making across much of the developing world throughout the 1980s and into the 1990s. The World Bank Report *Adjustment in Africa* identifies 29 Sub-Saharan African (SSA) countries that have undergone adjustment programmes with the World Bank. In fact, virtually every country in the world has been undergoing some form of structural adjustment. South Asia has the earliest and the latest adjusters in the developing world. Sri Lanka has been undergoing a form of structural adjustment since 1977, whereas India is a relatively recent adjuster, only starting the reform process during the early 1990s.

Together with IMF conditionality programmes, structural adjustment agendas have been designed to restore short-term macroeconomic equilibria ('getting the prices right'), but all of them have significant medium- and long-term implications that in earlier programmes were largely ignored, and have proved to be more persistent than initially thought. In many respects, these policies could harm the future economic prospects of these countries, by undermining existing market institutions without constructing alternatives.

This book is concerned with how developing countries can better implement policies that reflect the longer-term needs of the economy, specifically manufacturing industry, given the policy environment that currently exists under structural adjustment programmes. In particular, it argues strongly in favour of strengthening the meso level of economic institutions, specifically agencies providing support services to private sector industry. This meso level of agency involvement is critical in developing systematic competitiveness – that is, where competitiveness

1

is enhanced by moving away from systems of atomised, isolated firms and towards more complex networks of complementary institutions.

The central question posed by this book is: *what are the capabilities required by agencies to successfully enhance manufacturing?*

This relatively simple question masks several complex issues, not least questions surrounding the overall context of economic reform, the prospects and position of manufacturing industry, and the nature and quality of administrative reforms required under liberalisation. In addition, as the analysis shows, many of the crucial factors affecting capacity are external to the agencies, which in turn exist within a broader industrial governance system (Messner, 1997). It is this broader view of capacity that is the central concern of this study.

The history of manufacturing in Africa and South Asia has been distinctly mixed. Sri Lanka has effectively reinvented herself as a centre of export manufactures, particularly textiles, and India has a complex industrial structure encompassing all shapes and sizes of industrial activity. Africa, on the other hand, has had a disappointing industrial record (Riddell, 1990; Alemayehu, 2000). A long experience of inappropriate policy intervention has left a legacy of uncompetitive and technologically backward manufacturing industry. In this context, structural adjustment is designed to overcome these handicaps by introducing market liberalisation with the aim of allowing stronger firms to survive and the weaker ones to go into liquidation. This book will argue that one of the main failures of structural adjustment has been to see industry in these terms, i.e. firms as atomised entities rather than as part of a complex system.

An underlying thesis of this book is that industrial development depends on the creation of competitive systems, and that the meso, or middle, level of the economy is crucial to the operation of this system. Meso-level organisations, particularly government agencies operating at the public/private sector interface, are crucial to the internal communication of the system (networking). It is this level of the industrial system that is frequently ignored, at least relative to the more fashionable literature on entrepreneurship, or the more glamorous area of macroeconomic policy.[1] This study is primarily concerned with policy and capacity at the meso level.

Stabilisation and structural adjustment

The reforms posited by the World Bank and IMF have effectively set the parameters for policy, even though many countries have implemented the reforms to differing degrees and there are differences between the reform programmes themselves. Despite these differences there has been a policy core to most of the adjustment programmes (Toye, 1987).

In principle we should distinguish between *stabilisation* on one hand and *structural adjustment* on the other, although in practice there is some degree of overlap and it is usual for an adjustment programme to be implemented only when a stabilisation programme is in place (Stewart et al., 1992). *Stabilisation* is primarily associated with the IMF. It is designed to create short-term monetary equilibrium through reducing public sector and balance of payments deficits and controlling inflation. In contrast, the policy of *Structural adjustment* is primarily associated with the World Bank. Structural Adjustment Programmes (SAPs) are aimed at a more medium-term adjustment of the economy such as reforming financial markets, instituting property rights and reforming labour markets. Although there are some internal disputes between them, there is some homogeneity of policy and three main categories of reform have been present in most IMF programmes (Stewart et al., 1994): *demand* restraint, *switching* policies and policies relating to *long-term supply* or *efficiency*:

- *Demand restraint* policies aim at reducing aggregate demand in the economy with the objective of limiting expenditure on imports and releasing resources for exports. An integral part of this demand restraint is the control of inflation through the control of the money supply and reduction of public sector deficits. Particular emphasis is placed on the reduction of subsidies, mainly in state-owned enterprises (SOEs) where these are held to impair efficiency.
- *Switching policies* are part of the policy of 'getting prices right'. Devaluation and exchange rate liberalisation accompanied by liberalisation of domestic prices, including wages, are aimed at switching resources away from non-tradeables and into tradeables. This aims at constructing manufacturing sectors capable of growth and with export potential.
- *Long-term supply policies* are designed to make an economy more 'market friendly' in the longer-term. Trade liberalisation, reform of credit and financial markets, effective interest rate control and price reforms are all designed to reduce segmentation within the economy and eradicate restrictions to trade and production.

The World Bank SAPs exhibit a similar philosophical basis to the IMF programmes. All are extremely market-oriented and neoclassical in approach and stress 'appropriate' exchange rates, positive real interest rates, fiscal orthodoxy, monetary prudence and liberal trade and pricing policies. SAPs tend to stress a number of elements:

1. Liberalisation of trade through removal of quotas and limitation of tariffs. The removal of export disincentives and the establishment of export incentives including institutional reforms to support exports.

2. Fiscal, monetary and credit reforms aimed at mobilising domestic resources effectively. An integral element of this is the reform of SOEs, including wage liberalisation, the reduction of subsidies and improved financial performance aimed at increasing their efficiency.

3. Improvement of domestic resource use in the public and private sectors. Policy instruments include SOE reform and privatisation; price liberalisation; eradication of subsidies; increasing domestic and international competition; and the encouragement of foreign direct investment (FDI) and joint ventures.

4. Institutional reforms aimed at increasing the efficiency of the public sector in general and improving the institutional environment within which the private sector operates.

It is clear that many historical state interventions in industry have largely failed and structural adjustment is necessary, but instant and widespread exposure to markets may merely replace state failure with market failure, thus killing off activities which are potentially competitive.[2] Some industry in Africa and South Asia is competitive but the exceptions require selective interventions to overcome market failure in the short term. Most of these industries face learning (or 'relearning') difficulties which are long term and costly. Given that past 'learning' processes in many parts of industry were largely curtailed by inefficient public ownership, excessive protectionism, intervention, and the shortage of modern industrial skills, the chances of industrial market failure are extremely great. Structural adjustment as it is currently implemented increases the potential for market failure thus it is not surprising that the results of SAPs have been disappointing with regard to industry (Lal, 1995).

The new role of the state

The assumption that market exchange is 'natural' is not well supported by the available evidence. Evidence from real market exchange suggests that markets tend to work well only when they are supported by other kinds of social networks in addition to property rights (Evans, 1992: Granovetter, 1992). This idea has been explored by new institutional economics in various definitions of transaction costs, and has also been resurrected in much recent literature on 'trust' (Evans, 1992: Humphrey and Schmitz, 1996). However, the most succinct, and in many ways the most accurate, description of these supporting elements of market exchange have been summed up by the nineteenth-century French sociologist Emile Durkheim as 'non-contractual elements of contract'.

The World Development Report (1997) entitled *The State in a Changing World* is an attempt to revitalise the role of the state given the poor recent history of structural adjustment to produce the hoped for industrial growth in many countries, and in the light of a great deal of recent literature dealing with institutional aspects of markets (for example, Bates, 1981). The report outlines three main areas where the state may fruitfully intervene in markets: investment co-ordination; 'network-thickening'; and superseding markets. Collectively the authors recognise that markets do not always perform without an institutional framework and the state is integral, not only to the institutional framework at a high level, but also at the level of the entrepreneur where markets do not always function. For example, the World Bank crucially recognises that information does not circulate evenly in many countries:

> in underdeveloped markets with few participants, learning can be extremely expensive. Information, more readily available in industrial countries, here becomes a zealously guarded secret, impeding co-ordination and market development more generally.
>
> In theory, governments in such economies can act as brokers of information and facilitators of mutual learning and collaboration, and therefore play a market-enhancing role in support of industrial development. But whether governments can play this role in practice will depend, as ever, on their institutional capacity. (WDR, 1997: 72)

The central theme of this study is whether or not the state has the capacity to carry out these market-enhancing roles. The crucial agent within this process is not necessarily the state at an overall level. Ministries tend to set the institutions in a Northian[3] sense i.e. property rights, law and order, infrastructure, etc., whereas more specific agencies tend to carry out the meso-level market-enhancing activities required by entrepreneurs.

Many agencies within Africa and Asia have developed a poor reputation with regard to achieving their initial aims. Paramount amongst these agencies are the export-promotion agencies identified by Hogan, Keesing and Singer (1994). These organisations were said to have failed because of several reasons, developed by Hogan, Keesing and Singer (1994) into five central issues: poor positioning; inadequate human resources; lack of sustained intervention; weaknesses in design and process; and, bad advice and advisers. At the same time, the new directions in structural adjustment posited by the World Bank, amongst others, demand a set of new roles which need to be carried out by meso-level agencies which have historically suffered from these shortcomings. Thus the capacity of these agencies to carry out these new roles becomes the central issue.

Hogan's list of factors affecting capacities of agencies is, however, incomplete. A more comprehensive model is required to operationalise a research approach to capacity in agencies. The main factors affecting capacity may be divided into two main groups (after Batley, 1995): external and internal. The external factors affecting capacity may be divided into four main groups as follows:

Financial and economic conditions directly affect the ability to operate a service. The availability of finance is probably the most crucial factor in assessing the capacity of agencies to carry out their roles.

Civil–public interaction largely governs the relationships between the three main levels of the economy: the macro level of the government; the micro level of the entrepreneur; and the meso level of the agency.

Private sector development is a further crucial factor affecting the capacity of agencies to carry out their roles. The relative strengths and weaknesses of the private sector whose capabilities are being enhanced directly affects the performance of the agency concerned as well as the expected role. For example, if the private sector has been adversely affected by adjustment and is in decline then the agency has a more difficult task than in dealing with a growing, more successful manufacturing sector.

Lastly, *political interference* is notoriously difficult to measure and to gain any evidence for. However, an idea of the *rumours* circulating amongst the business community may be valuable research in itself. The power of rumour should not be underestimated within a market mechanism which relies partly on trust and expectation. Whether or not the rumours are true or not is somewhat immaterial. In a sense what really matters is what people *believe* to be true. In the business community this is particularly important in an atmosphere of uncertainty over policy, a feature of both Ghana and Zimbabwe.

These internal factors may be divided into three main groups, each one encompassing a wide range of factors. Firstly, *organisational and administrative structures* deals explicitly with the reason for being of the agency, its vision and leadership, and whether or not its internal structures reflect the task for which it was formed.

Skills and professionalism of staff examines the human resource base of the agency, staff numbers, appointment systems and rewards for performance. In addition, it also addresses the issue of the relationship of staff to the private sector entrepreneurs they are dealing with.

Lastly, the *availability of capital and financial control* considers not only whether there is sufficient funding for the tasks in hand but also whether there is sufficient capital and if this is controlled in any way.

State capacity is central to the issues of policy choice and outcomes, and at the meso level the capacity of the agencies is complicated by their dual requirement of internal coherence and external connectedness required to carry out their pivotal role in industrial development. This leads to a situation of embedded autonomy as identified by Evans (1992) when he states: 'It is the combination of embeddedness and autonomy that works, not either on its own' (1992: 179). The recognition of the importance of external and internal factors affecting capacity reflects this dichotomy.

The research question posed above may be worked into a hypothesis, given the discussion of the various factors affecting capacity. It follows that agencies are going to be faced with a series of 'critical constraints' to their capacity, defined by the factors outlined. A simple working hypothesis was that external factors will, in general, be the primary factors affecting the capacity of agencies, whilst the internal factors may also seriously affect performance, but are secondary to the external factors. There is one notable exception to this rule, which is dealt with below.

In practice, a more detailed analysis of the various factors is required. Financial and economic constraints are the critical factors in determining the capability of agencies to carry out their roles. In a sense it does not matter if staff are well trained, or if they operate in a hierarchical or horizontal management structure, if they do not have access to capital to carry out specific tasks then they will not be carried out. In addition, the availability of cash is implicit in the ability to reward and retain competent staff. In this way an external factor has a direct effect on an internal factor.

The exception to the rule is the skills and professionalism of personnel. An agency may be able to overcome most of the other problems if it has a pool of highly skilled and motivated staff. In practice, many of the private sectors where agencies are most required are weak (otherwise they wouldn't be needed). The experience of Zimbabwe shows that an agency may survive and prosper without political support as long as there is no direct adverse political interference. The experience of some agencies in Ghana and India shows that competent staff may overcome severe problems of civil–public interaction through establishing a track record and a reputation for impartiality.

In a sense these two elements *must* be present in any successful agency, whereas, if these two are present, most of the others may at least be tackled. The existence of competent staff and sufficient resources implies that the agency will be able to define its vision, define its own working practices and cope in whatever environment is provided for it. Services will be tailored to suit the external environment it faces. Whilst all of the other factors outlined above may affect capacity, they are secondary to the requirements of financial and economic conditions (resources) and the ability of the staff within the agency.

Central propositions arising out of the study are that:

1. The primary capabilities affecting the ability of agencies to carry out their roles are financial and economic conditions, which allow for the availability of sufficient resources for the task in hand, and the employment and retention of skilled and professional staff to carry out the roles assigned to that agency.
2. The capacity of agencies is further enhanced by the level of autonomy of the agency and its embeddedness in the industrial system.

All of the other capacity factors, whilst being important under specific conditions, are secondary to the two factors above. Any of the other internal or external conditions can, of course, affect capacity, but if either of the two primary factors are not present then capacity will be seriously compromised. In effect they act as the critical constraints on capacity. In addition, this thesis holds that internal organisational factors within the agencies are insufficient to explain the successful (or otherwise) performance of the organisation concerned. The emphasis is then placed on the impact of external factors on capacity.

Capacity and performance

The most problematic issue within the research related to the measurability of performance and the causal linkage between the performance of the agency and the performance of industry. For example, if investment increases within Zimbabwe, is this the direct result of the performance of the Zimbabwe Investment Centre or is it related to tax breaks for foreign investors, a lower interest rate or changes in the exchange rate?

Wilson's (1989) typology serves as a useful illustration of this problem within this research. He distinguishes between four basic types of organisation, depending on the measurability of their efforts and outputs. The typology serves to differentiate between types of organisational behaviour and the ability of bureaucracies to introduce meaningful incentive systems (Klitgaard, 1995).

In 'production' organisations, both efforts and outputs can be measured, thus the prospects for incentive mechanisms are strong (Klitgaard, 1995). At the other extreme, 'coping' organisations are not good candidates for performance incentives since efforts and outputs are not measurable. Wilson goes on to say that in 'coping organisations effective management is almost impossible' (quoted in Klitgaard, 1995: 21). There are two important strands of thought within this management analysis. Firstly, Wilson points out that in organisations where effort and outcomes are not measurable it is impossible for managers within the organisation to manage effectively since they are unable to measure performance accurately. Secondly, it is further implied that there is a problem within the principal–agent relationship since it is not possible to measure the effort of the agency and the success of the client – that is, the firm. However, it is clear that managers are doing *something* well within some coping organisations (Wilson, 1989). In terms of agencies this may be ascertained from the behaviour of the clients who, after all, have a choice over whether or not they avail themselves of the services provided. The opinion of entrepreneurs is therefore crucial in determining the performance of industrial support agencies.

There are two other categories in the typology: craft and procedural, both of which exhibit a mix of characteristics. When the army is not fighting a war, its soldiers perform standard operating procedures. That is; managers can observe what their subordinates are doing, but not the outcomes (if any) that result from it (Wilson, 1989). These managers are managing a procedural organisation – one in which the performance of the procedures is more important than the outcomes they produce.

Craft organisations are represented by the Corps of Engineers and the army in Wilson's analysis. When the army goes to war, it converts from a procedural organisation to a craft organisation. Managers who previously had been able to observe the every move of their subordinates are no longer able to relate directly to their subordinates due to the 'fog of war' (Wilson, 1989). The effort put into the fight may not therefore be directly measurable, but the outcome certainly will be. Craft organisations thus measure performance through outcomes, rather than through procedures followed.[4]

The four categories may be shown more clearly in Table 1.1.

Wilson's typology raises several issues for this research. Industrial support agencies are clearly coping agencies. They enable other actors to carry out activities which are governed by the market, which, by its very nature, is unpredictable and non-procedural, much like the crime rate (and the view of the police as a coping organisation). At the same time, the actors who are enabled are influenced by several additional factors outside the direct scope of the agency concerned – there is therefore a difficulty in establishing a direct causal linkage between the actions of the agency on the one hand and the performance of the target of the service on the other (much like the foreign service example given by Wilson). There is therefore clearly a problem in measuring performance.

Wilson's point about coping agencies being outside the scope of effective management is a problematic statement. Clearly there are well-managed police forces and foreign services. Just because the performance of industrial support agencies does not lend itself to analysis based upon 'hard' performance data, this does not mean that they are either not managed effectively, or non-measurable. There are various 'soft' approaches which may be taken into account.

Table 1.1   Wilson's typology

	Can measure effort	*Cannot measure effort*
Can measure outcomes	Production (e.g. internal revenue, social security, post office, FBI)	Craft (e.g. enforcement agencies, corps of engineers, forest rangers)
Cannot measure outcomes	Procedural (e.g. armed forces in peacetime)	Coping (e.g. foreign service, schools, police activities)

Source: Wilson, 1989.

The first, and probably the most obvious are the capacity factors present within each organisation. We may infer that an agency, which exhibits several capacity factors, may be more likely to be a good performer than an agency exhibiting fewer capacity factors.

Secondly, and in some ways more importantly, is the view of the clients of the agency: the firms. Entrepreneurs will not, as a general rule, use services unless they are of some use to their businesses (Farbman and Steel, 1992). The usage rates of particular services i.e. their reach, and their repeat usage by firms may therefore be a crucial measure of the relative success or otherwise of individual agencies. In addition, the *perceptions* of entrepreneurs may be crucial in measuring success. Most business relies upon networking. The business community is a narrow circle of entrepreneurs who interact regularly, frequently through business organisations. If a support agency is thus regarded as being useful then this information will find its way throughout the community very rapidly.[5]

Such indicators do not lend themselves to hard measurements but they *are* contributors to, or perhaps surrogates for, performance. Consequently, this research has endeavoured to find concrete, measurable evidence of performance, but reliance has had to be placed upon the analysis of capacity carried out within each institution and the views and opinions of the main clients of the organisations concerned: the entrepreneurs. The analysis returns to reliance upon a checklist approach and detailed analysis of the environment surrounding the agencies concerned. Hildebrand and Grindle identify a similar approach within their analysis of capacity:

> Because many factors affecting the outcome of public sector activities are beyond the control of particular interventions, indicators of capacity need to be identified in terms of a series of task-specific questions: Was the task effectively identified? Were appropriate actions put in place to achieve the task? Were skilled human resources assigned to accomplish the task? Were resources used efficiently to accomplish the task? Was the ability to accomplish the task sustained over time? (1994: 445)

Textiles as a 'tracer' industry

The focus of this study is on the meso-level agencies and their role in the industrial system. A comprehensive survey of all manufacturing in each country is beyond the scope of this study. As a result the study concentrated on the textiles industry as a window through which to examine the performance of manufacturing as a whole. 'Textiles' is taken here to include the manufacture of textiles (spinning and weaving, dyeing, processing, and finishing), and garments (apparel). This working definition covers a wide range of activities which were felt to be representative of many types of industrial activity. The key features of textiles as they relate to this study are:

- textiles production is generally held to be labour-intensive, particularly in garments; however, there are also capital-intensive subsectors such as fibre production and some textile weaving;
- small and medium-sized firms play a prominent role in the global industry. There is considerable scope for subcontracting arrangements with larger firms or production of high value-added items for niche markets;
- most enterprises employ a diverse range of capital stock, varying considerably in terms of vintage. At the higher end of the sector, intense international competition necessitates the use of high tech, modern equipment for spinning, fibre manufacture and, to a lesser extent, weaving. At the opposite end of the scale many garment manufacturers are able to employ second-hand machinery acquired from producers who are no longer internationally competitive;
- there is significant ease of entry into textiles production. Technology is available relatively cheaply at the lower level, there are openings for small and medium-sized firms, most lower-level production is labour-intensive and there are difficulties in enforcing (or in fact unwillingness to enforce) labour legislation. All of this means that a relatively modest amount of capital is required to establish an enterprise.
- textiles is a global industry. Although there is a significant amount of local clustering and subcontracting, textiles relies on international trade to create profits. In a sense textiles is the closest industry to the case for industrial districts connected by global commodity chains.

The global trade in textiles is governed by 'the most trade-restraining international agreement for manufactured products in existence'. The Multifibre Agreement (MFA) controls trade through a series of export quotas. This effectively means that the textile trade is very mobile, being able to shift international locations in order to circumvent quota restrictions. Despite the good intentions of the Uruguay Round of the

GATT negotiations with regard to liberalisation of the MFA over the next ten to 14 years, the prospect of increased protection amongst OECD countries and the spread of discriminatory trading blocs beyond the European Union (e.g., NAFTA), has led to a degree of export pessimism. The primary problems facing developing countries can be divided into two main groups.[6]

1. In the short term, how can national textile industries successfully operate within the MFA and successfully exploit any restrictions placed upon them, and how can the state introduce policies which will produce an environment in which textile production can flourish, and further, how can it aid domestic textile producers to move into higher value production and additional quotas?

2. In the longer term, is it realistic to have confidence in the international 'rules of the game' espoused by structural adjustment programmes and encouraging outward-oriented industrialisation? Again, what can the state do to enhance the competitiveness of domestic industries which wish to compete on the international market?

Historically, textiles has been regarded as a 'take-off' industry and also as a basic good. It has been subject to widespread and detailed government intervention from Edward III regulating wool imports into England in 1337, to the current Indian government which sets specific targets for the production of cheap cloth to clothe the poor.[7] There are two major issues facing the state here:

1. In the past, as we have mentioned above, governments such as that of India have treated textiles (and cheap garments) as a basic good and have subsidised the production of cheap, poor quality cloth. In the current climate there is a question mark over this style of intervention.

2. Given the long history of intervention, severe questions will be asked of existing textile producers. In a global market where competitive advantage is held primarily by transnational corporations (TNCs) the question whether domestic textile producers are able to compete, or enter the global trading chain at all has to be asked. Can domestic producers successfully export and what can the state do to encourage a modern, profit-generating industry.

All the questions raised above challenge existing forms of government support for industry. The emphasis is changing from direct industrial intervention to more indirect forms of industrial or business service provision and policy intervention. Institutional support for the textiles sector must be developed in such a way as to enhance the competitive advantage of domestic textile producers as well as channel foreign direct investment (FDI) into those areas where it can be of most benefit. In addition, if the domestic industry is not merely going to metamorphose into a large sweat shop, institutions must be aware of the techniques which are available to enhance and alter comparative advantage and thus enable industry to move into higher value-added production.

In addition, the wide range of industrial activity, from mass produced garments to small-scale production for niche markets, within the textiles sector makes it a useful tracer industry for examining the relationship between firms, meso-level industrial promotion agencies and government. It was expected before the research that textile firms would be in the vanguard of manufacturing in India, Sri Lanka, Ghana and Zimbabwe for all of the reasons cited above. As such, textile and garment firms should be amongst the biggest users of industrial promotion agencies. Ease of start-up and the lack of prohibitive initial costs encourage new entrepreneurs to respond to new opportunities, existing entrepreneurs to seek to expand and develop existing business, and many firms to seek to expand into exports. All of these sub-sections of the textile industry are potential clients of service agencies, they therefore represent a cross-section of the clientele of those agencies.

The structure of the study

This study is divided into nine chapters, including this introduction.

Chapter 2 moves on to examine the relationship between entrepreneurs and the institutions surrounding them. The analysis shows how the state fits in to the overall picture of business support and how public intervention at the meso level can facilitate private sector development. The analysis is developed further in the following chapter, with an analysis of the performance of manufacturing under structural adjustment programmes, including a detailed view of the textiles and garment industries, which are then used as a 'window', to consider the industry as a whole.

Chapter 4 constructs a picture of the existing business support systems within Ghana, Zimbabwe, Sri Lanka and India. This analysis traces support for manufacturing down several levels of government, but specifically examines the agencies that operate at the meso level.

This chapter leads in to the following three chapters, which consider three main trends affecting the meso-agencies included in the research. More specifically, chapter 5 looks at those that are currently becalmed or are stagnating, chapter 6 at those that are reinventing themselves, and chapter 7 looks at those agencies that represent innovative developments in business support.

Chapter 8 draws out the central issues related to the capacity of the institutions called upon to carry out specific support or development roles, and, finally, some overall conclusions are drawn that point to possible ways forward in developing business services.

2
Entrepreneurs and Institutions

Introduction

Over the past thirty years there has been a series of major shifts regarding the role of the state in developing countries. Throughout the 1960s and most of the 1970s there was a general consensus that the state ought to play a pivotal role in the post-independence period, particularly in the promotion of rapid economic development (Healey and Robinson, 1994). Towards the end of the 1970s this consensus began to break down and a new perspective began to dominate. The state came to be seen as the chief obstacle to development throughout the 1980s and into the 1990s, and there has been widespread criticism of the state and a new consensus that holds that the state should withdraw from the economic sphere, allowing markets to take over. In practical terms this has been central to the policy context defined by liberalisation, privatisation and structural adjustment (Healey and Robinson, 1994). There are signs that the idea of the state as a major cause of stagnation is changing, and the focus on reduction of state size is being replaced by a focus on the improvement of state capability to perform specific roles well (World Development Report, 1997).

This chapter begins by examining the changing view of the state as seen by the World Bank, a useful barometer of thinking on the role of the state. The World Bank drives a significant proportion of the reform process through structural adjustment programmes, and whilst it has not been the only driving force behind 'downsizing' the state, it reflects the dominant view in development policy thinking. The chapter then moves on to address some of the issues raised by the structural adjustment literature and places them in the context of a long-term view of industrialisation, entrepreneurship and, more specifically, entrepreneurial environments. The first section of this chapter charts the evolution of the role of the state encompassed by structural adjustment and goes on to place current thinking about the roles of the state within a longer-term historical context. The next section moves to addressing institutions specifically and to looking at some of the potential roles which the state may be asked to play. The following section then constructs a model of the entrepreneurial environment, which serves as a basis for locating institutions and examining their embeddedness. Finally, the chapter looks at these institutions in more detail and bisects the elements of capacity in order to facilitate further analysis.

The evolution of the state under structural adjustment

The writings of the World Bank on the economic position of the state have been remarkably vague (Herbst, 1993). In general they have tended to reinforce the neoclassical dichotomy of state and market, in which the state is reduced to patrolling the borders of the market, particularly through enforcement of property rights. In the 1983 World Development Report focusing on 'management in development', the Report outlines its negative approach to government intervention, but produces something which is far from clear:

> Markets may not perform perfectly because of insufficient information or because they do not take adequate account of indirect losses and benefits (the so-called externalities such as pollution or worker training). Nor can free markets handle public goods (such as public defence), where the cost of supply is independent from the number of beneficiaries, or natural monopolies. Finally, markets do not act to correct inequalities in income and wealth. Some market failures are so evident that they cannot be ignored; in addition, governments will always have legitimate non-economic objectives that can be pursued only by intervention. (WDR, 1983: 52)

This approach had not altered by the publication of *The East Asian Miracle* in 1993 which states:

> [governments] need to do less in those areas where markets work, namely the production sector, they also need to do more in those areas where markets cannot be relied upon. The appropriate role of government in a market-friendly strategy is to ensure adequate

investments in people, provision of a competitive climate for enterprise, openness to international trade, and stable macroeconomic management. (1993: 84)

Both of these statements mean little in situations where the market 'cannot be relied upon' which covers many areas of the developing world where information does not flow freely, infrastructure is inadequate, finance is scarce and the state is collapsing.[1] Structural adjustment programmes themselves represent and strong negative trajectory for the state, not a positive enabling one. 'Getting the prices right' involves getting states out of markets which may then allocate goods and provide incentives efficiently.

The 1997 World Development Report, *The State in a Changing World*, attempts to redefine the roles of the state further in the face of significant inconsistencies between the predominant theoretical view of separation of state and market, and the actually existing situation in many developing countries (WDR, 1997). The report changes the emphasis of policy away from state minimalism and towards an emphasis on enhancing the effectiveness of the state. Improvement may be attained through policies intended to 'reinvigorate the state's institutional capability, by providing incentives for public officials to perform better while keeping arbitrary action in check' (1997: 7).

However reluctantly, the World Bank has come to the view that markets do not always work well in developing countries (particularly in SSA). The underdevelopment of markets and the pervasive market failures in many economies are recognised as significant problems for a 'market-friendly' strategy for development. To emphasise again:

> in underdeveloped markets with few participants, learning can be extremely expensive. Information, more readily available in industrial countries, here becomes a zealously guarded secret, impeding co-ordination and market development more generally.
>
> In theory, governments in such economies can act as brokers of information and facilitators of mutual learning and collaboration, and therefore plays a market-enhancing role in support of industrial development. But whether governments can play this role in practice will depend, as ever, on their institutional capacity. (1997: 72)

In practice, the Report remains true to its origins and recommends only a 'light touch' by states. Even if markets perform poorly or do not perform at all then, in the eyes of the World Bank, this remains preferable to the state performing those actions. In terms of industrial policy there are three areas which the Report identifies as possible areas of intervention: investment co-ordination; 'network thickening'; and, superseding markets.

Investment co-ordination effectively speaks for itself. The aim is to develop organisations that can provide 'one-stop shops' for potential investors in terms of investment opportunities, partners for joint ventures and reducing the red tape accounting for much of the frustration experienced by overseas investors.

Network thickening represents a recognition that firms, particularly small firms, are more effective when acting together either in partnership or in subcontracting relationships. In addition, firms need a 'voice' along with other groups, therefore representative groups such as business associations become critical in having an input into policy.

Superseding markets recognises that markets do not exist in a number of areas for whatever reason.

- An absolute shortage of manpower and administrative expertise in both private and public sectors;
- An economy characterised by high transaction costs because communication lines are poor, infrastructure is crumbling and statistical and information services are poor;
- A governmental structure in which there can be no guarantee that public organisations will respond to price signals without political pressure;
- A government that does not look to the private sector for political support, but usually the public sector. Consequently there is very little trust between entrepreneurs and government due to former citizenship (Asians in East Africa, Lebanese in Ghana), ethnic group (white Zimbabweans), history (market traders in Ghana), or simply because they are successful;
- Capital markets are weak and financial systems poor. There is rarely a futures market – that is, a market for risk-bearing in conditions of uncertainty.

There are three additional 'stylised facts' which may be added to Herbst's (1993) list:

- An industrial sector where large-scale, lucrative production is dominated by foreign capital (Kennedy, 1988), or where export production is dominated by foreign capital and footloose industry (for example, Sri Lanka);

- A low level of technological innovation and research and development expenditure (Lal, 1995).
- There is a considerable possibility that certain parts of government may be unduly influenced by private sector groups, e.g. entrenched interests in dismantling trade protection in India.

In this context, serious questions must be asked of the ability of the market to operate adequately in terms of giving economic incentives to firms and its ability to provide adequate inputs to allow firms to respond to the incentives offered. The advantage of constructing such a list, however stylised, rests in its ability to illustrate failures in both the operation of markets in themselves and in the institutions surrounding markets. It also serves to illustrate the effect of those traditionally non-market transactions on market exchange, and consequently the false dichotomy between market and state which lies at the core of much neoclassical analysis, and some new institutional economic analysis, and, by implication, structural adjustment.

Given that economies are at least partially characterised by Herbst's list of 'facts', there are two central problems facing the analysis of industrial policy, as presented in WDR 1997.

Firstly, it still assumes a separation between market and state. There is no recognition of markets as being anything other than objectively efficient allocators of resources. I will return to this point later.

Secondly, there are problems when the practical recommendations are applied to situations of extreme market failure. In a situation where markets are relatively undeveloped, and where the private sector is non-existent, weak or reliant on protection, *and* when there are doubts surrounding the capabilities of the public sector to intervene, a 'light-touch' approach may be woefully inadequate in terms of stimulating a private sector. A more high-intensity approach is required to provide incentives for entrepreneurs to enter the economy productively – that is, to start manufacturing enterprises. This then is a paradox: high-intensity involvement is required, but the state may be incapable of delivering it.

Addressing these two problems involves a renewed emphasis upon the interdependence of markets and institutions, and the necessity for a recognition that states are embedded in markets. According to Evans (1992) this places the analysis firmly within the 'Third Wave' of thinking on the economic position of the state. The first wave was characterised by an optimistic view of the state as the main instrument of economic development and the second by the 'counter-revolution' and the utopian idea of the state patrolling the edges of the markets and allowing free market exchange. The third wave is characterised by a synthesis of these ideas. As Evans puts it: 'The ability to deal with specific problems like stabilisation and adjustment is rooted in diffuse general characteristics of the state apparatus and its relation to surrounding social structures and that these in turn are consequences of long term processes of structural change' (1992: 141). Like it or not the state remains central to the process of structural adjustment and recognition of this inevitably leads back to questions of state capacity.

Entrepreneurs and markets

The assumption that market exchange is somehow 'natural' and will optimise the use of scarce resources if the state withdraws may be a central pillar of the structural adjustment programme, but it is not well supported by the evidence. Studies of real market exchange suggest that markets work well only when they are supported by other kinds of social networks in addition to property rights (Evans, 1992; Granovetter, 1992). This is at the core of much of the NIE and literature on the concept of 'trust', but was summed up in a deceptively simple manner by Durkheim in the phrase 'non-contractual elements of contract'.

Markets are inextricably embedded in a matrix that incorporates cultural understandings, societal norms and social networks composed of polyvalent ties (Evans, 1992). Informal, non-contractual elements support contracts of exchange, and, in some cases, hierarchical organisations may internalise exchange relations (Williamson, 1975). If market exchange is embedded in a complex network of social structures, then neoclassical attempts to free the market from the state under structural adjustment may destroy the institutional foundations which enable the market to operate.

This is, of course, nothing new but part of a classic tradition of institutionalism, which emphasises the complementarity of state structures and market exchange, particularly relating to industrial promotion. This tradition lies with observers such as Polanyi (1944) who argued that the market is intertwined not only with social structures, but also the state. Max Weber held that large-scale capitalism could only exist within the kind of order that a modern, bureaucratic state could provide. He states: 'Capitalism and bureaucracy have found each other and belong intimately together' (quoted in Evans, 1992: 146).

Weber's view of a modern, stable bureaucracy underpinning capitalist development has been extended by later scholars. Gerschenkron's work on 'late developers' complements the Weberian approach by specifying the contributions of state organs to overcoming problems associated with the mismatch between the scale and complexity of industrial development required and the lack of scope of the complementary social networks (Gerschenkron, 1962).

Late developers faced production technologies and networks which required capital far in excess of what their private markets were capable of amassing. They therefore relied upon the state to mobilise resources and fill the gap. This active role is in excess of the Weberian framework role. Gerschenkron's analysis raises a further, crucial issue: risk. More advanced economies have institutions which allow risk to be spread across a wide network of capital holders. These institutions are lacking in late developing economies, and individual capital holders are unwilling to take on the burden on their own. It is therefore left to the state to act as an entrepreneur and shoulder some of the risk which would otherwise fall solely on individual entrepreneurs (Evans, 1992).

Gerschenkron's arguments are developed by Hirschman who takes up the emphasis on entrepreneurship and applies it to the 'late late' developers of the late twentieth century. Hirschman (1988) argues that capital, in the sense of a surplus available to invest, is not lacking in the global economy. What is lacking is entrepreneurship – a willingness to risk the available surplus by investing in productive activities. In turn, Hirschman's analysis is further refined by Baumol who explains entrepreneurial behaviour in terms of institutional environment.

The key to Baumol's analysis is the dissaggregation of entrepreneurship. If entrepreneurs have the capabilities to undertake activity, differing forms of institutions may lead to entrepreneurial behaviour which is unproductive or even destructive in certain circumstances (Baumol, 1990). For example, if an entrepreneur is born to a society where the most lucrative opportunities are available through the administration of assets, rather than in the private sector, then all of the institutional incentives encourage the entrepreneur to join the government, not the private sector.

Entrepreneurship may be defined as an individual who spots an opportunity and exploits it (Schumpeter, 1939). In turn, this general definition may be divided into three sub-categories: innovative, imitative and unproductive.

The *innovative entrepreneur* is the classic Schumpeterian entrepreneur who is able to exploit a business opportunity through developing a new technology, product and process (Tiffin and Osotimehin, 1988). In effect the innovative entrepreneur combines conventional business skills with additional technical or scientific skills. The innovative entrepreneur provides the generator for rapid economic growth in the private sector. Without innovation markets do not develop and grow and imitators have nothing to imitate.

Imitative entrepreneurs in the Schumpeterian sense play a secondary role of gradually eroding the profits made by innovative entrepreneurs through providing lower prices to consumers and forcing innovators to seek new rewards (Baumol, 1988). This role may be perfectly logical, and indeed valuable in itself, but it is somewhat misleading in the sense that it ignores the contribution of imitative entrepreneurs to the prosperity of their countries, albeit with a small time lag. Particularly for developing countries with relatively low research and development, economic welfare depends critically on techniques and technologies developed outside a country's borders. As Baumol himself states:

> Are there not 20 or 30 nations making extensive use of up-to-date semiconductors, computers, digital transmission of sound, optical fibres, 'intelligent' telecommunications switches, industrial robots and most other economically important inventions, say, 5 to 15 years old? Diffusion of such ideas, then, must be the order of the day. But if these ideas were disseminated and widely put into use, someone or some group of persons must have taken the required initiative. These are imitating entrepreneurs. (1988: 86–7)

This type of entrepreneurial activity has been effectively exploited by the newly industrialising countries of East Asia and the Japanese who imitated several western ideas with astonishing success, eventually transforming the environment for entrepreneurs into one where they became innovators themselves.

The third type of entrepreneur is the unproductive entrepreneur. From the Schumpeterian definition of someone who takes an opportunity when it is offered, it does not necessarily follow that that activity will be productive (Baumol, 1990). Even given the fact that the motivations of entrepreneurs are undoubtedly complex, we can assume that the pursuit of wealth and position are fairly high on their list of priorities, thus it follows that entrepreneurs will exploit any opportunity which leads to wealth and position, and this is determined by their institutional environment (Baumol, 1988). In a situation in which the returns to industrial activity are readily expropriated and the returns to military or political activity are high it is not difficult to see where their efforts will be concentrated. In other words, much of the activity in developing countries, which has been characterised as 'rent-seeking', is actually entrepreneurship which has been shaped by the entrepreneurial environment, it is just *unproductive* entrepreneurial activity.

It is widely accepted that there is no shortage of entrepreneurs in Africa or South Asia (Steel, 1994: Marsden, 1992). Given the institutional environment, in much of SSA in particular, it also appears clear that many entrepreneurs are engaged in unproductive entrepreneurship. The main hypothesis of this chapter is that the institutional environment may be changed by state involvement to switch incentives for entrepreneurs, encouraging them to leave unproductive activity and enter productive activity.

The Gerschenkron/Hirschman/Baumol vision renders the relationship between state capacity and autonomy (in the sense of 'insulation' from the private sector in the Weberian view) considerably more ambiguous than the neoclassical dichotomy, or even the neo-Marxist view of the relative autonomy of the state from the particularistic demands of individual capitalists (Rueschenmeyer and Evans, 1985). It is therefore necessary to recognise the interdependence between public and private sectors. Once this recognition is given, the simple dichotomy of state and market underpinning structural adjustment becomes less attractive as a policy mechanism.

The Weberian bureaucracy may be effective in enforcing law and preventing fraud, but the surrogate entrepreneurship demanded by Gerschenkron or the subtle changes in incentive systems for entrepreneurs demanded by Hirschman and Baumol require more than a simple administrative, bureaucratic and insulated structure. They require accurate intelligence, inventiveness, active agency and sophisticated responses to economic reality. As Steel states with reference to Africa:

> The challenge facing policymakers is to turn the miracle of survival into the miracle of growth, by investigating how regulators, financial systems, and other agencies can themselves become agents of change to support small entrepreneurs in transforming the economies of Africa. Africa's entrepreneurs can be agents of change and growth, but they cannot do it alone. (1994: 4)

The state as an actor thus requires the ability to improvise on the economic stage, in order to interact successfully with entrepreneurs. The dichotomy of market/state which has permeated much of the recent writings on the economic role of the state does not lend itself to rapid or even relevant provision of services for entrepreneurs. Work carried out on the phenomenon of industrial districts in Germany, Italy and Spain emphasises the importance of local service provision by bureaucrats who themselves are members of the business policy networks (Van Dijk and Marcussen, 1992: Humphrey and Schmitz, 1996). In this way, the government policy makers are not isolated from the business community but *are embedded in it* (Evans, 1992).

Embedded autonomy

The concept of 'embedded autonomy' is introduced by Evans (1992) as a means of bringing bureaucracy and clientele closer together. He argues in favour of focusing on state capacity as an important factor in policy choice and outcomes. More specifically, Evans challenges the tendency to equate capacity of the bureaucracy with insulation in a Weberian sense and points towards a combination of internal coherence and external connectedness which may be called 'embedded autonomy'.

The idea that an organisation, or a bureaucracy in this case, should be embedded into the institutional system within which it operates is not new. For several years analysts, including Evans, focusing on industrial development have examined the success of the newly industrialising countries (NICs), pointing to the close relationships which exist between government and business. Much of the NICs' success has been put down to the ability of the administration and business to act together to achieve common goals. Other trends within industrial development have also pointed to the close nature of local administrative systems and industrial growth, particularly amongst studies investigating clustering of firms and industrial agglomeration in Japan, Italy and Germany particularly (Scott, 1992; Storper, 1992; Best, 1990; Schmitz and Musyck, 1993).

In each of these cases, administrative organisations have become embedded into the local industrial system – the dichotomy of market versus state has essentially disappeared and they become two sides of the same coin. Participating in networks of this type reduces risk by enabling participants to shape their environment through networking with public and private organisations. From the point of view of an industrial support agency this embeddedness allows the agency to develop services in conjunction with the business community which are relevant to the specific clientele of the agency. It is precisely the pooling of know-how over a range of actors encompassing public and private sectors which comprises the advantage of networked systems over traditional, hierarchical decision-making structures (Messner, 1997).

Embedded organisations are therefore better able to serve the interests of the system as a whole than non-embedded organisations. Transaction costs are minimised, information transfer facilitated and an institutional advantage is gained through a collective decision-making strategy encompassing all stakeholders within the industrial system.

Evans (1992) goes on to warn against over-embeddedness, however, since he identifies a tendency for embedded organisations to degenerate into cartels, aimed, like all cartels, at protecting their own members from changes in the status quo. It is therefore crucial that the state is able to uphold the autonomy of the organisation. The autonomy of any arm's-length agency organisation is threatened not only by the state but also by the market, which can lead to concentrations of power which are difficult to control and which, in turn, may lead on to privileged organisations (Messner, 1997). These privileged organisations are able to influence policy for their own benefit or for the benefit of specific parts of the industrial system and to the detriment of the system as a whole (a form of 'prisoners' dilemma'). Autonomy is therefore necessary in order to maintain the integrity of the organisation and to ensure that the services provided are to the advantage of the industrial system as a whole, rather than for one particular interest group.[2]

Messner puts this institutional form into a broader context of the changing nature of the state:

> Analysis of the state confirms the operation of this development logic: the development of the modern state is first characterised by the emergence of a monopoly on power and the centralisation of political power within the state. As it expands, the state begins to differentiate internally and becomes a complex system consisting of many corporate actors who no longer form a single, integrated hierarchy. Externally, we see the successive emergence of policy networks specialised in specific policy fields; in them public and private actors work hand in hand. (1997: 185).[3]

Embedded autonomy thus represents a delicate balance between representing and interacting with the private sector, whilst maintaining sufficient integrity to maintain autonomy from individual power groups within the private (or public sectors). Embeddedness therefore allows organisations to reflect need, whilst autonomy allows them to act in the best interests of the industrial system as a whole.

Institutions, firms and entrepreneurship

Institutions here are used in the sense of the broad range of implementing agencies. Steel (1994) distinguishes between *facilitating institutions*, which influence how well markets perform, and *assistance institutions*, which support entrepreneurs through representative organisations or on a consultancy basis. In practice, however, many of these implementing agencies perform a broad range of activities and it is perhaps more practical to group them by sector activity i.e. financial, informational, human resources and technological.

At this point it would be useful to distinguish further between institutions. The sectoral institutions mentioned above should be distinguished from the contextual institutions, in North's sense, at the macro level i.e. property rights, rule of law, etc. (North, 1990b). The institutions of primary interest for this analysis are those at the meso or micro level which correspond to *organisations*.

The organisations with which this book is concerned are designed primarily to act within the market context assisting firms with dynamic changes taking place within the market system. In other words they are not concerned with making the market itself act more efficiently, but with enhancing the capabilities of firms in a situation where the market is inadequate and providing correct incentives where market prices are distorted. In a sense this is a false distinction since economies work on a systems basis. In other words it is important to recognise that it is insufficient to develop one aspect, such as credit, in isolation, without considering the system within which it operates (Steel, 1994). This is potentially dangerous since it could lead to a 'theory of everything', but it should be recognised and built into any analysis of the internal machinery of agencies which need to relate successfully with the external system.

The first major activity that the agencies need to address is that of entrepreneurship. The literature concerning entrepreneurial environments is a highly diverse one and has too infrequently focused on the needs of the entrepreneur, the chief beneficiary of a good environment (Gnyawali and Fogel, 1994). Furthermore it is so fragmented that it is of limited help in developing entrepreneurial promotion programmes, particularly in terms of determining the relative importance of linkages between various parts of the environment and the entrepreneurs themselves (Gnyawali and Fogel, 1994). Such linkages and the need for the development of a conducive environment are more pressing in developing countries, particularly SSA, where there is a relatively low level of entrepreneurial activity and often a hostile environment exists.

I have already mentioned above the dichotomy within the entrepreneurial environment between contextual and dynamic elements. The contextual element relates closely to the institutions of the economy in North's sense, that is property rights, rule of law, etc..., which form the socio-economic environment for entrepreneurship. An additional element of this would be the macroeconomic environment which, in this analysis, is assumed to be that of structural adjustment. The context of entrepreneurship within this analysis is therefore that of rapid liberalisation and its resultant effects.

The second element of the dichotomy relates to dynamic factors influencing the market. In general they are factors which change over time (hence dynamic) and are commonly cited as externalities or market imperfections. In addition they are frequently cited in the entrepreneurial literature as the main obstacles to firm growth (see, for example, Steel, 1994; Farbman and Steel, 1992; and El-Namaki, 1988). The dynamic elements are where the agencies which are the primary concern of this study operate. They essentially lend themselves to specific intervention to reduce distortions in prices and incentives, which are not addressed within structural adjustment. These elements may be usefully divided into four main groups:

Firstly, *technology* is by its very nature uncertain and oriented to the future, placed squarely outside the neoclassical view of the world. In point of fact the ideas of technological advancement and Pareto optimality are fundamentally opposed or even mutually exclusive (Metcalfe, 1995). Pareto optimality relies upon 'getting the prices right' through the allocation of resources according to marginal valuations of inputs and outputs. Technological innovation, on the other hand, relies upon informational asymmetries reinforced by patents. This allows the classic Schumpeterian entrepreneur to exploit his informational advantage and gain advantage over his rivals.

In the analysis of entrepreneurs above, it was pointed out that a crucial element of entrepreneurial activity is that of imitation rather than innovation. It therefore follows that the role of institutions in enhancing domestic entrepreneurship is to allow entrepreneurs to gain access to recent innovations, primarily from abroad, as well as enhancing research and development activity. Both of these activities are crucial to economic development and it should be recognised that whilst technology transfer is in itself important, higher, more value added areas of production will not be attained without domestic technological innovation (Tiffin and Osotimehin, 1988; Freeman, 1982; Lal, 1994). Tiffin and Osotimehin (1988) goes further and outlines several reasons why technological innovation support is important in an African context:

- it is effective, and possibly one of the most important sources of economic growth. Sweeney (1987) further postulates that technological innovation has been one of the most important factors leading to the development of the poor regions of the European Union;
- supporting technical entrepreneurship does not require extensive planning and the creation of much new organisational structure. Tiffin and Osotimehin (1988) further suggests that in Ghana and Nigeria respectively, the public infrastructure already exists;
- technical innovation strengthens the position of private sector firms vis-à-vis the state and other competing firms domestically and abroad.

The second major element is *information* which closely relates to the diffusion of technology mentioned above. If industry is not supported by a relevant informational infrastructure then any innovations that are developed domestically will not be made more widely available and imitative entrepreneurship will be hamstrung from the very beginning. The provision of information is particularly important for smaller businesses who find it difficult to gain access to critical information. Key agents of change have frequently been those which enable firms to fill a particular niche or to introduce a cost-saving innovation (Steel, 1994).

Such agents are particularly important in the African context where markets do not always convey accurate information. For example, US chain stores are extremely keen to buy Afrocentric and standardised products from Africa where lack of quotas makes garments relatively less expensive. However, agents express doubts over the ability of African firms to fulfil orders to a specified quality. Information is required on both sides. Firstly by the agents to put them in contact with relevant firms and secondly by the firms to improve knowledge of these market opportunities and to improve quality control measures of their products. Initially, there is scope for assistance agencies in this role, but once a track record is established this knowledge is itself a marketable commodity therefore any competent agency, in the long run has significant scope for cost recovery through sales of services (Steel, 1994).

The World Development Report 1997 singles out information as a potentially major area of state intervention. As the report states:

> in underdeveloped markets with few participants, learning can be extremely expensive. Information, more readily available in industrial countries, here becomes a zealously guarded secret, impeding coordination and market development more generally.
>
> In theory, governments in such economies can act as brokers of information and facilitators of mutual learning and collaboration, and therefore play a market-enhancing role in support of industrial development. But whether governments can play this role in practice will depend, as ever, on their institutional capacity. (WDR, 1997: 72)

Thirdly, technology and information are necessary, but without *human resources* these will not be exploited. The current weak base of human capital in SSA is well documented (Lal, 1992: World Bank, 1989). Despite a new emphasis on 'capacity building' within donor agencies this has been conspicuous by its absence in structural adjustment programmes. Many SSA industries would become increasingly competitive with relatively minor improvements in human resources (Lal, 1995). Human resource development is a critical issue but a large area. Education, for example, is crucial in increasing the supply of entrepreneurs and culture may be a barrier to groups of people (for example, women) becoming entrepreneurs but both are outside the scope of this study. Assistance institutions may directly improve the capabilities of firms through a number of measures including provision of services which are expensive for firms, building long-term capabilities and undertaking training. All of this suggests a long, laborious process, not shock therapy.

It should be pointed out here that there is a significant pool of basic skills that may be developed, for example, through the apprenticeship system, however, this is primarily geared towards passing on traditional skills at a relatively low technological level (Lal, 1995). Agencies established to enhance human resource capabilities would have to be highly specialised, filling gaps which are identified by the private sector. This is a clear area of partnership between public and private sectors since training programmes should be made relevant to the demands of industry and only a continuing dialogue can sustain this.

The last, and some would claim most important, element of dynamic support is that of *finance*. In terms of overall financial policy towards industry the World Bank provides the following guidance:

- increasing the rate of formation of enterprises;
- facilitating the transformation of small firms into medium- and large-scale firms, and the encouragement of subcontracting with larger firms;
- increasing the rate of domestic capital formation;
- increasing capital and labour productivity and reinvestment rates.

Red tape and inefficiency within the banking system mean that the transaction costs for both domestic and international investment are extremely high. The existence of stock exchanges, whilst a positive step in itself, has not generated significant sums of equity finance (Herbst, 1993: Faber, 1996). Furthermore, the overriding constraint of public sector deficit finance has led several governments to raise interest rates on Treasury Bills to well over 30 per cent in some cases leading to a capital flight out of manufacturing into financial speculation (Jackson, 1996: Dijkstra, 1996). This has exacerbated the general situation of manufacturing being low on most investors' lists of preferences which is economically logical in the short term, but disastrous in the long term (Faber, 1996).

There is a clear role for the financial support of industry. The establishment of venture capital or leasing companies and some form of directed credit or loan subsidy for manufacturing are all potential roles, or, adapting from the experience of the NICs, the establishment of specialised funds for specific purposes granting loans at preferential rates (Kim, 1995). At the same time, savings should not be ignored and should at least go hand-in-hand with credit (Steel, 1994). Mechanisms such as these are particularly important when there is little support from non-banking financial institutions: 4 per cent GDP in Ghana is provided by non-bank financial institutions, as opposed to some 30 per cent in Malaysia and 65 per cent in Singapore (World Bank, 1993). Given the poor history of African banks as agents of change, and of government influence across South Asia, and the lack of alternative financial institutions, the importance of new sources of risk finance cannot be underestimated and is probably the single most important ingredient for the successful formation of new enterprises and the sustainability of existing ones (Harvey, 1996).

The analysis presented above outlines four main areas where the state has potential for intervention in a dynamic sense – that is, facilitating change and assisting firms through dynamic market failures. The four areas are *technology, information, human resources and finance* all of which are well documented within the literature.[4] To examine further the roles and capacities of the institutions at the core of this study it is necessary to combine this analysis with the earlier work on entrepreneurship and to outline a conceptual framework documenting the position of these support mechanisms within an overall system of entrepreneurship.

Entrepreneurial environments and support mechanisms

There is a potentially infinite number of motivations for people to become involved in business. Vesper (1990), quoted in Gnyawali and Fogel (1994) identified four key elements in the creation of new enterprises: a profitable business opportunity; technical know-how of the entrepreneur; business know-how of the entrepreneur; and entrepreneurial initiative. In other words the entrepreneur should be able to spot a business opportunity, have the wit to exploit it (or be willing to take a risk to do so), and have the necessary capabilities to take advantage of the opportunity. Following Gnyawali and Fogel (1994), these may be categorised as 'opportunity', 'propensity to enterprise' and 'ability to enterprise'.[5]

Opportunity refers to the extent to which possibilities exist and entrepreneurs have power over the results of their own actions i.e. the macroeconomic conditions, government attitude to business, institutions, etc. Opportunities tend to be higher in situations where market forces are well developed and entrepreneurs face low barriers to entry and exit. Essentially this is the macroeconomic context of entrepreneurship.

The *propensity to enterprise* refers to the characteristics of the entrepreneurs themselves – background, education, social position, gender. The literature suggests that certain kinds of people are more likely to become entrepreneurs than others and that this likelihood is governed by the socio-economic background of the entrepreneur. For example, in several countries women may be more unlikely to become entrepreneurs for cultural reasons. The propensity to enterprise may be further enhanced by an entrepreneur's confidence in his or her ability to act as an entrepreneur.

The *ability to enterprise* refers to the sum of technical and business capabilities required to start and run a business (Gnyawali and Fogel, 1994). Without basic business or technical skills entrepreneurs may not be able to seize business opportunities available to them, proceed through the various preparatory stages, apply for loans and formulate business plans, and so on.

A crucial requirement in the process of business formation and ongoing management is the linkage and interdependence of the three elements of propensity, ability and opportunity. A positive correlation between all three elements is likely to contribute to a positive *likelihood to enterprise* (Gnyawali and Fogel, 1994). A schematic representation of an entrepreneurial environment is shown in Figure 2.1 at the core of the system. It can be seen from this that a key role of the entrepreneurial environment is to help entrepreneurs develop both the propensity to enterprise and the ability to do so (Gnyawali and Fogel, 1994). In addition, several studies have doubted the effectiveness of merely providing finance when there has been an absence of a likelihood to enterprise, using the language of the model (see, for example, Marsden, 1992). Thus the model incorporates financial assistance in terms of converting likelihood to enterprise into actual venture creation.

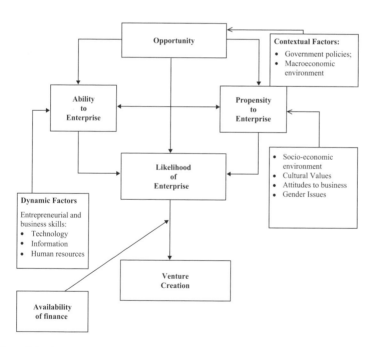

Figure 2.1   An integrative model of the entrepreneurial environment
Source: Adapted from Gnyawali and Fogel (1994).

The main propositions suggested by this model are sixfold (after Gnyawali and Fogel, 1994):

- the higher the opportunity, propensity and ability to enterprise, the higher the likelihood to enterprise;
- the more favourable the socio-economic factors, the greater the propensity to enterprise;
- the greater the entrepreneurial and business skills, the greater the ability to enterprise;
- the more favourable the government policies and procedures, the higher the opportunity to enterprise;
- the higher the likelihood to enterprise, the higher the new venture creation;
- the higher the likelihood to enterprise and the greater the availability of financial and non-financial assistance, the higher the new venture creation.

This model has important implications for public policy. The public sector can clearly have an impact in opening up opportunities for entrepreneurial activity through 'market-friendly' approaches to macroeconomic management, the implementation of 'entrepreneur-friendly' laws such as patents and copyrights, and minimising the transaction costs of doing business by reducing red tape and improving the enforcement of contracts. At this same contextual level, government has a role in influencing the socio-economic environment for entrepreneurship. This has been a historical problem in Africa and Asia, where many regimes were brought to power on socialist or anti-business platforms and the private sector consequently suffers from a relatively low social position relative to the public sector. It also suggests that providing financial support for entrepreneurs will be unproductive if the ability and propensity for enterprise is low.

Structural adjustment addresses the contextual question, seeking to improve the position of the private sector, liberalising markets and creating opportunities for business. At the same time, liberalisation brings with it a depoliticisation of several existing programmes, many of which have been perceived by entrepreneurs as being 'anti-business'. Many governments which had previously been opposed politically to private enterprise are now publicly embracing it (Hailey, 1992). Whilst structural adjustment addresses the contextual issues, the relatively neglected element remains the development of capabilities of entrepreneurs and firms to exploit the opportunities offered to them. Furthermore, financial repression which is an integral part of structural adjustment, and particularly of IMF conditionality, is cutting off the supply of finance even to those entrepreneurs who exhibit a high propensity and ability to enterprise (de Valk, 1994). Structural adjustment is therefore addressing only part of the entrepreneurial environment shown in Figure 2.1, thus liberalisation may be distorting the incentive systems facing entrepreneurs, or at least not providing the means by which business can respond to the new incentives offered to it.

In essence, therefore, liberalisation, and structural adjustment in particular, deals with the right-hand side of Figure 2.1, i.e. contextual factors such as 'institutions' in the Northian sense, and the macro- or meta-level environment which determines the propensity to enterprise (e.g. socio-economic environment, cultural values, attitudes to business and gender issues). The emphasis of this study is on the left-hand side of the model, particularly on the dynamic factors and the availability of finance (e.g. technology, business skills, information and human resources). This definition of the area in which agencies operate fits neatly into the division of agencies between *assistance institutions* and *facilitating institutions* (Steel, 1994). Facilitating institutions are those that help the market operate. These are closely related to the Northian institutions affecting the propensity to enterprise. On the other hand, the assistance institutions are the focus of this study i.e. those which directly affect the ability of entrepreneurs to engage in entrepreneurial activity. These agencies provide support services such as finance, information and training.[6]

The entrepreneurial model discussed above may be incorporated into an overall model of the policy environment facing firms (Figure 2.2).

Figure 2.2 should be seen as complementary to Figure 2.1. It attempts to place entrepreneurs in a policy context. In this stylised diagram the economy is divided into four main levels:

- micro: firms and entrepreneurs;
- meso: the 'middle' level of the economy representing the interface between public and private sectors and incorporating government agencies who work at a tactical rather than a strategic level;
- macro: the national, strategic level i.e. government policy; and
- meta: the 'big picture' of sociopolitical, economic and cultural institutions which provides a framework for the other three levels.

In terms of the entrepreneurial environment model shown in Figure 2.1, the macro level in Figure 2.2 corresponds to the opportunity provided for entrepreneurs, the meta level provides the propensity for entrepreneurial activity and the meso level is the level most closely

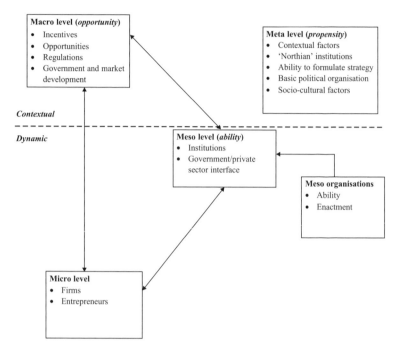

Figure 2.2   Stylised model of economic levels

associated with the ability to enterprise, or at least to enhance the existing abilities of entrepreneurs at the micro level. It is at this level that entrepreneurs are able to receive information, technology dissemination, training and finance, and it is here that government agencies have a significant impact. The basic assertion is that firms are unable to exist on their own, but must be embedded in the right environment.

Messner (1997), amongst others, uses this quadruped structure to elaborate a method of *systematic competitiveness*. Arising largely out of work carried out by the German Development Institute, Messner uses the interaction of the four different levels of the economy to explain competitiveness of industries within industrial districts. As he states:

> an economy's competitiveness is first based on targeted and inter-
> linked measures at three system levels (the macro-, micro- and
> mesolevels). The activity and specific dynamics at these levels, and
> their interplay, are shaped by different institutional structures specific

to individual countries, organizational patterns, the ability of groups of social actors to learn and adapt, and their integration within specific normative value concepts. The macro-, micro- and mesolevels are embedded in these social dimensions (the metalevel). Competitiveness emerges in firms, though it cannot be reduced to their activities; international competitiveness can be understood only within the context of social patterns of organization. (1997: 10)[7]

Competitiveness is therefore not merely a matter for entrepreneurs, but also the environment within which they operate. Medium- and long-term industrial development therefore depends upon the level of embeddedness of firms within the economic system, which in turn depends upon the level of interaction between the different levels of the economy.

In the African context there have been significant breakdowns in this 'system', particularly between the macro and the micro levels (Herbst, 1993). Historically, there have also been political problems with incumbent regimes not deriving their political support from the business sector and in some cases being directly hostile.[8] In addition, I have already claimed that structural adjustment and financial repression, which operate at the macro level, have adversely affected many enterprises lacking the ability to respond to the new incentives offered and in some cases the incentives have been distorted due to a flawed institutional environment (which would include inadequate markets). Given this analysis the institutional element at the meso level takes on increased significance as the bridge between the macro and micro levels in terms of enhancing abilities (including enabling enterprises by providing the finance to turn likelihood to enterprise into actual enterprises), and acting as an information conduit.

The integrated model of entrepreneurship shown emphasises the interdependence of the contextual and dynamic factors in enhancing entrepreneurial capabilities. I have already postulated that structural adjustment is positively addressing only a portion of the model, and have suggested that a more integrated approach should be taken to develop capacities to respond to these new incentives, in other words developing the ability to enterprise and turning likelihood to enterprise into actual enterprises. I have also argued above that there is no shortage of entrepreneurs in Africa or South Asia (the meta level, or propensity) but, particularly in Africa, they are moving out of manufacturing, in many cases into trade, because of the relatively low entry costs and lack of finance for longer-term manufacturing projects. Both of these elements point clearly to the need for changes in the incentive systems to encourage those entrepreneurs that do exist to take advantage of the new opportunities opening up and enter manufacturing. This adds additional importance to the meso level, the level which has been most neglected in the economic development literature. In viewing industrial development as a system, the development of systematic competitiveness requires all elements of the model to be functioning and, certainly in Africa and to a lesser extent South Asia, this is clearly not the case.[9] There is thus a case for the development of enabling institutions at this level designed to enhance the abilities of entrepreneurs and also to facilitate the working of the system.

There remains a critical question with regard to this form of intervention. That is, whether weak states have the expertise to develop entrepreneurial ability, and if not, how could they work towards this set of skills. We will address some of these issues below.

Enabling institutions and entrepreneurship

The history of state involvement in these areas, in general, has been mixed. In the case of Africa there is a sizeable literature on state failure and considerable distrust and scepticism amongst entrepreneurs, and in the case of South Asia, there is a huge literature on the state and government failure (Marsden, 1992). Wolf (1988) outlines four main types of government failure:

> 1. Public agencies may fail to supply goods at socially desirable prices due to budgetary or political pressure, retention of information or over-employment;
> 2. Public agencies may supply poor quality goods due to lack of competition or an inadequate benchmark;
> 3. Public agencies may deliberately misallocate goods to satisfy particular constituencies;
> 4. Public officials may view agencies as ways to make money by extracting rent.

These four main public sector failures draw a mainly negative picture of the public sector in developing countries. This is the position taken by Hogan, Keesing and Singer (1991) in their analysis of the role of support services in expanding manufactured exports. They identify several main reasons for 'ineffective support services in developing countries':

Firstly, the legacy of import substitution in developing countries has increased the complexity of the effort required, particularly in changing deep-rooted attitudes, in particular:

- The wrong skills and abilities – ability to survive under import substitution relies upon the ability to seek rents and circumventing controls, not the abilities of innovation, competitiveness and marketing;
- The wrong production base – copycat products, not exportables;
- Lack of export know-how and experience;
- Vested interests embedded within previous regulatory systems (i.e. import substitution regimes)

One of the lasting legacies of import substitution has been that it has left a large component of the workforce and management inadequately equipped to deal with the market. Enhancing exports in particular is a 'people business' (Hogan, 1991). Above all, it requires an ability to understand the requirements of the marketplace and the productive capacity of the producer, and to be able to bring them together constructively. There is a marked lack of such human resources within the public sector in Africa since most people so skilled are snatched up by the private sector and they are in short supply.

Secondly, the neglect of the supply aspects of exporting. There has been a significant deficiency in provision of advice on export production and the related task of upgrading the capabilities of firms. Recent donor innovations have attempted to provide some of these services, but most of the skills required need to be brought in from advanced economies. In manufacturing there needs to be a close relationship between production and marketing. For those firms seeking to export, an ability to produce goods on time, in sufficient quantity and of sufficient quality is crucial. The supply capabilities of firms are therefore paramount in expanding exports and currently there are significant deficiencies. Related to this is a lack of recognition that exports are in effect a partnership between government, which sets the rules, and the private sector, which does the business. Given, the historical situation in which entrepreneurs mistrust government and vice versa, agencies which have been perceived as being close to the government and lacking autonomy have met a sceptical or even hostile response on the part of the private sector. Agencies which typically are located within historically poor and inadequately funded ministries such as trade and industry ministries, have been particularly handicapped as the partnership has completely broken down (Hogan, 1991).

Lastly, support for the expansion of exports has frequently been provided through inappropriate delivery mechanisms, usually a sole organisation which provides a whole range of services free of charge. This policy has not proved to be effective. An additional problem has been that public sector agencies have frequently been established as monopoly providers of information to firms at little or no cost i.e. they provide their services for free. Since many agencies in Africa perform their services badly, the fact that their services are provided free of charge does not automatically crowd out the provision of private sector services, but it may slow down this development (Hogan, Keesing and Singer, 1991). On the other hand, the monopoly position of many of these agencies is directly harmful, particularly when it is accompanied by a hostile environment to foreign competition in service provision. Allowing development of a private sector in these services coupled with the introduction of charging for services provided by the public sector agency may provide incentives for that agency to improve its services in order to justify its own existence (Hogan, Keesing and Singer, 1991).

Keesing and Singer use trade promotion organisations (TPOs) as their main example of an executive agency. Their concern is primarily to outline the characteristics of poor performers. They have developed a checklist of characteristics of ineffective TPOs as outlined in Figure 2.3 (Hogan, Keesing and Singer, 1994). Six factors in particular have contributed to the ineffectiveness of public service TPOs:

- The unsuitability of government employees to the task, particularly in supplying services to commercial enterprises. Their fundamental attitudes are geared towards administration not business, and business frequently has low credibility within the public service;
- Inflexibility of government procedures and red tape may significantly slow response times in an area where flexibility and rapid responses are necessary for success;
- Confusion of purpose, particularly in a multifunctional agency. For example, agencies which regulate as well as promote may not be trusted by business to do either because they do both;
- Perpetuation of the wrong attitudes and strategies through ignorance of staff within the agencies – not least by encouraging business in its misguided belief that successful exporting merely requires a few business contacts;
- Misguided even-handedness in the face of the outright discrimination of export markets which are highly specialised;
- Neglect of the development of commercial services. Since TPOs tend to perform badly, the fact that their services are free does not itself prevent private entry into the market. What does, potentially, is red

tape, and government's discouragement of foreign firms who could provide those services. Critically, the policies of developing countries frequently limit the access of local firms to commercial service providers in advanced countries.

Figure 2.3   Characteristics of ineffective business support organisations

---

Origins

- Set up initially on donor advice and with donor funding, not as a result of demand by entrepreneurs.

Planning and objectives

- No corporate planning, individual targets, or measurable departmental objectives;
- Planning starts with the funding allocated by government;
- Its role is that of carrying out a 'national strategy', policy advice, admin. tasks, etc...
- No consistency in focus;
- Has never conducted formal subsector studies of potential exporters or growth industries.

Relationship with government

- Strong cultural [and political] divide exists between public servants and the business community;
- Business community needs coaxing to take participate in activities such as trade promotion;
- Agency retains information as a bargaining chip rather than distributing it;
- More services are provided to government than to business.

Missions and trade fairs

- Missions and trade fairs represent the only significant impact of the organisation;
- At least one-third of trade missions consist of TPO staff;
- Other participants are selected using non-economic criteria;
- Overseas missions use at least one third of their time seeing government officials;
- Missions rarely generate orders;
- There is no effective follow-up.

Relationship to other donor agencies

- Organisation is effective at resisting reform;
- Organisation is effective at playing donor agencies off against each other.

Management

- Executive officers are appointed by the Ministry and not an independent board;
- Most managers have no commercial experience;
- Organisation has no effective control over overseas commercial posts.

Staff

- Public servants are paid so badly that they have second jobs;
- Many spend 80 per cent of their time at their desks;
- Organisation is overloaded by clerical staff who doze at their desks most of the day;
- Senior staff are looking for a way out, preferably in a well-paid donor agency.

Source: After Keesing and Singer, 1991.

What capabilities are required in an entrepreneurial environment?

Given the rather negative prognosis delivered above and given the crucial position of agencies within the entrepreneurial environment it is clear that agencies must develop a new set of characteristics which allow them to carry out the roles – some of them new roles – which are required within the entrepreneurial environment elaborated above. While identifying the areas where such agencies have failed is relatively easy, identifying those areas of success is more problematic simply because there are so few successful exceptions to the rule. Simply to write off such agencies as a waste of resources as Keesing and Singer have a tendency to do is to ignore the evidence from the Organisation for Economic Co-operation and Development (OECD) and from the NICs. Any analysis which tries to identify the capabilities required for a successful agency in this area is hampered by the problems inherent in trying to build up a quantifiable and causal link between improved manufacturing or export performance and the operations of the agencies. Precise data is virtually impossible to collate and agencies which are regarded as successful, such as many in Western Europe, are seen as being successful because government and the private sector believe that they are so (Hogan, 1991).

Hogan asserts that organisations themselves need to become more demand-led than supply-driven. An important way to achieve this is to charge for services, the theory being that if the service is valuable then firms will be willing to pay for it. However, there are problems with this approach: the level of prices may be beyond some enterprises which need the services but cannot afford them. An additional issue is that of monopoly in the delivery of the service. If the public service provider is the sole distributor of information then it has no incentive to provide complete or useful information even if the service is paid for (Hogan, 1991).

Organisations delivering complex support systems such as finance or information require complex internal management procedures. The provision of loans, for example, requires internal financial management and accountancy, loan tracking systems, approval systems, application assessments and portfolio management, all of which are relatively new skills to the traditional bureaucracies found in many public services. The lack of skilled personnel within the public sector to staff these agencies is a critical issue. These skills are extremely marketable and once staff have developed them the chance that they may leave for more lucrative employment in the private sector is great.[10] Indeed, promotion agencies are frequently only a small step from the private sector themselves. Staff skill development and retention become crucial issues within agencies if they are to sustain a high level of service provision.

Enterprises operate in an environment largely determined by external factors, particularly the condition of the macro-economy. Agencies, if they are to provide relevant services to these enterprises, must therefore be aware of and be able to cope with the external environment and evolve over time. This in itself involves a considerable amount of knowledge, and good linkages with firms and complimentary organisations providing similar services such as community organisations, business associations, NGOs, financial institutions and credit agencies. To borrow an analogy from North:

> To be a successful pirate one needs to know a great deal about naval warfare; the trade routes of commercial shipping; the armament, rigging and the crew size of the potential victims; and the market for booty. Successful pirates will acquire the requisite knowledge and skills. Such activities may well give rise to a thriving demand for improved naval warfare technology by both the pirates and the victims. (1990: 77)

The analogy is clear: it is not enough to know about how to run your ship, you also need to know about the sea and other vessels sailing upon it.

Internally, the organisation should be able to learn from its experience and adapt to changing conditions. It should have a clear vision of its role, which is effectively transmitted to its staff, and it should have adequate human resources to carry out its functions and be able to select, train and retain this staff. In addition, the organisation should be financially accountable and have adequate financial management systems (as well as adequate funding). Sound financial management would include control and information systems, portfolio management and project management and appraisal. Any organisation needs to be able to transmit its objectives internally to its staff, to plan, establish norms and procedures and to evaluate performance. The list is almost endless.

The experience of the 1980s in Africa has shown that the failure of many programmes designed to stimulate industrial development has been caused by internal management failures of the implementing institutions. This pattern may also be seen in many of the wide range of agencies established in South Asia, particularly India. Many of these agencies continue to exist even after their original raison d'être has ceased to be a major issue.[11] Developing the internal capacity of organisations providing support services is therefore crucial to the sustainability of manufacturing growth.

The elements of capacity outlined above suggest that any theory of capacity could rapidly turn into a 'theory of everything'. As Hildebrand and Grindle note: 'By suggesting that capacity building is almost synonymous with development itself, it makes operationalising the concept in a meaningful way almost impossible' (quoted in Batley, 1995: 9). On the other hand, an analysis of an organisation which has one foot in the government camp and one in the private sector would be inadequate if account was not taken of the external factors impinging on the internal structures and performance of that organisation.

The initial step in the analysis of capacity is amongst the most difficult: defining 'capacity'. Hildebrand and Grindle provide a general definition of 'the ability to perform appropriate tasks effectively, efficiently and sustainably' (1994: 10). Campbell and Fiszbein disaggregate this rather broad definition into two main elements. Firstly, the organisation's 'ability to optimize the use of ... resources in the production or provision process ... as well as the ability to respond to needs' (1994: 1). Secondly, they elaborate by saying that capacity is 'the existence of those tools that make it possible for ... government to perform [its roles] successfully' (1994: 2). In terms of this analysis an agency involved in industrial support should be able to galvanise and optimise resources with the aim of enhancing the capabilities of manufacturing enterprises and entrepreneurs to facilitate a positive response to the new set of incentives offered by liberalisation of markets.

To elaborate, any business support agency must have a capacity for productive efficiency, allocative efficiency and adaptive efficiency. *Productive efficiency* optimises the use of resources available for the task in hand. This would require knowledge of budgetary incentives and maintenance of a 'hard' budget constraint, but also, in the case of industry, knowledge of how to raise suitable investment funding for industry and how to use it. *Allocative efficiency* effectively means the ability of the agency to respond to the needs of its consumers – that is, firms. This requires a constructive dialogue between agencies and firms which has not been an obvious feature of African industrial development until recently. In addition, institutions involved with the market should be able to evolve with it, in other words should exhibit *adaptive efficiency* which is defined by North as the 'willingness of a society to acquire knowledge and learning, to induce innovation, to undertake risk and creative activity ...' (1990: 80). Accurate measurement of adaptive efficiency may be the most problematic of the three to measure accurately but indicators would be the continuing relevance of the agency to its major consumers, whether or not it is a 'learning organisation', or if it proved capable of changing policies over time in response to changes in market circumstances.

Numerous scholars have outlined a number of elements which are held to be crucial for a successful agency, or at least serve to contribute to a model for comparative purposes (see, for example, Farbman and Steel, 1992; Hogan, 1991; and Batley, 1997). These may be conveniently grouped into two groups around internal coherence and external connectedness outlined by Evans (1992), or internal and external factors outlined by Batley (1995).

External factors affecting capacity

External factors allow the organisation sufficient leeway to carry out the tasks assigned and also allow them the resources to do so. External factors condition the feasibility of services by delimiting the overall resource endowment and also constrain the ability of organisations to use resources efficiently and in a responsive fashion. In addition the external environment to a large extent influences the quality of dialogue and interaction by determining the entrepreneurial environment. Hildebrand and Grindle identify external factors as being both important to the analysis and also as a frequently ignored element. They state: '... organisations and trained individuals do not perform in a vacuum; their ability to carry out assigned responsibilities is deeply affected by the broader context within which they operate' (1994: 443). They go on to say: '... in some countries, performance problems diagnosed at the organisational or individual level may be so deeply embedded in economic, social, and political deficiencies that efforts to improve performance must focus primarily on these conditions' (1995: 443). There is a potentially never-ending list of factors requiring some degree of delimiting for the purposes of analysis (see, for example, Batley, 1997).

Firstly, *financial and economic conditions* are probably the single most influential factor affecting the performance of any agency aimed at enhancing the private sector since they directly affect the performance and capability of that sector. This group of factors includes budgetary constraints, availability of additional finance from government, donors or the private sector, the macroeconomic environment and local conditions affecting costs. The financial conditions are instrumental in setting the budget line of the organisation which in turn determines the ability to recruit and maintain staff, buy materials, and undertake programmes. In SSA, this is probably the overriding constraint on the operation of government services. Retrenchment and financial repression have decimated government budgets and the private sector is unable to raise capital through a conservative banking system and underdeveloped capital markets.

Secondly, *private–public interaction* is particularly important in the provision of support services for business. To be effective it is crucial for an agency to have the confidence of both the private sector and government. Government must have confidence that the organisation is good value for money and the private sector must have confidence that needs to be primarily earned through successful operations and service (Hogan, 1991). In many SSA countries the fact that the agency exists within a public sector which has historically opposed the private sector means that agencies are off to a bad start. The confidence held in the agency may crucially rest with the quality of the staff employed, the 'vision' and autonomy of its leadership and its freedom from political interests. Unless entrepreneurs identify these staff as commercially competent then obtaining their confidence will be virtually impossible (Hogan, 1991).

A lack of 'voice' for the private sector and its lack of self-confidence after years of repression may also hinder a process which is, by its very nature, that of a partnership. Many SSA governments do not derive their political power from the private sector and have been ideologically opposed to it. As a consequence private–public relations are characterised by mutual mistrust, particularly where there are ethnicity issues at stake (e.g. Lebanese in Ghana, white Zimbabweans). Many former pressure groups, such as business associations, have become discredited due to their associations with previous regimes. There is thus a lack of trust between the public and private sectors in SSA, compounded by a largely discredited partnership infrastructure. Successful agencies incorporate business into their structure, perhaps by appointing prominent businessmen to the controlling board (Hogan, 1991). In addition, the participation of private sector businessmen in an organisation which is designed to enhance the capabilities of private sector business serves to maintain the relevance of the services provided.

Thirdly, the effectiveness of agencies may be affected by *political relationships*, particularly with regard to staffing issues. Appointment systems may severely limit the planning horizons or room for manoeuvre of leading staff or officers. For example, appointments made as 'payment' for political loyalty will constrain the efficient working of the organisation through introducing unproductive entrepreneurial behaviour or rent-seeking and impede the organisation's ability to achieve overall aims as opposed to the aims of the individuals concerned. A link between political patronage and the democratic system may be particularly damaging if each political party appoints its own political supporters to agency positions after each election increasing uncertainty, wasting skills and demotivating staff. In addition, political patronage within agencies may lead to the government 'printing money' to pay wages in a situation of financial repression which in turn adversely affects the economy as a whole through higher inflation and more financial repression.

Lastly, *legal and administrative frameworks* determine the framework within which the organisation operates. Statute in particular is important in formulating the roles and scope of the organisation as well as the overall objectives and autonomy. This could be positive in terms of providing a clear objective or negative through giving an ambiguous one. The existence of a clear set of 'rules of the game' will provide stability to both the agency and the private sector with whom it operates.[12] In addition, the institutions surrounding judicial independence and strength and the establishment and enforcement of property rights are critical for the survival of any private sector development. Government agencies historically have been identified in many countries as being organisations 'above the law', i.e. having the ability to enforce their own property preferences over others. An ability to work with another grouping, i.e. the private sector, must be partly determined by some degree of equality under the law between the two groups. Property rights are central to the establishment of this relationship.

Internal factors affecting capacity

There is a degree of overlap between some of the internal and external factors and in a sense it is a false dichotomy since many of the internal factors directly influence the relationship between the agency and its consumers as well as the technical efficiency of service provision to entrepreneurs.

Any successful organisation must have a *'vision'*, a basic set of principles that guides the work of the agency (Farbman and Steel, 1992). Such a 'vision' emanates from its leaders and is transmitted to all staff so they have a clear idea of what the agency's principles are. In addition, an agency which purports to act in the interests of business must to some degree emulate their clientele and be flexible. In order to do this the leadership of the agency must have autonomy (Hogan, 1991).

Autonomy does not necessarily mean independence. A public body must operate within a framework set by government, but must be able to take decisions, which are outside the traditional bureaucratic administrative framework and reflect the commercial considerations of industrial markets. In western economies the most successful agencies are those which are responsible to their boards of directors and chief executives without outside interference (Hogan, 1991). Haggard and Webb (1993: 152) also point out that autonomy may insulate the reform process from interest groups when they state: 'politicians can fortify their commitment by delegating authority ... this reduces the capacity to reverse their decisions in response to short-term considerations'.

'Independence', on the other hand, implies that an agency is completely separate from the state. This clearly cannot be the case where services are being provided by the state for particular reasons, and are not being provided by the private sector. Business services, for example, are provided to overcome market failures of two types: firstly, they are required but are not always present or there is no incentive to provide them, e.g. information and training; and, secondly, the private sector, for whatever reason, is not providing those services to firms. Government agencies providing these services require autonomy since their decision-making does not lend itself to hierarchical structures, but they cannot be independent since they are government agencies. In addition, independence implies that an organisation may be able to become embedded into the micro element of the industrial system. In order for a system to operate effectively, however, an organisation at the meso level must be able to embed itself in *both* the macro and the micro levels. Thus the organisation is autonomous from firms and government, but not independent from them because it is embedded in a system.

Possibly the most important factor contributing to success is adequate *staffing*. Good staff make good organisations, and a lack of adequate staff renders most organisations ineffective. Across most of SSA there is a shortage of people qualified to staff a support agency. Many suitable graduates occupy positions in subsidiaries of international companies which in turn means that agencies must undertake training programmes of their own (which in turn requires time and money – both in short supply). Agencies required to supply support services should be able to take a longer view than entrepreneurs. This requires considerable expertise as well as a commitment to 'where we are going'. Staff also require motivation through the culture of the organisation, transparency of decision-making and boundaries around responsibilities.

Closely linked to adequate staffing is the availability of *finance and capital*. Reward systems and the availability of capital such as computers directly affect the ability and motivation of staff. Particularly in situations where staff may be dealing with a private sector that sometimes may be able to pay more, competent staff may be poached by firms. Government agencies face the common problem of attracting competent staff and then retaining them. The only way to achieve this is to provide higher, or at least comparable, financial incentives to the main competitor for their services.

There are a considerable number of forms of funding, the most common of which is government grant. The advantages of this are that agencies are relieved of the burden of raising revenue and have an inflation-proof income, however in an environment of reductions in public sector deficits and political interference, many agencies in Africa have become reliant on donors for funding of substantive activities which increases doubts over long term sustainability and reduces planning horizons. A preferable alternative source of financing identified by Keesing and Singer (1991) amongst others, is user charging which has the advantages of increasing autonomy of the agency, focuses the programme on services which are perceived as valuable by consumers and strengthens the commercial aspect of the services provided. In addition, if services provided are directly related to exports, it is possible to raise a levy on the value of exports gained directly through use of the services provided. There are arguments against this form of funding such as that it raises the cost of exports and it is inequitable since exporters pay for something that benefits everyone (increased exports), but the most powerful argument in favour of levies is that the most successful trade promotion organisations use them whereas the weakest are government funded (Hogan, 1991).

Raising the funding is only one side of the coin, the other is using it efficiently. Successful agencies will have effective internal financial systems, providing clear incentives and budgets for staff and activities. Staff implementing activities will be aware of and will work to those budgets and account for expenditure and there should be some form of financial accountability for managers.

This links with the fourth main area of internal capacity, *internal policies and practices*. As well as financial accountability there should be managerial accountability and responsibility. In particular, managers should be made accountable for mistakes, in the same way as their contemporaries in the private sector, at least nominally, are.

Effectively this is the least quantifiable of all of the internal capacity factors because such an integral part relates to 'culture' of the organisation. There are some tangible elements to this area, however, which would include the existence of work procedures, evaluation of personnel, clear objectives for staff, motivations, style of management, customer responsiveness, changes in structure and fragmentation and information.

Clearly, there are many factors which could be incorporated into a definition of capacity which could be applied to business support agencies. Keesing and Singer provided an initial analysis of agencies though the medium of a list of 'Characteristics of ineffective business support organisations' (Figure 2.3). Having begun to develop the idea of capacity, the next step perhaps would be to build up a model of 'Characteristics of effective business support agencies' to act as a juxtaposition of this initial model. Putting the internal capacity factors into Keesing and Singer's framework we can build up the framework shown in Figure 2.4.

Of course, not all agencies will fit snugly into either the negative or the positive model, and most will be somewhere between the two. The main questions addressed by this study are: where do many of these institutions exist within this spectrum and what capacities do they have?

Conclusion

African and South Asian economies in general have under-performed since independence, although Sri Lanka and, latterly, India have seen some improvement in economic performance. Most of them are characterised by *both* market *and* state failure. The legacy of several years of state intervention in the industrial sector, coupled with the dominance of multinational companies in large-scale production, has led to a lack of confidence and a shortfall in the capabilities of African entrepreneurs in the sense that there is a lack of experience and tools with which to build a market economy, and, perhaps, a lack of confidence amongst South Asian entrepreneurs – particularly those who have grown close to the state over the last 40 years of protectionism. The change from a state-dominated economy to an internationally competitive market economy requires a significant change in the mindset of those operating within the economy. Any realistic analysis of business support must begin by looking at these agents of private sector development – the entrepreneurs – and their environment.

Figure 2.4   Characteristics of effective business support services

Origins
- Set up initially on advice from all stakeholders, including business and government.

Planning and objectives
- Corporate planning, individual targets and measurable departmental objectives.
- Planning derives from the needs of clients and demands of 'customers' as well as government policy.
- Its role is clearly defined and some of degree of responsibility allocated for attainment of objectives.
- Consistent year-on-year focus, building up 'regular customers' and providing long-term advice.
- Surveys of potential and existing customers are an integral part of targeting specific areas of potential growth.

Relationship with government
- Government trusts the agency and allows it sufficient autonomy to make decisions in favour of business.
- Government makes funding available and allows [and encourages] financial autonomy through charging for services.
- Government carries out related reforms which complement the operations of the agency e.g. trade reforms, export licensing, etc.
- The agency does not represent an 'employment agency' for political allies.

Relationship with business
- Many staff recruited from the business community. The agency acts more as a partnership between government and business.
- Business community willing to participate in activities to the extend that they are willing to pay for services.
- The agency sees provision of information as a central strategy.
- Services are provided to entrepreneurs and to government.

Activities
- Activities are wide-ranging, both geographically and in terms of scope.
- The vast majority of participants in activities are from business.
- Participants are selected on commercial merit.
- Activities are useful and to the point. Missions spend their time making business deals and getting orders.
- Effective follow-up, assessment and evaluation of all activities with participants.
- Unsuccessful activities are acted upon and successful activities improved.

Relationship with donors
- Agency is open to proposals for reform, but is not merely passive.
- Organisation has a long-term relationship with a small number of donors so a direction of reform is sustained over time.

Management
- The chief executive officer is appointed from the business community by an independent board.
- Top managers have extensive commercial experience.
- The agency has control over staff – that is, they are not 'owned' by another Ministry.

Staff
- Staff are highly motivated by good pay and conditions.
- All staff are available 100 per cent of the time and are known to their client base.
- Most staff are qualified professionals with a realistic ratio to support staff.
- Senior staff want to work for the agency and set high standards for their subordinates.

The public sector that does exist in Africa has had a poor history of results. Bureaucracy in a Weberian sense is *under-* not over-supplied (Herbst, 1993). There is an abundance of administrative or rule-making organisations, but most are incapable or unwilling to pursue collective, coherent goals and Weberian bureaucracies are in small supply (Evans, 1992). In addition the state's ability to perform administrative functions should be regarded as a scarce good. Expansion of administrative tasks leads to a vicious circle. State capacity grows at a slower rate than the expansion of tasks leading to an administrative diseconomy of scale. This reduces performance and undercuts legitimacy, which makes it more difficult to claim resources which further reduces capacity and the gap between tasks and capacities grows ever wider. Almost all African states do too much and perform poorly.

There is some degree of contrast here with South Asia. Both India and Sri Lanka have formidable reputations for bureaucracy, and it would certainly be difficult to argue, as Herbst does for Africa, that the Indian bureaucracy does too little, not too much. The danger facing Indian industry is the history of protectionism and the lack of international competitiveness with regard to some industries.[13] Many traditional manufacturing industries, for example the textiles sector, are concerned that the withdrawal of government protection against cheaper imports, before they have a chance to upgrade technology, will put many of them out of business. The historical protection of the handloom industry in India is a glaring example of this, as is the continuing support for ailing state corporations such as NTC Mills.[14]

The underlying theoretical base adopted by this analysis is said to be characteristic of the 'third wave' of thinking on the state and economic development, the first of which was the optimistic view of the state as the instrument of development, the second a utopian view of free markets and minimalist states and the third a synthesis of both, relying on their interdependence (Evans, 1992). This in itself is not a new phenomenon but relates to a classic political economy tradition emanating from Weber and Polanyi and developing through observers such as Gerschenkron, Hirschman and Baumol. The Gerschenkron/ Hirschman/ Baumol synthesis renders the relationship between state capacity and autonomy considerably more ambiguous than the neoclassical or neo-Marxist dichotomy which underlies structural adjustment. The above analysis emphasises the idea of the state as entrepreneur, willing to shoulder some of the risk and enable other entrepreneurs to enter productive activity. This emphasis on entrepreneurship forms the basis of any realistic theory of state involvement in industry.

Baumol (1990) uses a tripartite structure to examine entrepreneurial behaviour. Entrepreneurs are collectively defined in a Schumpeterian sense as individuals who recognise and exploit opportunities to make profits. Baumol, however, disaggregates this broad definition into three groups: innovative entrepreneurs, who invent and exploit; imitative entrepreneurs, who follow innovative entrepreneurs and enter new markets; and unproductive entrepreneurs, who carry out entrepreneurial activity which is not economically beneficial to anyone except themselves. It is not difficult to predict where an entrepreneur will go given a situation where the private sector is persecuted and the public sector offers patronage, power and money. This analysis is particularly applicable to many developing economies, some of which have been characterised by widespread unproductive entrepreneurship such as rent seeking. There is no shortage of entrepreneurs, but many of them are engaged in unproductive activities. The chief determinant of the type of entrepreneurial activity entered into is the institutional environment.

In analysing the provision of support services to business, some degree of caution is needed not to assume that the demand for such services is adequately known, even by the entrepreneurs themselves (Farbman and Steel, 1992). In addition, there has been little analysis of the way in which entrepreneurs and support agencies interact in a system. In order to examine this further it is necessary to view the system as a whole and begin to tease out those areas where institutional intervention may be most beneficial. In a sense a model is required that marries entrepreneurial literature with much of the industrial literature. The core of the model adopted in this analysis is essentially a simple, common sense model of how enterprises come into being adopted from Gnyawali and Fogel (1994). This may equally be applied to enterprises facing radical changes in institutional circumstances such as structural adjustment.

The entrepreneurial environment model itself consists of three core elements: opportunity, ability and propensity. When each of these elements is fulfilled then there is a high likelihood that an enterprise will be formed, but in order to bring this enterprise into being finance is required to enact any plan. In terms of relating the institutional literature to the model, the propensity to enterprise largely derives from the socio-economic environment, culture, attitudes and education of the population, and the opportunity is given by the 'bigger picture' of structural adjustment. Both of these elements are therefore contextual in nature and are primarily concerned with institutions in North's sense.

The other elements of the model form the focus of this study, which contends that they have been under-studied or ignored in much of the literature. Both the ability to enterprise and the likelihood to enterprise are influenced by dynamic factors – those that change over time, frequently rapidly. These represent a bundle of elements, including finance, technology, information and skills. It is in this area that there is a real and constantly changing interface between government and the private sector and it is here that institutions may have a beneficial effect in facilitating change and enhancing entrepreneurs capabilities, but it is precisely this area where the history of state intervention has been historically poor. There have been numerous reasons for this, including (after Keesing and Singer, 1991): unsuitability of public employees to the task; inflexibility of red tape; confusion of purpose; perpetuation of misguided beliefs; misguided even-handedness in uneven markets; and, neglect of the development of complementary services, both internal sales at commercial rates and the development of external competition. This does not however mean that there have not been success stories (the NICs stand out in this respect) but the rent-seeking literature adopted by the World Bank is better at explaining failure than explaining success (Chowdhury and Islam, 1993).

It is clear from the model of the entrepreneurial environment outlined above that industrial development involves an interactive system, not a series of atomistic firms merely responding to price signals. There are many more variables than a simple neoclassical model can comprehend. The relatively new influence of NIE, emphasising the institutional role in reducing the transaction costs and uncertainty arising from market exchange replaces the neoclassical dichotomy of state and market with a more integrated approach in which the two cannot be separated. Firms should be seen as one element within a virtuous system which generates 'systematic competitiveness' (Messner, 1997). This more integrated approach to industrial development requires a new level of state involvement in facilitating firms to overcome short-term market failures and enhancing entrepreneurs ability to enterprise through supporting human resources development, finance, technology and information.

State involvement within a competitive system should not be simply seen as a dimension of comparative statics, i.e. fixed. The role of the state is not only to overcome short-term static market failure, but to provide a longer-term strategy, a stable macro economic environment and to overcome *dynamic* market failures.[15] This style of involvement in industrial systems requires a new approach and a new set of institutional capabilities. The internal management capacity of organisations, and external factors impinging on their ability to carry out these new roles is therefore of paramount importance. The experience of the last decade points to internal weaknesses in implementing organisations as a contributory cause where projects have failed or fallen short of their objectives. Taking a systematic view of industrial development suggests that external constraints on operations are just as important. It becomes crucial to develop a holistic approach to industrial development which encompasses a complex web of inter-relationships between agencies, government and the private sector – a 'governance' system (Messner, 1997).

This leads to the central theme of this study: have business support agencies at the meso level in Africa and South Asia got the capacity to enhance entrepreneurs' response to the incentives offered by market liberalisation? In order to look at this highly qualitative issue I have attempted to build up a model of characteristics of successful business support agencies to act as a juxtaposition to Keesing and Singer's model for unsuccessful support agencies. In reality agencies will lie somewhere between the two extremes, the question is, where?

There are several complicating factors to the analysis which involve a more complex analysis of capacity in order to disaggregate exactly what is being examined. The central problem with this, following Hildebrand and Grindle (1994), is that 'capacity' can effectively be defined as 'everything'. Using analyses from Batley (1995), Hildebrand and Grindle (1994), Farbman and Steel (1992), Sahley (1995) and Hogan (1991), a basic division of capacity between external and internal factors, each with four subsections, has been made. External factors affecting capacity include financial and economic conditions, private–public interaction, political structures and practices and legal and administrative structures. Internal factors affecting the capacity of agencies include: vision and leadership, human resources, financing and financial systems, and internal policies and practices. This analysis allows the analysis of agencies both internally as management structures, but also externally as agents acting within an integrated system of industrial development and as elements in the entrepreneurial environment. The analysis of agencies points towards a combination of internal coherence and external connectedness which Evans (1992) terms *embedded autonomy*. It is the combination of embeddedness and autonomy that is effective, not either on its own.

3
Adjustment and Manufacturing: The Structure of Entrepreneurship

Introduction

This chapter provides a brief overview of the progress of economic reform programmes within India, Sri Lanka, Ghana and Zimbabwe, contrasting their various reform experiences and time involved with the process. In short, Ghana and Sri Lanka may be taken as early adjusters, whereas India and Zimbabwe were both late in introducing IMF- and World Bank-inspired reforms, even if they had developed their own forms of liberalisation before then.

The position of textiles within the analysis was explained in the previous chapter, but this examination of adjustment broadens out to include all industry, and manufacturing in particular. This chapter discusses the context within which the private sector operates. It deals with the external factors affecting the capacity of business support agencies.

All four countries considered in this chapter have a common history of colonialism by Great Britain, and consequently followed much of the structure and practice of private industry throughout the British Empire in terms of law, business practice, management style and association. In addition, many of the same types of support organisation, in terms of associations of industry, chambers of commerce and government organisations for standards and so on, exist in all four countries. At the same time, the history of all four since independence has largely been one of increasing government controls with decreasing effectiveness of those controls. Each of these governments adopted the dirigisme criticised by neoliberal such commentators as Deepak Lal (1994).

This chapter seeks to analyse the framework within which entrepreneurs work in these four countries. It begins with a discussion of reform processes within each country, and the history of the reforms. It then goes on to look at the performance of manufacturing, and specifically textiles, within this reform period. The financial and economic conditions surrounding agencies are probably the most influential external factor affecting capacity, and in all four countries, the economic agenda is set primarily by the reform process. These reforms have not only set the 'rules of the game' for firms, but have also exposed the robustness, or otherwise, of markets in these countries. An understanding of the reform process, and its effects, is therefore crucial in comprehending the external constraints within which firms, and the agencies that support them, operate.

The textiles sector before reform

Ghana up until 1983

The general picture of the textiles industry in all four countries reads like a spectrum from poor in Ghana, through not quite so poor in Zimbabwe, to mixed in India and developing in Sri Lanka. The textiles sector in Ghana shared the fate of much Ghanaian industry throughout the 1970s, reaching a high point of production in 1970 and then entering free fall until the start of the reform process in 1983. The industry suffered perhaps more severely than most for two main reasons. Firstly, the costs of leaving the industry, particularly at the cheaper end, are comparatively low, and, secondly, the collapse of the currency meant that imported inputs such as dyes became prohibitively expensive. In addition, the development and rapid growth of the second-hand clothing market effectively undermined much domestic production, and the expansion of textile production and export from East Asia significantly reduced the opportunities for developing export alternatives to the small domestic market.

The structure of the Ghanaian textiles complex was designed by government in the 1950s as a vertically integrated sector from cotton lint production to garments. The chief activities of the sector surround cotton, although some synthetic textiles production does take place. The principal outputs are clothing, school uniforms,[1] bed linen, traditional African prints[2] and household fabrics (such as curtains and towels). Before independence, the sector barely existed other than in traditional cottage industries for *kente* cloth. At independence, President Nkrumah instigated a policy of import substitution by large private and public firms, many of which were foreign (for example, Ghana Textile Manufacturing Company (GTMC) is only 20 per cent Ghanaian).

By 1970, the textile sector's share of manufacturing value added was around 15 per cent and it accounted for around 27 per cent of total manufacturing employment (UNIDO, 1989: 40). Around the same time, capacity utilisation hovered around 60 per cent, declining throughout the 1970s, until bottoming out at 10 per cent in 1982. Between 1977 and 1982, per capita textile consumption fell from 2.95 kg to 1.44 kg, virtually halving the domestic market (Ntim et al., 1991).

At the same time the Cotton Development Board, the main controller of domestic cotton production, collapsed, producing only 5 per cent of the needs of domestic producers in 1982. Even if the Board had been able to secure sufficient domestic cotton, the market for textiles had contracted so much that the ability of textiles firms to pay would have been questioned. The rational response of the Board was to look for export markets, which it has been able to find, much to the chagrin of domestic producers, who now have to import cotton. By the time of the introduction of the Economic Reform Programme (ERP) in 1983, the 'textiles pyramid' was in a state of collapse, unable to generate new markets and unable to pay for imported inputs.

Zimbabwe up until 1992

This picture is repeated in Zimbabwe, with the exception that there is a significant domestic market for textiles. In fact, the survival of the majority of domestic producers historically relied upon heavy state protection against cheap imports and second-hand clothes. In the mid-1990s, the textiles sector employed around 4 per cent of total formal manufacturing employment (around 42 000 people). This does not include the very large informal sector in Zimbabwe that knits and sews for local markets and for the tourist trade. This is estimated to employ around 350 000, but this is almost certainly an underestimate (KSA, 1996). Only 1 per cent of the clothing companies employ more than 700 people, 8 per cent over 400 and 10 per cent over 200. The remaining 77 per cent are employed in small-scale enterprises.

Most companies in Zimbabwe were established under the UDI[3] period to produce for the domestic market. This enforced import substitution was supplemented with exports to the then Rhodesia's main ally, South Africa. In the early 1990s only about 11 per cent of Zimbabwean firms were engaged in export production, only a handful of which produce large volume runs for export. In the spinning and weaving sub-group there are only six firms, and two of these account for around 75 per cent of the fabric supplied to the domestic clothing industry.

The smaller firms engage in a wide range of activity from repair work, knitting, crocheting, dressmaking and tailoring. Around one third of firms employing fewer than 50 people are clothing manufacturing companies (McPherson, 1991). Many of these engage in 'Cut-Make-Trim' (CMT) contracts with larger firms where the larger company provides raw materials, and perhaps uses subcontractors to supply the domestic market where the rest of its own production is exported. One of the main problems facing Zimbabwean firms is the lack of flexibility in production. With the exception of only a few firms engaged in CMT contracts, there is very little subcontracting within the industry, the main objection coming from smaller firms who feel they are 'exploited', or whose internal financial management is so poor that they are unaware of whether or not the larger firm is covering their costs.

Zimbabwean industry is also characterised by a high degree of firm concentration tending towards monopoly/oligopoly. One half of all the manufacturing sector's products are produced in monopoly conditions, whilst 80 per cent of the remaining products (about 40 per cent of the total) are produced under oligopoly (Gunning, 1994). In 1992, the Zimbabwe Monopolies Commission reported that some 69 per cent of manufactures originated in industries where the four largest enterprises account for at least 80 per cent of the output. In addition, the economy exhibits several facets of dualism: black and white; formal and informal; urban and rural. All of these features have their roots in the colonial period and were sytematised during UDI period.

India before 1991

The Indian textile pyramid is probably the most complex in the world. In common with Ghana, textiles attracted much government attention after independence with the passing in 1948 of the Industrial Policy Resolution and the Cotton (Textiles) Control Order. These ordinances strove to develop the larger Indian textile mills and so achieve rapid growth, but at the same time to protect the rural handloom sector, which was perceived to have suffered from textiles imports and from organised mills under colonial rule. A bewildering number of regulations was reinforced and added to constantly throughout the entire period, regulating everything from sectoral capacity and variety of production through to areas and acreages for cotton production.

At the beginning of the period, the organised mill sector was concentrated in the major cities of Bombay, Ahmedabad and Coimbatore, with a smaller number of mills in the cities of Calcutta, Indore and Kanpur. The handloom sector, in contrast, was more decentralised across the countryside and incorporated an estimated three million looms. Its production was predominantly for the domestic, rural populations and operated very much on a local level. The mill sector, on the other hand, produced for a national and international market. The thrust of policy at this time was undoubtedly to protect the handloom sector from mills, and, more recently, the powerloom sector. Ironically, it was this last group that thrived under the regulations, particularly the banning of virtually all textile imports. Some imports of manmade fibre yarns were allowed, but only under a draconian regulatory regime.

Eventually, during the early 1980s, the Indian government concluded that the series of regulations introduced over the three decades since independence, including a freeze on loom expansion, restriction on varieties produced, prohibition of non-cotton yarns, statutory requirements for the supply of controlled cloth at uneconomic prices, and compulsory supply of hank yarns, had become counter-productive and had led to an expansion of the powerloom sector at the expense of the handloom sector – the very sector they were designed to protect. In additon, the mill sector had not flourished under the regime. In 1985, a new comprehensive policy was formulated that consisted of five central elements:

1. Removal of unnecessary controls such as allowing for equality of treatment under fiscal measures, removal of barriers to entry and exit, freedom in the use of cotton and manmade fibres.
2. Closure of non-viable units without nationalisation of 'sick' companies.
3. Progressive reduction on fiscal levies on manmade fibres.
4. Recognition and support for the textile sectors' export potential.
5. The importance of cotton to be recognised and supply guaranteed at reasonable prices.

The overall aims of these measures were to ensure the overall growth of all three textile sectors and the development of balanced competitiveness within all three. The collection of measures introduced in 1985 represented the beginnings of a reform process in India that continues to advance to this day. The fundamental building blocks of liberalisation were put in place in terms of private sector management (except in public sector undertakings (PSUs)), technological modernisation through the 'Textile Modernisation Fund', liberalisation of imports directly related to exports and the facilitation of research to enhance competition.

Again, the state of the Indian textiles pyramid illustrates a complex mixture of vertically integrated units moving right through from cotton production to the delivery of finished garments. It encompasses a wide variety of materials, including manmade fibres, silk and cotton, and consists of three distinct production streams: handlooms, power-looms and mills. Its history, in common with Zimbabwe and Ghana, has been dominated by excessive regulation and government interference. Its access to a vast domestic market has facilitated the survival of all three sectors, where, in different circumstances, perhaps the handloom sector in particular, may have declined due to imports from East Asia. This has produced a political effect, with the growth of a significant lobby based on the continuation of protectionism against what is usually described as 'unfair competition' (i.e. charging lower prices). The existence of such pressure groups, concentrated not only in major urban areas, but also spread across rural constituencies, may have significant political effects in terms of the reform process.

Sri Lanka before 1977

Sri Lankan economic history since independence is markedly different from the three other core countries. In particular, the early post-independence period of Ceylon was oriented towards private sector participation in both industry and agriculture. The role of the state was essentially defined as one of promotion and facilitation rather than direct involvement in the running of the sector. By July 1957, however, there was a significant policy shift in economic policy that led to a change in the role and style of the state. The new policy followed the fashion and clearly identified certain key industries that should exist within the public sector. These included iron and steel, cement, chemicals, fertilisers, mining, sugar and power. A further 23 secondary-level industries were identified for joint state and private sector involvement, and this latter group included textiles.

At around the same time, Sri Lanka's terms of trade began to deteriorate in line with deterioration in commodity markets, and the government embarked on a protectionist import substitution policy incorporating strict import and exchange controls. In spite of a brief attempt at liberalisation during the late 1960s, this overall policy effectively remained unchanged until 1977. The private sector was not recognised as being central to national industrial development and, consequently, was not supported. With public sector enterprises being subject to high protection, a small domestic market and strict exchange controls, the opportunities for private sector development were few and far between.

The situation worsened throughout the 1970s, as the Sri Lankan government began to take a more active role. For example, the Business Undertakings (Acquisition) Act of 1970 gave government the right to acquire any business employing more than 100 people. This type of legal provision had the effect of greatly reducing the confidence of the private sector, along with investment in new or expanding enterprises.

By 1977, the import substitution policy had run out of steam, and with the private sector unwilling to engage in investment activities, the economy stagnated, creating a balance of payments crisis and a rising level of unemployment. Structurally, the economy remained an agricultural one. Manufacturing industry was small, technologically backward and inward looking. In addition, the factories that did exist were characterised by low levels of productivity and substantial under-utilisation of capacity.

The process of economic reform

All four core countries have certain characteristics in common – that is, the high level of government intervention at some point in the history of manufacturing. In fact, all four have had dominant public sector attitudes for some years: Ceylon and Ghana since 1957, India since 1949 and Rhodesia since UDI in 1965. Zimbabwe and India both developed 'corporate' styles of manufacturing industry with a partnership between public sector activity and private sector management and capital, whereas Ghana and Sri Lanka pursued vigorous nationalisation policies. It is no accident that Zimbabwe and India have relatively large domestic markets, allowing the private sector to produce for domestic consumption. Even though import substitution policies pursued by all four led to industrial stagnation in all cases, India and Zimbabwe at least had the ability to develop some private industrial infrastructure. Ghana and Sri Lanka's internal markets were so small that they were unable to even develop this rudimentary level of industrial production, and so the stagnation led to a situation of industrial stand-still.

The stagnation of industry in all four countries has led each one to embrace the reform packages promoted by the World Bank and IMF. Although Sri Lankan liberalisation predated structural adjustment as a policy instrument, the basic features of the reforms are virtually the same. With one or two minor differences in timing and specific measures, the overall thrust of the reform is remarkably similar. Although not all structural adjustment programmes are the same, there is a number of measures that form a recognisable core of the programmes. In all four countries this would include:

- Unification and successive devaluation of exchange rates in line with market value.
- Liberalisation of international trade in line with comparative advantage.
- Dismantling of price and distribution controls and distortions, including subsidies.
- Broadening the tax base and improvement in tax collection and enforcement.
- Encouragement of foreign investment.
- Encouragement of foreign companies.
- Development of export markets.
- Elimination of state monopolies.
- Broadening and deepening of the financial sectors.
- Lowering barriers to entry and exit for manufacturing.

The retreat from direct provision

An integral part of structural adjustment programmes around the world has been the privatisation of nationalised productive organisations. In many cases this has involved returning assets back to their original owners, as was the case, for example, with Unilever in Ghana. Certainly in Ghana, Sri Lanka and Zimbabwe, divestiture of state-owned assets has been an integral part of the reform package, and even in India, where many interests with regard to trade unions, managers and politicians are entrenched and powerful, the divestiture of state enterprises and increased private sector involvement (sometimes through joint ventures) have accelerated.

The situation in Ghana became critical with the introduction of the Economic Reform Programme (ERP) in 1983. The state-owned enterprises (SOEs) were not only in debt to the state, but were also in debt to each other, creating a huge financial black hole and an untenable financial situation. An ambitious programme was launched involving around 70 enterprises along with a further 42 Cocoa Board enterprises. The performance of this divestiture programme, realistically, may only be described as poor. By the end of 1989, only 30 companies were said to be 'substantially completed', but only six had reached the approval stage, and 19 had effectively been liquidated. The effect of divestiture was therefore to liquidate all of those companies that were uneconomic, contributing greatly to the large number of firm exits throughout the 1980s. The lack of success of this programme has left an economy still dominated by the state. Around 300 SOEs dominated the economy throughout the 1990s, and they still benefit from a range of legal-administrative advantages, particularly with regard to tax. In 1995 they accounted for around half of total production in the 'modern' sector and well over half of total industrial employment. At the same time in 1993, the private sector was said to account for only 3 per cent of GDP, with the public sector contributing 97 per cent (Herbst, 1993).[4]

The lack of success of the privatisation programme and its associated slowdown after 1987 have sent negative signals to the private sector, in turn discouraging private sector participation in the process (Development Researchers Network, 1994). At the same time, despite much publicised liberalisation within Ghana, the public sector remains one of the largest in SSA. As a result, further divestiture remains a pillar of current donor programmes in the country.

The ESAP introduced in Zimbabwe in 1992 included the privatisation of state-owned industries as one of its most prominent features. In fact, privatisation within Zimbabwe has not been the mainstay of the economic reform programme, even though state-owned enterprises are present in several key areas of the economy. Ownership as a broader issue is far more crucial to the success of the economy as a whole, than just state ownership. In fact Zimbabwe has always had a strong, private sector economy existing alongside the state-dominated one. This is a peculiarity of Zimbabwe's economic and political history.

A complete analysis of ethnicity in Zimbabwe is beyond the scope of this book, but the issue is so critical in determining the structure of the economy that it demands some attention. In brief, under the Rhodesian government, blacks were exploited as a source of cheap labour, and were restricted in terms of where they could live and work. Whilst this no longer exists in terms of law, the more subtle control of capital remains in the hands of many whites and, to a lesser extent, Asians. This is exacerbated by the continued existence of strict zoning laws forbidding some informal sector activities in certain areas. This has the overall effect of leaving the black population dependent on the formal, white-owned sector for employment.[5]

The Zimbabwean Central Statistical Office (CSO) estimates the distribution of firm ownership to be as follows (1994):

African	40 per cent
Asian	16 per cent
European	41 per cent
Others	3 per cent

Europeans, who comprise 1.5 per cent of the population, control some 41 per cent of industry. In Harare and Bulawayo, the main urban centres, Europeans and Asian own around 74 and 78 per cent of firms respectively (Gunning, 1994). The central problem for the government since 1980 has been the dichotomy of business: on one side a well-developed industrial sector for the minority, and on the other, an underperforming one for the majority. One of the central aims of the government has been to bridge this gap by constructing an 'indigenous' economy without alienating the white minority. This relationship has, however, deteriorated in the late 1990s because of increasing economic pressure on the government and frustration among the majority population about the slow pace of economic growth.

The paradox of 'socialism' under the current leadership, and one of the reasons why the economy is now under such pressure, is that instead of building up a small business sector to compete with the existing corporations, those corporations thrived, grew stronger, diversified and soaked up all of the best human resources. Socialism effectively strengthened private sector oligopoly within Zimbabwe by protecting it from competition.

The reforms undertaken in Sri Lanka in 1977 and again in a second wave in 1989, were partially designed to open up the economic space given to the private sector. Many of the reforms were initially aimed at halting 'crowding out' rather than out and out privatisation, specifically to encourage private investment. During the period 1977 to 1989, and in the second wave of reforms after 1989, privatisation gained ground. All reforms were aimed at enhancing the private sector orientation of the economy, including a reduction in the number of public enterprises, increasing the efficiency of those that remained, privatising state-owned plantations and streamlining Foreign Direct Investment (FDI) procedures. In addition, the Greater Colombo Economic Commission (GCEC) was transformed into a national investment promotion organisation (a Board of Investment). The new role of the GCEC was to increase the international competitiveness of manufacturing and its export orientation and improving the private sector's willingness to invest.

In the period 1987–90 the Sri Lankan government launched a comprehensive adjustment programme, described in a Policy Framework Paper supported by the IDA and the IMF (World Bank, 1993). Central to this programme was a desire to reduce the size of the public sector. Divestiture was guided by a Presidential Commission, formed in 1987, and later, in 1989, renamed the Commission on Peopleisation.[6] The criteria for choosing enterprises for privatisation was markedly different from that adopted in Africa. Enterprises had to be profitable and obviously commercial, conditions that did not really exist, certainly in Ghana. In addition, enterprises had to be small enough to be divested on the domestic market and not sensitive to political interference.

The privatisation process consisted of three distinct phases: the conversion of corporations into public companies; restructuring viable enterprises; and privatising selected public enterprises. In view of experience, these three stages have been merged into one for smaller enterprises.

The institutional framework for privatisation has been through periods of rapid change. In particular, the Commission on Peopleisation was disbanded in January 1990. Following this development, the Commercialisation Division (CD) of the Ministry of Finance was placed in charge of the process.[7] The CD handles smaller privatisations, and at the time of writing was involved with about 16 projects. Larger privatisations involving foreign investors are dealt with by the Public Investments Management Board (PIMB) formed in September 1989 (becoming a company in 1990). The PIMB also handles government equity in converted public enterprises.

The privatisation experience in Sri Lanka involved a wide range of enterprises and has received constant support from the government since its inception. In addition, compared to the experiences in Africa, privatisation in Sri Lanka does not appear to have been seen as an excuse to unload inefficient companies. Companies due to be privatised frequently received restructuring advice and support in order to make them profitable in the private sector. In 1989/90, the successful sale of the two largest textile mills, Thulhiriya and Pugida, generated considerable confidence in the privatisation process, something that has continued through the 1990s.

The changing regulatory environment

One of the central elements of the reform process in all four countries has been the reform of regulations and the regulatory environment.

The government of Ghana has been particularly successful in altering the regulatory environment for industry. Much progress has been made, for example, in reforming the legal and regulatory practices governing enterprises. Under the auspices of the Public Sector Advisory Group (PSAG) working with USAID, several of the legal requirements governing transfer of assets, calculation of income tax and establishment of new companies have been relaxed or simplified.

A similar process was followed in India, with the deregulation of most industries. Problems have arisen with the withdrawal of so many regulations across India. In particular, the enforcement of liberal provisions has been lax, and sometimes deliberately scuttled by errors and omissions. The reservation of 22 articles covering various fabrics covered by the Handloom Act of 1985 was reinforced with new provisions. Sectoral interests managed to obtain a stay of operation for seven years until the matter was decided in favour of the handlooms by the Supreme Court. This has been a common pattern during several legislative reforms.

Although several regulations have been dismantled to bring about inter-sectoral parity, the mill sector, in view of its size and expected operational efficiency, is called upon frequently to support the handloom sector through, amongst other things, a subsidy on yarn prices. When the price of cotton fluctuates, the mill sector effectively absorbs the loss incurred by the more inefficient handlooms. Consequently, the mill sector has been lobbying for the 'level playing field' of liberalised markets. Despite this, the distortions remain.

Price controls have long been a feature of Zimbabwe's economy. A legacy of economic policies under UDI, the systems of price controls have increased in complexity since 1980. The price controls include setting maximum and minimum prices on specific products, fixed mark-ups on commodity prices, price setting, ministerial approval for some price rises (e.g. newspapers, iron and steel), and specific mark-ups for wholesalers and retailers. All of these regulations were strictly enforced by an inspection system and a series of fines. For the larger firms, these regulations, coupled with trade protection, strengthened their position by providing stability, but also by restricting access to the formal system, for example, by the imposition of foreign exchange quotas, for new, smaller, firms.

One of the main aims of the ESAP has been to unbundle these regulations. By 1992, most price controls had been removed (exceptions being seeds, iron and steel and batteries), and at the time of writing the number of goods requiring a pricing formula has been reduced to vehicle parts, agricultural chemicals and equipment and lubricating oils. Generally, price control has been replaced by price competition through trade liberalisation.

Generally, over all four countries, the number of regulations has fallen dramatically under the reform programmes, but whilst the number may have reduced, deregulation has sometimes been weak, particularly in view of the delaying tactics used by sectoral interests in India and their use of the judicial system to delay implementation.

Investment

One of the main aims of liberalisation has been to generate increased foreign investment. All four countries have attempted to liberalise their investment environments. In particular, the approach in all four has been to reduce the number of organisations that an external investor needs to deal with in terms of buying a domestic company, investing in a joint venture or starting up a new company. In Sri Lanka, the GCEC was established as a 'one-stop shop' for foreign investors, a pattern also adopted by the Ghana Investment Promotion Centre (GIPC) and the Zimbabwe Investment Centre (ZIC).

Even the vast economy of India has created a 'single window' clearance facility for foreign investment, although the success of Indian FDI policy has been mixed. Over 80 per cent of FDI approvals have been in the priority sectors of power generation, oil refining, electrical equipment, chemicals and export-related sectors. In the case of textiles and garments, foreign investment has been minimal, partly due to the lack of clarity surrounding current investment policy and procedures.

FDI has been identified as a priority for the textile industry, since foreign investment could help satisfy the considerable scope for building export markets and upgrading technology. A small beginning has already been made with regard to modernisation, with tie-ups with foreign companies enabling improved international competitiveness. The current tie-ups are limited to quality production in around a dozen mills in the formal sector producing textiles for the US, Europe and Israel. Clearly, to build on this start, increased clarity and opportunity for foreign investors are required.

In both Zimbabwe and Ghana, the introduction of 'one-stop shops' has led to increases in investment activity. However, in both countries, the main beneficiaries, in common with India, have not been manufacturing industry. Whilst the Indian beneficiaries of power and utilities have not attracted the expected interest due to the limited scope for profit, the chief beneficiaries have been the natural resource sectors, despite huge domestic markets for manufactured goods. In Ghana, the bulk of investment has gone into gold extraction and timber, whilst the Zimbabwean mining industry as well as some agriculture (particularly tobacco) has gained from foreign investment. Ghana in particular has suffered from a perception that government has not been consistent, clear or transparent in its passing of enabling legislation for investment. This view has not been limited to international investors, but has also been expressed by domestic entrepreneurs. Certainly, the fact that many domestic investors do not have confidence in the government discourages overseas investors.

Sri Lanka is one of the best-known stories of investment liberalisation. The imaginative and widespread use of export processing zones (EPZs), culminating in the creation of the entire economy as a virtual EPZ, has led to a rapid growth of foreign investment in manufacturing, particularly in the textiles sector, where labour is cheap and regulations few and far between. The government has pursued a complementary set of policies involving the liberalisation of capital and stock markets, the liberalisation of portfolio investments, the commercialisation of state-run banks and the relaxation of credit allocation guidelines, along with the overall reduction of excess liquidity within the system and consequently, of inflation.

Reconstruction of financial services

Reconstruction of financial markets, the development of a market for risk and the constitution of a domestic market in stocks, shares and investment is critical to the development of a thriving manufacturing sector. In particular, there are a number of common features of financial markets that are important to industrial development:

- Reliance on market forces in the determination of interest rates and the volume of credit. In all four countries this has, to varying degrees, incorporated deregulation of interest rates, divestiture of state owned banks, abolition of credit ceilings and the encouragement of overseas banks.
- Provision of extensive financial support for the banking system, frequently through complementary adjustment programmes, for example in Zimbabwe, the financial sector has its own programme (FINSAP) aimed at addressing the particular problems of the financial sector in adapting to the more general economic adjustment programme.
- The establishment of capital markets and stock exchanges, with the liberalisation of exchange rates and regulations and the development

of a market for risk, e.g. insurance companies and institutional investors.

However, in the countries studied this framework is often subordinated to short-run financial stability resulting in substantial financial repression through high interest rates. IMF programmes seek to control inflation primarily through higher interest rates and controls over the printing of money, but one of the most obvious means of regaining financial control is to reign in the substantial public sector deficits built up in the era of import substitution.

Public sector deficits may also, however, be dangerous to liberalised financial markets. In Ghana, for example, the government's main method for financing its substantial deficit is to issue Treasury Bills. This has the effect of soaking up a great deal of capital on the Ghana Stock Exchange Company, an already small market dominated by Ashanti Goldfields and Unilever, as investors take the safe option of a guaranteed return over a more risky investment in manufacturing. The stock exchange in Zimbabwe has been more successful, but is subject to huge swings in fortune due to its reliance on agricultural companies and the Old Mutual Building Society (where many commercial farmers keep their savings). If there is a bad harvest, the market immediately crashes. This has serious implications for long-term investors in activities such as manufacturing. Both of these examples illustrate the problems of liberalised capital markets in small domestic markets (with a few big fish), but also in the more general problem of rational investors choosing shorter-term, guaranteed returns over the more risky and longer-term returns of manufacturing investment.

Trade reforms

With the start of the World Trade Organisation compliance in 1995, India has flung her doors wide open to imports through a system of tariff reform. Despite protests from textiles interests at home, India has undertaken to be a disciplined member of GATT. Despite the progressive phase-out of the MFA, India has opted to introduce liberalisation on a far faster timetable. Most textiles were under the 'restricted list' and imports were allowed under special import licences, whilst fibres, yarns and industrial fabric imports were allowed within open general licences to the trade. In the case of textiles, special import licences are issued to exporters at a specified share of their export value and these licences are tradeable in order to facilitate the free flow of imports.

The main features of market access for textiles in India are the opening of markets for almost all fibres, yarns, fabrics, made-ups and garments, the progressive reduction of tariffs, and a provision to discourage low-priced imports through temporary rates of duty. Such policies were also followed by Sri Lanka, although the Sri Lankan liberalisation was earlier and deeper than that in India. The first wave of reforms in 1977 included substantial trade reform aimed at reducing import quotas, coupled with a move to reduce general tariff levels. These policies were reinforced in the second wave of reforms in 1989, when import duties were significantly simplified by introducing a four-band system, with the maximum tariff rate not exceeding 50 per cent. Progressive sets of reforms have created a very open trade environment in Sri Lanka, with the policy of EPZs effectively being applied to the whole island.

Similar trade liberalisation policies have been pursued in both Ghana and Zimbabwe, although the policy has been more limited in Zimbabwe. Ghana has been particularly effective in implementing 'stroke of the pen' reforms such as abolishing import licensing, but gives little support to longer-term and sustained reforms such as providing information on international standards in industry or facilitating exports. Trade is less important to the Ghanaian economy than to equivalent countries. In fact, the sum of imports and exports reached the equivalent of 37 per cent of GDP in 1992 (Development Researchers Network 1994), which is considerably lower than other countries with similar resource bases. In addition, if overseas aid is subtracted from this figure, the rate decreases to 35 per cent of GDP, compared to 70 per cent in Zimbabwe and 133 per cent in Côte d'Ivoire.

This poor performance of Ghanaian trade has been worsened by a decline in non-traditional exports in the 1990s, particularly in activities not including the extraction of natural resources. Despite a set of export incentives, including rationalisation of the tariff structure, abolishing quantitative restrictions, reducing bureaucracy and introducing duty drawback, exports still remain depressed. This picture is partially repeated in Zimbabwe. Reforms in lifting export restrictions were not linked with lifting excessive duties on the imported inputs relied upon by the textiles industry. The structure of the industry and the pre-reform history, mean that much of the dye and even much of the raw cotton lint used by the garments industry for example, needs to be imported. High duties directly affect the competitiveness of the resulting exports.

Currency reform

Itself frequently a source of distortion, the price and availability of foreign currency has played a critical role in the development of most industry across most of the developing world. In Zimbabwe, the relatively arbitrary policy of periodic foreign currency allocation has meant that some firms have machinery that is not 100 per cent compatible because it was bought at different times, when foreign currency was available. All four countries have undergone significant foreign exchange liberalisation with varying side-effects. Domestic inflation and continuing public sector deficits in Ghana and Zimbabwe have led to continuously declining exchange rates that have had significant knock-on effects for industry. Many of the raw materials used by the industry are imported, consequently the price of producing one garment has increased radically throughout the period. Despite being countered by cheaper exports, competitiveness is severely undermined by import price increases. The lack of reform in terms of maintaining foreign exchange bank accounts in Zimbabwe has also worsened the situation since importers need to engage in expensive exchange transactions.

Fiscal policy

Liberalisation has generally been accompanied by changes in fiscal policy, particularly tax reform. Whilst many of the tax reforms themselves have been complex, the general policy is relatively simple, and consists of several interlocking elements. In general, in all four countries, the thrust of fiscal (and, indeed, trade) policy has been (in addition to trade reforms mentioned above):

- Progressive reduction of import and export duties.
- Reduction and simplification of corporate rates of income tax.
- Some degree of decentralisation of tax collection and charging.
- Changes in the personal rates of income tax.
- A switch in emphasis from increasing tax rates to improving tax collection.

Human resources

A more general point relating far more to Zimbabwe and Ghana than to Sri Lanka and India is that of shortages of skilled human resources. Zimbabwe is a good example of this problem. The country has a good education system producing some highly educated people, but Zimbabwean industry suffers from a severe shortage of artisans. Prior to independence there were only two technical colleges and most technical education was for the white population. Many strategic posts were taken up by South African or British citizens. The situation has eased since 1980, but of the current 10000 students, around half are undertaking 'business', rather than technical, training.

This pattern is repeated in Ghana, where entrepreneurs find it difficult to recruit semi-skilled and technical staff. For example, one entrepreneur told me that she found it easy to recruit a skilled (and expensive) tailor, or a completely unskilled labourer, but that it was virtually impossible to recruit someone who would just sit there and use a sewing machine. There are a number of reasons for this, including the mismatch of education and technical needs, but one of the main problems for the private sector (and the public sector) is that in a small economy with scarce skilled labour, domestic firms lose out in competition for human resources with international NGOs and multinational companies because they can afford to pay more.

The reform experience of the textiles sector

The reform process includes a set of similar elements across significantly different economies. Examining the effect of reforms on the capacity of government support agencies requires some knowledge of the effects of reforms on the environment for business. Consequently, this section outlines the general trend of the textiles sector and its responses to the structural adjustment process. This does not pretend to be an exhaustive study of the textiles sector in all four countries. Many volumes could be (and have been) written on the Indian textiles sector alone, let alone the experience of Sri Lanka. The overall aim of this section is to provide a picture of the kinds of pressure affecting the textiles industry as a whole, aiming at pulling out features or trends that can be generalised across manufacturing industry as a whole. The purpose is to improve our understanding of whether or not government agencies have the capacity to help business. An understanding of what has happened to business throughout this period is therefore critical.

Across Zimbabwe and Ghana, the story of textiles under structural adjustment has been one of struggle. In India, the story is one of shifting balances within the sector. The Sri Lankan industry has effectively had adjustment constructed around it, and the establishment of EPZs specialising purely in garment exports has provided a significant boost to industrial production.

Of the four countries, the Indian story is by far the most complex, largely due to the large domestic market for yarn and spun textiles. The Indian spinning sector is, in fact, the largest in the world and has expanded under structural adjustment, in stark contrast to the contracting weaving sector. The mill sector in particular has provided the main thrust of modernisation and restructuring within the sector, with the capacity utilisation of mills increasing from 77 per cent in 1980–81 to around 81 per cent in 1994–95. This has been supplemented by some 417 new spinning mills, established under the second wave of reforms, i.e. since the early 1990s. Modernisation has also resulted in better usage of new equipment. An increase in yarn production from 1298 million kg in 1980–81 to 2090 million kg in 1994–95 has been achieved whilst the number of installed looms has fallen from over 200 000 to around 140 000 during the same period. This has been due to improved use of existing equipment and the installation of newer, more efficient looms.

The mills do not, however, perform well in terms of exports of yarn. Between 1980 and 1995, the export of cotton piece exports increased from 312 square metres to 459 square metres, a decline, in proportional terms, from 70 per cent of total cotton piece goods export, to just 28 per cent. The mills have been largely displaced by the power-loom sector, whose growth has been spectacular. The powerloom share of exports in cotton fabrics, for example rose from 10 per cent in 1980–81 to around 67 per cent in 1994–95. This replacement of mill-produced fabric by the powerloom sector is largely a function of their lower unit costs. The powerlooms had an increase in unit costs from Rs. 4.30/ sq. m in 1980–81 to Rs. 14.76/ sq. m in 1994–95. This compares to increases of Rs. 5.8 to Rs. 26.16 in the case of the mill sector and Rs. 9.72 to Rs. 40.71 in the handloom sector. The low unit value of much of the powerloom sector reflects on the low end of production and on its quality. Out of the main varieties of sheets, drills, twills, and canvas cloth, for example, over 70 per cent is exported in its grey (unprocessed) state.

The growth in powerloom exports has been mirrored by rapid growth in production. In fact, this has been part of a long historical trend. Regulations on the mill sector, designed to protect the labour-intensive handloom sector effectively provided a gap in the market that was filled by the powerlooms, with their decentralised structure and power operated looms, they were able to undercut the mills and the handlooms. Consequently from 23 800 looms in 1951, the sector had grown to 0.6 million in 1980, 0.9 million in 1989 and 1.36 million by 1995.

One of the great advantages of the powerloom sector is its broad composition. With both small and big units, flexible production practices and variable production runs, the powerloom sector has advantages of flexibility over the mill sector and economies of scale over the handloom sector. Flexibility and variety have costs, however. The decentralised nature of the industry, and its history in 'filling in' for the other two sectors, has led to a chaotic production structure, with a multitude of production possibilities, prices and capabilities. Much of the growth has been achieved by new entrants buying surplus or second-hand equipment, which comprises a relatively cheap start-up cost. Most of this machinery is in urgent need of upgrading and modernisation. Market forces have created a market for the powerlooms, but not for finance for their operators who are predominantly small-scale businessmen and, therefore, not influential within government.

Despite the rapid increase in the share of exports produced by the powerloom sector, this remains a small proportion of the sector's total output. In 1995, exports were only 10 per cent of production, as compared to 40 per cent of the mill sector and 2 per cent for handlooms. There is clearly scope for the powerloom sector to increase exports, but the lack of modern technology, could guarantee consistency of quality in production, prevents further expansion into this area.

The Sri Lankan story is one of success, sustained over a long period of time. From the initial reform process in 1977 to 1995, the value of exports from the garment industry increased from US$10m to US$1395 in 1994, accounting for some 45 per cent of the volume of total national exports. Taking advantage of incentives, tax concessions, low cost labour and export quotas, most of the garment production has been generated by 'footloose' international firms investing in EPZs. Most of the garments are exported to the big international markets of the USA (60 per cent), EC (33 per cent) and secondary markets including Canada, Japan, and Australia.

The high value generated by this sector is, however, not indicative of its value to the economy, since the net foreign exchange generated amounts to only 33 per cent of the total value of exports. Around 95 per cent of the fabric requirement is sourced from overseas, mainly from Hong Kong, China, India, Pakistan, Bangladesh and Malaysia. This has a knock-on effect of preventing Sri Lanka from benefiting wholly from the Multi-Fibre Agreement quota system (it would benefit if the cloth used was produced domestically).

Despite this, the sector has grown far more rapidly than the other two main sectors within the textiles pyramid: yarn and fabric. The average annual growth rate between 1986 and 1994 was 9 per cent for yarn and 5.8 per cent for fabric, compared to 11 per cent for garments. This is reflected in the marginal contribution made by yarn and fabric producers to overall textile exports. The analysis of the composition of exporters is interesting. Of 591 firms exporting in 1995, 87 per cent had export values of less than Rs. 50m, whilst 5 per cent had exports within the range Rs. 50m–Rs. 100m. Only 5 per cent of firms had export values in excess of Rs. 200m. This means that a small number of firms account for a majority share of the export earnings in Sri Lanka.

With regard to policy, one of the main features dominating textiles in Sri Lanka is the withdrawal of the MFA. Since 1989, one of the main changes within the export sector has been the switch in balance between quota and non-quota exports. The USA is the largest export market for Sri Lankan garments. In 1989, only 3 per cent of exports were non-quota items. By 1994 this proportion had risen to 22.5 per cent. Given the withdrawal of the MFA quota system, this reduction in reliance on quota exports seems like a sensible policy.

The Ghanaian textiles industry can only aspire to this Sri Lankan success. Since the introduction of the ERP, the sector has been subject to a significant number of firm exits. This exodus has been concentrated in the large- and medium-scale sector. In 1987, there were 78 firms employing more than 30 people, but by 1995 this had declined to 32. Figures in the small-scale sector are virtually impossible to estimate exactly, but according to the Ministry of Industry, of the 1508 firms registered in 1987, only six remain in production. This reduction in small-scale firms may not, however, be the result of liquidation, but rather the result of firms opting out of the formal registration system, a system that is not effectively enforced.

The decline in productive enterprises has been particularly marked amongst the large- and medium-scale enterprises originally established under the import substitution policies of the 1960s and 1970s. Problems with the Cotton Marketing Board and an inability to buy imported cotton at cheap prices, due to the shortage of foreign exchange, resulted in a lack of competitiveness in the textiles industry in Ghana. The years of protection further eroded any competitive potential by allowing firms to survive with inadequate technological bases, which resulted particularly in problems with consistency in quality (Lall, 1994). Competitiveness is yet again undermined by the industry's dependence on imported inputs that progressively became more expensive with devaluation.

Above all, however, the domestic industry has been undermined by an inability to compete in domestic markets with three main competitors:

(a) Raw cotton lint could be imported more cheaply from China than it could be produced domestically.

(b) Traditional producers were hit by the import of cheaper, mass produced cloth from Côte d'Ivoire, including printed (as opposed to woven) *kente* cloth.

(c) The domestic market has been swamped by the import of cheap second-hand clothes from the West. Domestic garment producers lost their market, and textile producers lost their customers.

The decline of mass-produced textiles in Ghana has resulted in a shift away from formal, large units and towards smaller, more informal, flexible units. One side-effect of this has been to significantly reduce the influence of trade unions. The picture is not all one of devastation, however. There are two areas deserving of further attention: foreign investment and small-scale entrepreneurs.

The foreign influence is present in Ghana, not only through the historical British relationship, but also through Chinese and Lebanese capital. Historically, the Lebanese have been involved in trading activities within the country, and this has been expanded through the presence of a sizeable Lebanese community involved mainly in the service industries and trade, but also, albeit to a lesser degree, in manufacturing industry.

Within textiles, the most prominent group of foreign investors is Chinese. China has developed a relatively close relationship with Ghana. Much of the machinery employed in the textiles industry is of Chinese origin, and around 40 per cent of the formal textiles industry is foreign-owned, or subject to joint venture arrangements, virtually all of which are Chinese. Volta Garments has been generally regarded as one of the success stories of this new textiles industry. Existing within its own virtual EPZ at Akosombo, this factory imports virtually all of its inputs, and then re-exports finished goods. The Ghanaian government has granted permission for a number of other manufacturing units to follow Volta's example in importing part-finished tee shirts, sewing them up, and then re-exporting.

Whether this has benefits in the short term, it has long-term implications with regard to the sustainability of the textiles sector within Ghana. In particular, many current Ghanaian enterprises are stopping their own manufacture, clearing their shopfloors of machinery and leasing premises to traders and Chinese import/export agencies. This is considerably easier and less risky than being involved in manufacturing. In the longer term, the reasons for this Chinese investment will disappear. With the phasing-out of the MFA, the severe quota restrictions will be removed on exports from all countries. Ghana is currently not subject to any quota, hence the reason for moving there. Most of the Chinese firms are involved in quota avoidance, but with the removal of quotas on, for example, Sri Lankan exports of tee shirts, why should the Chinese continue to locate in Ghana?

The second area of development is far more positive. There has been a growth in small-scale firms, not only producing, for example, school uniforms, but also producing for export. Most of these firms are controlled by market-oriented, well-trained women entrepreneurs who have experience in textiles design, frequently gained in Europe. This dynamic group produces 'Afrocentric' goods for the US market and, increasingly, South Africa (for detailed analysis of the US market see Biggs et al., 1994). US buyers, such as Pier 1, have a high profile within Ghana, drawing on the rich mixture of textile designs and styles ranging from Nigerian *splash* to Ghanaian *kente*. The firms predominantly consist of a permanent core of staff, with an additional group of temporary workers brought in to produce larger orders. Perhaps unsurprisingly, these entrepreneurs were positive about the reforms' effects in making labour markets more flexible and trade more open.

Whereas the story of Ghanaian textiles is one of decline with occasional bright spots, the Zimbabwean industry has enjoyed (or endured) an fluctuating history under the reform process. More accurately, the industry has experienced a down then up history. An initial downturn in fortunes with the introduction of foreign competition was followed by a partial recovery. However, this recovery came to a rapid halt with the onset of drought in 1992 and a trade dispute with South Africa involving the South African government protecting its own industry by raising tariffs. Consequently, some Zimbabwean exporting firms lost around 70 per cent of their markets. The sector is also import-dependent, with over 60 per cent of inputs being imported, usually through South Africa. By the mid-1990s, the recovery remained weak, with the number of firms failing to reach the 308 present in 1990.

Around 20 per cent of the industry's 300 firms are engaged directly in export, a handful of which produce large volume runs for foreign markets. Typically, around 70 per cent of production of these firms is exported. By contrast, the remainder of the firms are producing predominantly for the domestic market, with less than 25 per cent of their production being exported. Clothing exports have actually increased throughout most of the 1990s, despite the collapse in the South African markets (this has been partially remedied following the conclusion of a new agreement).

In the spinning and weaving sector there are only six firms, employing around 12 000 people. Two of these firms provide over 75 per cent of the fabric used in the domestic market, a legacy of the initial vertically integrated system. Historically, the textiles sector has been highly protected, somewhat enforced during the UDI period, consequently, the system moves from cotton farming through to the supply of garments to the sizeable domestic market. This has left a legacy similar to that of India, of poor and outdated technology and a lack of competitiveness. In addition, the Zimbabwean system has been highly unionised and, consequently, highly inflexible in terms of the international market. This is exacerbated by a lack of subcontracting relations between firms, and particularly between the larger firms and the extensive small-scale sector, that tends to manufacture products for highly localised markets.

The historical legacy of supplying predominantly the domestic market has led to further problems with the increase of imported second-hand clothing. It has been estimated that second-hand clothing from Europe accounts for around 40 per cent of domestic consumption (KSA, 1996). This has been a particular problem for the Zimbabwean industry because the very sector they compete in is mainly the lower end of the market – precisely the end being squeezed by cheap imports. Main competitors include Turkey, the Czech Republic and most of Southern Europe. Compared to these, Zimbabwe is currently more expensive, less productive and less market-oriented. In addition, investment ratios are relatively low, and there is a shortage of human resource skills, particularly in design and marketing. Quality control is also a serious problem for the Zimbabwean industry, with most firms typically reporting 85 per cent of deliveries being late – an unsatisfactory record on the international stage.

Conclusions

Overall, the experience of all four countries, in terms of reforms and the resulting industry histories, covers a wide spectrum. All four reform packages have a set of common elements incorporating exchange rate liberalisation, the relaxation of trade regimes, the reduction of price controls, the encouragement of foreign investment, tax reform, retrenchment, privatisation and deregulation. Adjustment programmes set the background framework within which the entrepreneurial environment exists. Above all, the background of liberalisation provides a completely new set of incentives for entrepreneurs to respond to. The test of strength for an economy is therefore the ability of an industry to respond to these incentives.

The four countries examined represent radically different economic structures. The Ghanaian textiles industry has virtually collapsed, the Indian textiles industry has a variety of experiences in terms of restructuring, the Zimbabwean industry is struggling to cope with international competition and the industry in Sri Lanka is regarded as a model for development, but has its own problems.

In short, the task facing the Ghanaian industry is firstly to cope with the radical restructuring within the industry, particularly the collapse of the medium- and large-scale mass textile producers. At the same time, the government needs to take responsibility for supporting an enabling environment for both the foreign investment that is finding its way to Ghana, and, perhaps more important in the long term, the small-scale firms competing in international markets and exporting high-value, niche products to the lucrative US and European markets.

The Zimbabwean story is slightly different. Whereas in Ghana, there has been a history of hostility between public and private sectors and the public sector remains dominant, the Zimbabwean private sector consistently contributes around 30 per cent of GDP, and a spirit of 'peaceful coexistence' has existed between the government and the predominantly white-owned manufacturing sector. The besieged nature of the Zimbabwean private sector means that a degree of coherence has been retained with a plethora of business organisations and representative bodies. In contrast to Ghana, the relative strength of the private sector acts as a positive background for industrial promotion activities. It should also be noted that the Zimbabwean trade union movement has become closely allied to the business community, in a form of unholy alliance against the government. Many textiles firms are able to stabilise their production over a period of time by negotiating pay deals in advance with trade unions, and in general, union officials tend to be supportive of business claims that government is hampering industrial development.

The main challenges facing Zimbabwean industry are related to an inability to cope with international competition. The historical structure of the industry, established to serve a protected domestic market, has meant that existing firms lack competitiveness and the modern technology that would enable them to compete on an international stage.

The Indian industry is far larger than that in any of the other countries considered here, but there are clear similarities in its situation. In particular, the emphasis on import substitution, admittedly for a huge domestic market, has led to a similar position to that of the Zimbabwean industry. The textiles sector can be split into three distinct groups: mills, powerlooms and handlooms. Of these, the mill sector was deliberately discriminated against, the aim being to benefit the rural handloom sector. However, the history of this set of policies is that the powerloom sector has been the one section of the industry to benefit. Effectively filling in for the lack of production due to restrictions on the mill sector, the powerloom sector has been able to provide supplies of textiles at lower prices than either of the two other sectors.

The spectacular growth of the powerloom sector has not been mirrored by a spectacular growth in exports, even though they have increased since the 1950s. This illustrates clearly the powerloom sector's role in filling in for domestic demand. The ready availability of second-hand machinery and the Indian capacity for improvisation, has produced a sector that cannot compete with the international market without a significant increase in funding for modernisation. The requirements of the international market, particularly with regard to consistency of quality, demand that textiles can be produced to order. Currently, the powerloom sector does not produce cloth of sufficiently high quality to compete with, for example, the Hong Kong textiles industry. One of the main challenges facing the Indian textiles industry is to help build this domestically successful industry into an international force.

The Sri Lankan story is almost exactly the opposite of this. The textiles industry barely existed in Sri Lanka in 1977, at the beginning of the first stage of reform. Since then, it has grown at spectacular speed into an international industry supplying all of the main markets of the world. The driving force behind these developments has been international capital striving to circumvent the quota restrictions of the MFA, and seeking the financial safety of EPZs. The challenge facing the Sri Lankan industry is to apply the skills developed in the international industry to the domestic industry. The long-term development of the Sri Lankan textiles industry relies on the government and private sector acting together to develop backward linkages to match the success of the outward ones.

Having examined the business environment and response, I will now move on to look at what government support agencies can do about them.

4
The Structure of Business Support Systems

Introduction

This chapter outlines the background and structure of the business support systems that exist in each of the four countries. Its starting point is the inherent weaknesses within the private sector and moves on to examine the organisational responses to them. Many of the weaknesses have already been touched upon in previous chapters, but not articulated as a clear list of problems and needs faced by the sector. The aim of this analysis is to outline the main areas of government intervention required by the private sector itself, and then to move on and identify areas where the state has in fact intervened. Analysis of the responses of government to private sector needs provides a framework for analysing the external factors affecting the capacity of business support agencies. The final section of this chapter examines these external factors in detail.

Structural weaknesses in the private sector

I have already outlined the basic experiences of the textile industry across all four countries. In undertaking the research, extensive interaction with managers and entrepreneurs revealed a series of basic recurring 'structural weaknesses' (see also Development Researchers Network, 1994; PEF, 1996; Gunning, 1994; Slater et al., 1997). These imply a series of market failures that, in turn, imply a series of potential interventions by government in support of manufacturing industry. In a sense, they also imply a failure of the institutions to address the issues adequately and reflect the attitude that once the incentives have been changed, industry will merely respond (Lal, 1995).

Firstly, there has been a *lack of incentives for medium- and long-term investment*. This has been exacerbated by a degree of 'crowding-out' by the public sector and excessive regulation in the case of India (particularly in the mill sector). The vastness of the Indian market, the measures designed to curtail the mill sector in favour of the handloom sector, and the availability of cheap second-hand machinery, have all acted as disincentives for the most efficient sector, the powerlooms, to invest in improved productive techniques.

Investment has also been affected by the severity of financial repression under adjustment. High inflation, devaluation and punitive interest rates,[1] have all militated against long-term investment strategies. Persistent public sector deficits in Ghana and Zimbabwe have also prevented financial markets providing ready sources of funds for investment, by dragging finance into government bonds with shorter maturity periods and guaranteed returns, and the inter-bank market. In such a market, the longer term, more risky course of manufacturing is bound to lose out.

There is a general tendency for banks to be risk-averse in their lending strategies. This has tended to particularly affect the smaller enterprises – those expected to construct a new industry after the older, larger firms have exited. Alternative sources of finance are difficult to come by, unless, as in the case of Sri Lanka, there is a deliberate strategy of out-sourcing on the part of multinational companies. The lack of financial depth is a feature of Ghana and Zimbabwe, where it is difficult to raise finance for machinery and expansion. Even the financial market in Zimbabwe, which is relatively well developed, is reliant on the vagaries of the weather and harvests through its reliance on Old Mutual (Harvey, 1996). This has led to a situation where companies have been unable to pay credit interest, even when profits have been rising.

Across all four countries there is a *lack of clear government support* for the reform process, and for the private sector in particular. Confidence is a fragile thing, and the private sector needs to be supremely confident in the reform process before investment is likely to take place. Ghana is a particularly good example of this. The Ghanaian private sector talks frequently about the lack of clear government signals of its commitment to private sector development. Despite efforts to build bridges between the public and private sectors, a gulf remains, resulting from decades of hostility towards the private sector. Lack of confidence has not been helped in Ghana by:

- A slowdown in privatisation and a perceived lack of transparency.
- Perceived delays in cost-cutting at the central government level.

- Delays in controlling inflation.
- Perceived centralisation of services by government.
- Lack of political commitment to private sector development.

All these perceptions, whether true or not, serve to adversely affect the confidence of the private sector. In many ways, the situation is far worse in Zimbabwe, where the ethnic issues surrounding private business serve to add fuel to the fire, providing government with a ready-made and often-used political target.

There are a series of issues relating to timing of the reforms and a *lack of preparation for adjustment.* Many of the enterprises subject to divestiture, for example, have gone out of business, and even when divestiture has been successful, the reduction of protection has resulted in a high rate of business failure. This was outlined above in the textile sector, where the number of closures of Ghanaian firms, for example, has been spectacular. There has been a lack of an 'adjustment period' in order to allow industry to alter practices in line with international competition, and to allow businessmen to adjust their attitudes and knowledge base in order to be properly prepared. This has been exacerbated by a lack of skills, experience and capital to compete with international companies used to operating in world markets.

An additional example can be taken from Zimbabwe. The export incentives put into place at the beginning of ESAP were removed in January 1994, which coincided with an improvement in the domestic market (despite 'dumping' and second-hand imports). Several of the large firms that had previously been exporting, returned to the domestic market, where they could sell their products with relative ease, putting out several indigenous firms which had moved into manufacture for domestic markets, but could not compete against larger firms with better access to credit and raw materials (Zimconsult, 1995).

The powerloom sector in India has been growing rapidly as a result of its domestic competitiveness, but still exports only a small proportion of its output. As a result of lack of technological investment, quality control and human resources for marketing, the industry has suffered from international competition. Whilst many of the larger mills have developed international contacts and have attracted investment, the smaller units in the powerloom sector have not, as yet, been successful in working together to pool skills and resources to facilitate international competition, or break out from either low value, or niche markets.

One of the most frequent problems cited by entrepreneurs was *lack of credit*.[2] Even those sources of investment currently available have not been easy to access, or very transparent. Banks give little credibility to loan applications for all of the reasons outlined at the beginning of this section. The Business Assistance Fund, which was set up by the Ghanaian Government to facilitate the provision of credit to industry, appears to have been used to prop up failing businesses rather than encourage new ones.[3] In addition discussions within the Ministry of Trade and Industry (MTI), and with groups of small-scale entrepreneurs in the textiles sector, pointed to the fact that most of this money was going to large-scale factories which were in danger of going out of business, rather than encouraging new industries to grow, something echoed loudly in Zimbabwe where the banking sector is notoriously conservative, restricting credit to those with positive credit histories. Even in India, with relatively developed financial services, larger mills find it easier to access credit than the smaller powerloom operators.

If asked, most entrepreneurs will cite lack of credit (even at a commercial rate) as the main constraint facing them (see, for example, Jackson, 1996; Slater et al., 1997). In addition, the Private Sector Roundtable Group of the Private Enterprise Foundation (PEF) in Ghana cites the lack of finance from both the bank and non-bank financial sectors as the single most serious constraint facing the private sector (PEF, 1993). The lack of a non-bank financial sector is a serious constraint on investment. As a benchmark measure the World Bank estimates that non-bank finance in Ghana amounts to only 4 per cent of GDP. This may be compared with 30 per cent of GDP in Malaysia and 65 per cent in Singapore as an indicator of lack of financial depth (World Bank, 1993). The fact that a stock exchange has been established is a positive long-term development, however, since its inception it has failed to raise significant funds other than for investment in gold (and Unilever). There is a lack of capital for investment.

In response to the lack of domestic investment, all four countries have attempted to attract foreign direct investment (FDI) within sectors other than in natural resource extraction (which is an area of are well funded, traditional exports). To achieve this all the governments included in this study have changed the roles of their respective investment organisations from those of control and regulation to one of promotion. In addition, legislation provides simpler investment codes and additional incentives such as corporation tax relief and repatriation of earnings. However, Ghana has been slow in implementing the new law and this delay weakened confidence within the investment community

(EC, 1994). The delay has prompted the World Bank to say: 'Unless more vigorous steps are taken, Ghana may miss the opportunity to exploit FDI in support of economic growth' (1993: 63).

International experience has shown that FDI tends to increase in line with domestic investment. Unless indigenous entrepreneurs are willing to invest, it is doubtful that foreigners will (World Bank, 1993). The key to raising investment is thus to provide incentives for Ghanaians, Indians, Sri Lankans and Zimbabweans to invest in their own economies. Sri Lanka has managed to find a way to buck this trend to a degree, but its reliance on overseas 'footloose' investment, is providing its own set of problems. In particular, with the phasing-out of the MFA, there is some concern that some of this investment will leave the island and return 'home'. The reliance on just one chief product, apparel exports, has also led to some concern within the Government of Sri Lanka with regard to dependence and inflexibility (Slater et al., 1997).

To a degree, but perhaps most in frequently Sri Lanka, Zimbabwe and Ghana, industry suffers from a *lack of capacity in business planning*, sometimes due to the fact that entrepreneurs find it difficult to think ahead due to financial constraints and uncertainty. Lack of working capital and credit prevent long-term planning and, in many cases the ability to take up contracts with foreign buyers over medium and long term periods. Numerous examples were cited in interviews (see Jackson, 1996). For example, one firm in Ghana which was going out of business had an order for various garments for the US but the bank refused to loan the money to buy the inputs required. Many larger firms cite uncertainty over inflation and the accompanying interest rates as major obstacles to any long-term planning.[4]

Zimbabwean firms suffer particularly from a lack of marketing skills which is partly a result of their historical legacy. In addition, there is a shortage of strong indigenous design capacity, which is not the case in Ghana. Zimbabwe has no equivalent to *kente* or *splash*; thus the kind of lucrative niche markets which are open to Ghanaian exporters to the USA (and increasingly South Africa) are not open to Zimbabwean firms. Similar problems are present within the Sri Lankan industry (Slater et al., 1997). Entrepreneurs cite a whole series of managerial problems directly affecting the industry, including:

- Lack of suitably qualified managers and operators, particularly machinists, foremen, supervisors and middle-managers.
- Non-existent marketing function.

- Lack of design skills.
- Rigid labour laws, and inflexibility in the labour market.

Sri Lanka's textiles industry, for all its success, remains a tailoring industry, not a fashion industry. Sri Lankan firms do not take part in the high-value activities of design and marketing, they just manufacture. This is very similar to the situation in Zimbabwe, where the design function is extremely weak and marketing has traditionally been poorly handled.[5]

The chief exception to all of this is India, which has a multitude of skills. Unfortunately they tend to be concentrated in the mill sector, not the powerloom sector. The most effective producers within India, therefore are caught in the same trap as those in Sri Lanka. They produce low-value, low-quality textiles, rather than building on their advantages and moving more up-market into design, fashion and niche markets, where their shorter print runs, increased flexibility and speed of production could be used to their most advantageous.

There are common problems of *low operating capacities and productivity* stemming from low wages, poor working practices and limited access to modern technology and skills. Many of the entrepreneurs interviewed cited the problem of a 'missing middle' in the labour market. For example, one of the firms visited in Ghana had no problem getting qualified tailors (who, of course, demanded qualified tailors' wages), or people off the street who could be trained up, but there were no workers available with any experience of working with a sewing machine on a production line. The problem is primarily lack of skilled artisan labour but this is compounded by a lack of middle management skills such as marketing, quality control and sourcing (Biggs et al., 1994). This pattern is repeated in Sri Lanka, where the highly skilled tend to move into the international firms, and there is a shortage of middle management.

Poor working practices have led to inflexible working systems particularly in terms of inter-firm linkages. Subcontracting is an important element of most international textile and clothing businesses and yet it is relatively undeveloped in both Ghana and Zimbabwe. In both cases there are two main problems. The larger firms are not designed in such a way as to facilitate the use of subcontractors, a function of both the historical legacy of Taylorist work patterns, and also the high transaction costs of enforcing contracts with other firms, and, secondly, the smaller firms resent being placed in a 'subordinate' relationship to the larger firms, preferring their own independence. This lack of a 'production network' severely compromises the flexibility in production required to climb the value added chain in international markets. It restricts the capacity to compete for anything other than poor-quality, low-profit-margin mass-produced garments.

Subcontracting and flexibility can have their disadvantages, however. Sri Lankan firms frequently produce for large international firms, but, consequently, fail to develop themselves. There is an overall low level of backward integration, specifically referring to weak links between the garments industry and accessory industries that produce items such as labels, hangers, buttons, zip fasteners, etc. This is primarily because of weaknesses within the subcontracting industries themselves in terms of poor quality, limited production capacity, high cost of production (hence the relative cheapness of importing), and poor institutional structure for sub-contracting (Kelegama, 1986).

Quality control is a specific issue in international markets with regard to textile exports. The wide availability of cheap, high-quality and consistent textiles has been a problem for all four countries (Sri Lanka to a lesser extent). India in particular has been said to have gained relatively poor performance in textile export markets primarily due to poor quality of its exports (Misra, 1993). In addition, importers of Indian yarn in the EU and USA regard the number of faults, defects, damage and stains to be unacceptable. They also complain of higher shrinkage rates during wet processing, and lack of reliability, and consequently, regard imports from China, South Korea, Hong Kong, Peru, Colombia, Brazil and other competitors as being superior to the Indian product (Misra, 1993). In other words, the Indian export industry needs to expand beyond price, into non-price determinants of trade competitiveness.

Most firms across the sector in all four countries use *poorly maintained or outdated technology*. Historically, there has been a lack of credit to replace machinery or even to buy spare parts for existing machinery. Second-hand machinery is readily available for garment manufacture and weaving, but entrepreneurs claimed that historically regulations had prevented them getting hold of it, and that at present, price was also a chief prohibiting factor. In fact second hand machinery is available even in more up to date technology. One group of garment manufacturers in Accra was grouping together to purchase a computer-aided design tool (CAD) which could be shared by a group of companies. The main problems were lack of finance and access to space, both of which could have been facilitated through the Business Assistance Fund, but were not. One of the larger firms interviewed further added the point that even where the machines were in place, if anything happened to them then spare parts were difficult to obtain.

Problems in Zimbabwe have been exacerbated by haphazard access to foreign exchange. Perhaps one year a firm would be granted a certain allocation of foreign exchange but be denied it the next. By the time the next allocation was granted the technology had changed. Firms were therefore left with a mixture of sometimes incompatible machinery within the same factory unit.

Many entrepreneurs in Ghana feel that the government places technology and research and development too low in its list of priorities (Private Sector Roundtable Group, 1993). There are poor links between the technology institutes and business; and those organisations which have met with some success are constrained in their activities due to lack of funding (for example, Ghana Regional Appropriate Technology Transfer Services (GRATIS) which has an excellent reputation within its narrow field but is constrained through lack of money).

Even in the market closest to the international trade, Sri Lanka, the inadequacy of capital means that many firms cannot modernise their technological base. Slater et al. (1997), also describe a technological backwardness with respect to specific sectors of the textiles industry, including lack of use of open-ended machinery and the continued use of shuttle-less wearing machines. Design capabilities are further hampered by a lack of modern design technology and cutting tools. CAD tools not only improve the accuracy of design and cutting, but can also reproduce exactly the same features over and over again, thus improving the consistency of quality of production. A desire to move up the value chain from low-quality, cheap production into higher-value industrial development must be matched by new technologies to facilitate competition with international companies.

Even India, with its relatively highly developed high-tech industries, has failed to update its older industries such as textiles. Lack of modernisation has been regarded as one of the major contributory factors of 'sickness' in the Indian mill sector, although the reverse may be true, with poor financial management prohibiting upgrading of machinery (Misra, 1993). In fact, widespread upgrading of those mills producing for the domestic market did not make economic sense, since the real cost of labour to the economy is so low, the costs of introducing labour-replacing machinery may be greater than the benefits. Modernising the export sector, however, is the only option for expansion into lucrative export markets.

There is *inadequate infrastructure* particularly for export; roads, rail, ports and airports all need further development. In addition, even where they do exist there is usually insufficient storage space or premises. The main focus of the World Bank's financial aid in Ghana has been infrastructural redevelopment, but even then, the World Bank representative believes that it will take several years of investment for the road network to attain the level at which it was operating in 1957.[6] Textile firms in Zimbabwe and Ghana report infrastructural deficiencies in almost all areas of infrastructure. The worst are undoubtedly telecommunications, water and electricity. The textile sector uses considerable amounts of both electricity and water in its processing of cloth and any interruption (particularly unannounced) leads to significant lost production and therefore cash.

The story is repeated in Sri Lanka, where outside the EPZs, infrastructure is regarded as being poor (Slater et al., 1997). Inadequate infrastructure in telecommunications, electricity and transport are the root cause of the lack of competitiveness in much domestic industry.

There has been *low capacity/credibility (in government) of business associations* to represent the sector as well as carrying out tasks such as marketing and information exchange. The Association of Ghanaian Industry (AGI) in Ghana represents 'old' industry and is largely discredited amongst its members.[7] The whole issue of dialogue between the government and business in Ghana is a problematic one given the turbulent history and the government's historic dislike of business. In Zimbabwe the situation is more complex in that there are parallel organisations for representation of business, the Confederation of Zimbabwean Industry (CZI), which is the historical organisation originally associated with white businessmen and the Zimbabwe National Chamber of Commerce (ZNCC), established to represent indigenous business after Independence. This said, industrial representation is still dominated by the CZI, which has an excellent reputation amongst the business community and is active in terms of dealing with and providing information to, government.

The Indian picture is far more complex, with an intricate web of representative organisations at local and national level. The main issue is the lack of representation of the powerloom sector, and the sheer size of the groups being represented. Perhaps more than most, those industries that are small and far away from the centres of textile power in Ahmedabad, Bombay and Coimbatore (the 'ABC' of the mill industry), do not feel represented. The situation is not helped by the fact that many of the representative organisations and associations are regarded as amenable to control and 'guidance' by the Ministry of Textiles (Slater et al., 1998).

Lack of information, particularly with regard to export markets, competitors and quality is a potentially fatal flaw in any competitive system. Most indigenous manufacturers are handicapped by a lack of information dealing with the complexities of foreign retailing organisations. Many firms, except perhaps in Sri Lanka, fail to establish direct links with foreign retailers and thus are unaware of packaging, labelling, printed material regulations, as well as several buyer specifications (Biggs et al., 1994). The failure of Ghanaian and Zimbabwean firms to develop overseas distribution networks through agents could severely dent their export potential. Against that, several US firms, such as Pier 1, regularly visit their suppliers in Ghana and fieldwork showed that several smaller firms exporting garments maintained regular distribution networks via agents or directly with foreign retailers. In fact, since Ghana has developed a reputation for African designs and prints and its firms have delivered on contracts, other US firms now appear to want to deal directly in Ghana. Without the advantage of market niches, Zimbabwe competes in the cut-throat export market of mass-produced garments along with most of East and South Asia as well as India and Sri Lanka. In such a market, information, particularly with regard to opportunities in the lucrative European market is crucial and being able to market properly doubly so.

The dependence of Sri Lankan firms on their foreign contractors is partly a function of their lack of information about international markets. Increased information would not only allow them to find alternative selling solutions, for example through agents, but also to shop around for improved supplier deals. Particularly if the work was of sufficiently good quality, a reliable subcontractor could be worth a considerable fee. This is, of course, a risky strategy in a cut-throat market. In fact, the need for Indian firms to form alliances and link-ups with international firms is primarily to gain access to information networks as well as markets (Misra, 1993).

Quality control has already been touched upon above, but remains sufficiently important to merit a reinforcement. Many of the small firms involved in the industry have a core of 10–20 regular employees with additional labour being called in to fulfil larger orders. With a lack of reliable machinery this can lead to significant differences in quality and product specification (size, number of stitches). In addition, a lack of recognised, qualified staff can also lead to differences in quality due to lack of training and experience, inadequate skills on particular machines, etc. Effective standards boards could play a crucial role in improving the quality attained by exporters in terms of providing information, holding quality control workshops and training courses and in encouraging the development of International Standard IS9000 attainment within firms. India, amongst others, has identified this element of non-price competition as being crucial to the expansion of export markets and instrumental in the poor history of exports relative to East Asia (Slater et al., 1997).

Quality control can be enhanced by technology, but one of the primary reasons why quality remains inconsistent is a lack of qualified personnel to manage the quality process. All four countries have inadequate training facilities for their textile industries. In addition, standards sufficient for export are difficult to achieve within the environment and with the technology available to the powerloom sector in India. This could be an important constraint the powerloom sector's continued growth throughout the 1980s and 1990s.

The response of the state: institutional frameworks

Given this comprehensive list of weaknesses, the scope of government intervention in the form of either deregulation (intervention through withdrawal) or constructing an enabling environment is extremely broad and complex. It is clear that entrepreneurs find it increasingly difficult to respond to the new set of incentives provided by structural adjustment programmes and the rigours of the international market. All of these factors are produced by institutional inadequacies, in the Northian sense of institution, and virtually all of them may be overcome by some form of support service, whether inspired or provided by the state. The institutional environments in all four of the core countries are different. Thus this section outlines the institutional structures currently existing within each of them in turn, with the aim of informing the debate surrounding external factors affecting capacity.

Institutional responses in Ghana

What is missing across most of SSA, including in Ghana, is an institutional network providing a comprehensive industrial system. Most firms in SSA exist as atomistic producers, not as elements in an integrated system. In addition, the obsession with macroeconomic stability has produced an institutional environment in which firms are relatively unimportant. For example, private banks have no incentives to invest in small firms, no matter how successful they are, because they can make more money speculating on government bonds with prevailing high interest rates. High interest rates in themselves restrict the availability of capital, but one interesting comment from a successful Ghanaian entrepreneur was that she could not get hold of any capital even at a commercial rate.

The GOG has historically taken over ownership of productive assets rather than taking on a facilitating role and enhancing private sector production. As a result there is a relative shortage of economic development agencies in the economy. There are a number of more recent meso-level agencies established with the aim of enhancing particular aspects of economic development. For example, there is an Export Promotion Board, the Ghana Standards Board (GSB), the National Board for Small Scale Industries (NBSSI) and the Ghana Investment Promotion Centre (GIPC). The lack of historical enabling agencies and the financial repression and government budget-cutting throughout the 1980s has produced a dearth of public economic agencies, but at the same time there have been a number of donor-funded initiatives, particularly EMPRETEC, funded by DFID,[8] the Private Enterprise Foundation (PEF), funded by the DFID, and the Association of Small Scale Industries (ASSI) funded by the United Nations Economic Commission for Africa.

The chief perception amongst entrepreneurs in Ghana is, however, that the impact of such agencies has been limited. Many agencies established to remedy the weaknesses in traditional forms of public administration suffer from problems of isolation and limitation (Spath, 1992). In many cases larger, more established firms in urban centres have benefited. In the case of Ghana this has effectively meant that finance has been channelled into failing enterprises. Smaller firms, frequently successful exporters, cited problems in gaining access to some of these services, largely due to risk-averse bureaucratic procedures and qualifications for aid. In addition, there have been problems of lack of communication between organisations. A good example of this is represented by the statistical problems faced in compiling information on small firms. Each organisation has different statistics and there has been no attempt to co-ordinate any of this information. In short, many agencies in Ghana have not only failed to become embedded within the manufacturing sector, but also to network with each other.

The lack of agencies and their relative ineffectiveness outside their immediate groups of firms, has led to an atomistic structure of production in Ghanaian manufacturing. Although most of the industries were established as vertically integrated structures, the demands of international competition mean that flexibility is required not only vertically but also horizontally. The central relationships running through the larger, established firms still remain, but several links in the chain have become unproductive, unreliable or non-viable so they have effectively ground to a halt. At the same time their rigid relationships exclude smaller, more dynamic firms for entering the productive chain. The problems faced by newer entrepreneurs are exacerbated by the lack of help with their capabilities in terms of access to training, marketing, accounting and quality control, the lack of access to finance, and the lack of access to 'natural' markets for small scale producers such as subcontracting to larger firms, something which is almost entirely lacking in Ghanaian manufacturing.

The institutional environment in Zimbabwe

In contrast to Ghana, Zimbabwe has had a long history of establishing meso-level economic development agencies designed to facilitate the private sector. Donor involvement tends to be channelled through existing agencies, much of it directed at small-scale industrial development. The main institutions can be divided into two main groups: government-established institutions and private sector institutions.

The tradition of the public institution in Zimbabwe mainly dates from the UDI period when the then Rhodesian government established several agencies to help the growth of white-owned industry under sanctions. Several of the agencies, such as the Industrial Development Corporation (IDC) and the Zimbabwe Standards Board (ZSB), date from this period. Many of the organisations founded in Zimbabwe exhibit signs of establishment of partnership between the private and public sectors. IDC, for example, was established with private and government money with the aim of spearheading industrial development. The IDC ventured into greenfield projects and built them up until they were operating at a profit. In this way the IDC took on the early risks of business start-up and successes could be used to provide capital for further ventures. After independence the new government attempted to mirror several of these institutions with the aim of separating off indigenous development from the white-dominated system. This has led to the establishment of parallel organisations such as the Zimbabwe Development Corporation (ZDC) which competed for funds with IDC. The experience of the IDC, its successful track record and the fact that it no longer represents only the white community, has entrenched it as the more successful of the two agencies considered.

There are a number of agencies which were established at the time of independence such as the Zimbabwe Development Bank (ZDB) and the Small Enterprises Development Corporation (SEDCO) to complement the existing agencies, but there has been a rapid development in enterprise agencies since the introduction of ESAP and a more outward-oriented manufacturing policy. These organisations include Zimtrade, the trade development organisation, the Zimbabwe Investment Centre (ZIC), the Venture Capital Company of Zimbabwe (VCCZ), the Credit Guarantee Company (CGC) and the Scientific and Industrial Research and Development Centre (SIRDC).

Of these, only ZIC and SEDCO are wholly owned by the GOZ. Zimtrade was established as a joint venture between the public and private sectors, the VCCZ was established as a trust with trustees from the industrial sector, financial companies, the Reserve Bank, the International Finance Corporation and the Commonwealth Development Corporation, and the CGC was established as FEBCO (Pvt) Ltd well before independence as a finance trust for white businessmen. Zimtrade and CGC also benefit from long-term donor support. In the case of Zimtrade, there is an EC programme funding consultants, and in the case of CGC, CIDA has been involved in funding programmes such as those encouraging women entrepreneurs.

There is also a successful company established specifically to provide help to small, black firms. The Indigenous Business Development Centre (IBDC) provides access to capital and represents the indigenous sector to government and aims at the establishment of an enabling environment for small business. The Business Extension and Advisory Service (BESA) section provides business advice nationally to any Zimbabwean seeking assistance and works closely with Zimtrade on potential exporters.

Zimbabwean industry is fortunate to have a relatively coherent and eloquent business sector. It is greatly helped in this by the Confederation of Zimbabwean Industry (CZI), the main historical representative organisation. CZI has an excellent reputation amongst Zimbabwean business and has been supported by USAID in establishing the Zimbabwe Enterprise Development Centre which provides a business link programme to encourage networking and subcontracting amongst Zimbabwean entrepreneurs (Zaaijer, 1997).

As with many agencies established during the UDI period, the CZI has an equivalent established after independence. The Zimbabwe National Chamber of Commerce (ZNCC) was designed to represent indigenous businessmen. Unfortunately for ZNCC, the combined effects of recession and the success of CZI has meant that ZNCC has tended to lose out to its sister organisation in terms of membership.

The meso-level institutional environment for business in Zimbabwe is relatively well developed and comprehensive. Private organisations such as CZI are well respected and public organisations are transforming themselves as ESAP progresses. There is an increasing number of different organisational arrangements present, particularly those which involve public and private sector in some form of partnership, such as trusteeship like CGC or joint ventures like Zimtrade. In terms of this analysis this would initially indicate that Zimbabwean institutions are more embedded in the private sector than Ghanaian institutions.[9]

Furthermore, many have changed themselves as ESAP has progressed and far from becoming less involved in a flourishing private sector, most have become more involved in a still flourishing private sector. For example, Gunning (1994), taking a conventional World Bank neoliberal line, wrote:

> Zimtrade was mentioned several times as only a poor substitute for going abroad yourself, which was difficult because foreign exchange for business travel was rationed. So we expect that the use of a number of these institutions will decrease with the progress of ESAP. (1994: 184–5)

This has not happened, and in fact Zimtrade was spoken about in glowing terms by virtually everyone interviewed during the fieldwork. Zimtrade has expanded its customer base and the services provided. More importantly it has maintained a core of 'regulars' with which it has built up a strong relationship. In addition, many more firms are prepared to pay for services available through Zimtrade (which is no longer a monopoly).

The relevance of each institution is partially shown in usage figures provided by Gunning in his 1994 survey is shown in Table 4.1. Although incomplete, this survey does provide a useful indication of the relative usage of the institutions covered. In particular, it shows that ZIC, Zimtrade, CZI and ZNCC tend to reach a higher proportion of firms than most other organisations (closely followed by NGOs). The Commodity Import Programme was a specific programme established by GOZ, which is now discontinued. It also reveals a lack of funding for smaller organisations such as SEDCO and IBDC at this time, both of which receive many requests for assistance but are only able to help a small proportion. This may be a reflection of the firms using the services

Table 4.1   Usage of business support services in Zimbabwe, 1994

Institution	Assisted	Not assisted	Never heard of
SEDCO	11	174	16
IBDC	8	178	15
NGOs	37	136	28
CZI	84	96	21
ZNCC	46	139	16
Zimtrade	69	112	20
Commodity imports	55	87	59
ZIPAM	35	143	23
Financial institutions	31	144	26
African enterprise	1	44	156
African project	2	61	138
ZIC	41	138	22

Source: Gunning, 1994: 183.

i.e. larger, older firms tend to use the larger organisations and make more use of services in general (Gunning, 1994). In addition, there does not seem to be strong sectoral or locational differences in usage of services.[10]

The institutional environment in India

As, perhaps, we would expect, Indian textiles are governed by a complex web of organisations and institutional arrangements. The Ministry of Textiles controls matters related to the production, distribution and development of textile industries, including handloom, powerloom, ready-made garments, silk and fibres (other than man-made fibres). The Ministry is headed by a minister of state and a secretariat, in turn headed by a senior civil servant. The important element of this is that a minister of state does not carry cabinet rank. As a result, the Ministry has retained a relatively low profile and remained fairly small. Despite this, there are still a number of divisions within the structure, covering all of the main areas of production: cotton, jute, silk, manmade fibres, policy and co-ordination, woollens and powerlooms and export promotion. All of these divisions are subject to the tortuous hierarchy of the Indian bureaucracy.

In addition to this structure, within the textile bureaucracy there are three major subordinate offices, each having its own secretariat and infrastructure. These cover handlooms, handicrafts and textiles production in Bombay. Apart from its formal structure, the Ministry also oversees several autonomous statutory bodies related to textiles, including the Fashion Institute of Technology, the Indian Institute of Handloom Technology and the Textile Committee. There are also a number of public sector corporations, including the National Textile Corporation, the Jute Corporation of India and the Cotton Corporation of India.

The Ministry also performs supervisory functions with respect to a number of boards and councils. Within this group, the following are subject to direct control by the Ministry:

Boards

● Central Silk Board
● Cotton Advisory Board
● All India Handlooms and Handicrafts Board
● All India Powerloom Board

Advisory Development Councils

● Central Advisory Council for the Textile Industry
● Jute Manufacturers Development Council, Calcutta
● Development Council on Modernisation of the Textile Industry
● Standing Council on Modernisation of Textile Industry
● Co-ordination Council on Textile Research Associations

In addition to these, there is a large group of export promotion boards and local associations that does not come under the direct control of the Ministry, but is subject to considerable influence. For a start, each board and council is allocated under a division of the Ministry, and the minister of state decides which board is placed under which division.

The functions of the Ministry are largely regulatory, although there is some intervention in terms of controlling the public sector corporations. The role of the sub-offices of the Ministry in terms of the Office of the Textiles Commissioner (OTC), amongst other agencies, is broader. Originally established in 1943 to regulate and enforce legal requirements and to deal with domestic shortages of fabrics for the war effort, the OTC has become the main conduit for national regulation of the industry. In addition, the OTC, which has a number of subnational offices, is responsible for collecting statistics on textile production and acts as an advisor to the Ministry. As such, the OTC represents an important element of the state framework governing the textiles sector.

Many firms within the textiles industry, however, feel that the OTC has been primarily concerned with the policing of the textiles sector (Slater et al., 1998). This has been to the detriment of a comprehensive development approach. Given this, the OTC has been far more restrictive than constructive, hence many managers within the larger textiles firms feel that the OTC has retarded the growth of the sector. This is perhaps not surprising since much of the job of the OTC has been to regulate the activities of the mill sector, and it does leave open a number of possibilities for future supportive interventions, including acting as an arbiter for fair competition, monitoring international trade, and providing support on quality standards.

There are a number of areas where there have been long-term support agencies in place, in particular, research and development, and human resource development. The Indian textiles industry is the second largest in the world, and, as such, has been subject to a great deal of research and development activity over a number of years. Given the enormous size and geographical spread of the industry, the R&D support has been decentralised into regional institutions, specifically regional textile research associations.[11] These associations carry out comprehensive research activities with package programmes on inputs, machinery and upgradation of technology. These include advice on international standards, cost reduction, quality, and so on.

The activities of these four main institutes are supplemented by a series of specialist institutes that address specific areas of production within the industry. These include the Silk and Art Silk Mills Research Association (SASMIRA), the Man-made Textile Research Association (MANTRA) and additional associations for jute (JIRA), handloom technology (IIHT/DCH), woollens (WRA) and the Central Silk Board (CSB). All of these organisations not only carry out research but also offer consultancy services to the industry. The CSB, based in Bangalore, also formulates programmes for the entire sericulture industry. There are four research and training institutes providing support to sericulture, and several technical service centres providing in-house training in technical issues.

The human resource requirements of the textile industry in India are enormous. Considering the apparel sub-sector on its own, there are currently around 5 million people employed making clothes. This has been increasing steadily since 1990, amounted to some 4 million in 1997, and is expected to reach 6 million by 2003, of whom around 25 per cent are expected to be women.

The garments sector in India has been identified as a major growth area for Indian exports in particular, and total garment exports are expected to double over the next five years. The vast domestic Indian market is also changing with a switch from tailor-made to ready-made garments. The main issue, given the liberalisation of trade in garments, is producing apparel to a sufficiently high level of quality. This expansion and quality improvement will undoubtedly rely upon a vast improvement and increase in the workforce available to the industry.

Currently, there are a vast number of training institutes providing courses in textiles and garment production. These can be broadly divided into two main groups: those dealing with technical and production issues; and those training in design and fashion. Within the former group, most institutes provide a mixture of shorter-term technical 'job-oriented' courses, and longer-term vocational training similar to apprenticeships. The number of institutes providing these courses is huge and the variation in quality also enormous. The total number of such institutes in 1991 was as follows:

	Postgraduate	*Degree*	*Diploma*
Northern Region	70	225	680
Western Region	20	150	545
Southern Region	23	110	782
Eastern Region	—	30	180
Total	**113**	**515**	**2187**

Source: Slater et al., 1998.

The main complaint of the industry with these institutes is that they are not producing the style of training required by the firms. There is believed to be a bias towards theoretical as opposed to practical solutions, and the industry feels that teaching new research on new technological developments is pointless in an industry dominated by resource scarcity, use of conventional, frequently aged machinery, and a virtual absence of technology research. Quality control and consistency in learning is also a critical area, where government intervention may become important.

The fashion trade demands creativity and flair of art, together with the technical knowledge base that is vital to production. In addition, the rapidly developing Indian fashion industry demands increasing professionalism. Management of production and marketing are critical building blocks in constructing a fashion industry that is competitive and economic, rather than merely mercurial. The industry consequently has a large demand for trained professionals in design, merchandising and production management. In order to meet the anticipated growth in demand, to become more competitive and to provide professional expertise to the industry, a number of public and private institutes have grown up across India.

Organisations such as the Pearl Academy of Fashion in Delhi, the JD Institute of Fashion and the franchised Fine Arts College Miami, USA offer places in courses such as fashion design, clothing technology, merchandising, fashion technology and production management. The government itself has also got into the act, with the establishment of two prominent institutes: the National Institute of Design in Ahmedabad, and the National Institute of Fashion Technology (NIFT) in Delhi. NIFT has expanded into a series of regional centres in Bombay, Madras, Calcutta, Hyderabad and Gandhinagar.

Currently, although the training in fashion is increasing steadily, there remain several gaps in the market. In particular, training in foot-wear, accessories, make-up, fashion shows, photography, jewellery and headgear are necessary to complete the fashion picture in India. To date, there has been no significant breakthrough into the world fashion scene, and whilst Indian fashion has been making some headway, the basic training of potential designers needs significant investment.

Institutional support in Sri Lanka

Contrary to the received wisdom of Sri Lanka as a free market example of comparative advantage in action, the state has been a key player in the development of the textiles industry in the country for a number of years. The '200 Garment Factory Programme' within Sri Lanka also serves to guide the investment made by the private sector into wider social and economic objectives. Introduced in 1994, this programme serves to extend the generous concessions made to investors in the Free Trade Zone (FTZ) through the Board of Investment (BOI), to investors across the island. By the end of 1994, this programme had supported around 160 new enterprises, employing some 70 000 workers and generating around 50 per cent of all BOI company export earnings.

The 200 Programme fits into a more general institutional framework serving the textiles industry. Broadly, the main organisations working within this sector can be classified into two groups: those government agencies directly involved in the administrative and support services within the sector; and other technical organisations dealing specifically with support services such as training, testing and research.

The first category includes agencies such as the Board of Investment (BOI), the Export Development Board (EDB), the Ministry of Industrial Development (MID), the Department of Textile Industries (DTI), Lanka

Fabrics Ltd (LFL), the Ministry of Finance and Planning (MFP) and the Textile Quota Board (TQB). The second category is represented by a wide range of government and semi-government organisations such as the Clothing Industry Training Institute (CITI), the Textile Training and Services Centre (TTSC), the Textile and Clothing Technology Dept. (TCTD) of the University of Moratuwa, the National Institute of Business Management, the Foreman Training Institute of the Open University of Sri Lanka, and the Sri Lanka Standards Board (SLSB).

These organisations can be further classified into three different groups in terms of the degree of government control over their activities: ministries; departments; and, non-departmental public bodies (quasi-government organisations). Currently, the Ministries of Industrial Development, Finance and Planning, Plan Implementation, Womens' Affairs, Transport and the Environment are all responsible for the policy management of the public sector industries and the regulation of private sector activities. Departments are primarily responsible for servicing specific industry sectors such as textiles, powerlooms, etc. Finally, non-departmental public bodies (NDPBs) perform and deliver specific services. The NDPBs enjoy a different status from the rest of the public sector. In particular, they have more autonomy in their operations and their staff are outside the restrictions of civil service pay scales.

Since the 1950s all of these types of organisation have played a dynamic role in the economy. Industrial development has been a cabinet-level subject since independence, and, after 1977, the textiles sector, after having been under the Ministry of Industries and Scientific Affairs, became a separate portfolio. With the change of government in 1993, the textile portfolio again became combined with the Ministry of Industrial Development.

Presently, policies and regulations are determined and enforced by the Ministry of Industrial Development (MID). There are a number of organisations that fall directly within the remit of the MID, including the Textile Quota Board, CITI, TTSC, DTI and LFL.

The Textile Quota Board (TQB) was established as an inter-agency committee, with responsibility for maximising utilisation of export quotas under the MFA. Currently, Sri Lanka has bilateral textile agreements with the USA, the EU, Canada and Norway. Quotas are distributed evenly by the TQB and are allocated on the basis of performance quotas and pool quotas. Since quotas have dominated the industry until now, the allocation is critical to the competition within the sector. There are two main methods of allocation:

1. *Performance quotas* are allocated primarily on the past performance of exporters in earning and re-earning quotas through utilisation of export amounts. It is customary in the garment trade – which is characterised by seasonal merchandise – for firms to place orders for exports several months in advance of the actual shipment. Given this, quotas based on past performance provide continued stability and predictability for the exporter as well as the buyer.
2. *Common pool quotas* consist of those quotas remaining unallocated under the performance criteria. They are publicly advertised in the press, and firms are invited to apply for a pool allocation.

To provide flexibility within the export industry, the firms are allowed to transfer performance quotas on a temporary basis during one particular year. Such transfers will be credited to the original holder if the transferee fulfils the order. Payment of export levies on a regular basis is a prerequisite for the utilisation of both performance quota entitlements and common pool allocations. Failure to comply with these requirements incurs a penalty quota.

The DTI has undergone substantial reorganisation since 1990 in response to the a number of important changes. For example, several handloom workshops were handed over to devolved local councils in 1990, and powerlooms and finishing plants previously owned by the department were sold, also in 1990. In 1994, it was decided that the department should curtail all commercial activity, including silk production. Its current role is to improve the quality and productivity of the handloom sector through various support activities such as training and sales promotion. At the same time, LFL has remained a publicly operated commercial company engaged in the marketing of handloom fabrics and the sale of yarn to the handloom industry.

The BOI and the EDB were both established as arm's-length agencies for the promotion of business activities. The BOI was set up as a 'one-stop shop' for all investors, both foreign and domestic. In 1977, the government established the Greater Colombo Economic Commission to handle all inward investment connected to export industry, and it was this board that the BOI replaced in 1990. Formed as an autonomous statutory body responsible to the President, the scope of the BOI has expanded to cover a number of tax and regulatory functions as well as control of support services to a number of companies. In many ways the EDB is a similar organisation, but primarily oriented towards providing export plans, disseminating and gathering information and carrying out market research. At the same time, the EDB also provides direct support to exporters through product development support, market promotion and problem solving for exporters.

Alongside the plethora of government organisations, there are a number of associations involved in representing the firms themselves. The two most important, from the point of view of the textiles industry, are the Apparel Exporters' Association (AEA) and the Ceylon Textile Manufacturers' Association (CTMA). Both of these organisations act as effective channels of complaint from the private sector to government, and have both become powerful and respected lobby groups. For example, a 1977 government decision to allow BOI firms to dispose of 20 per cent of their product in the domestic market after paying a concessionary duty resulted in significant lobbying from the Chairman of the CTMA. He objected on the grounds that this excess stock would kill the domestic production of textiles through excess supply in the domestic market, and, in addition, directly affect a number of firms that rely partly on sales of their high reject rates in the domestic market in order to flourish. The CTMA won the argument.

Conclusions

Briefly, we can state already that there are significant similarities across all four countries in terms of the organisational arrangements used in the promotion of business. Whilst there has been significant change in terms of reform and liberalisation of the respective economies, there has been little innovation in terms of organisational support, rather, the organisations that have existed have either reverted to earlier roles, or taken on new ones. Even relatively new organisations such as the export and investment boards, are hardly innovative in terms of organisational structure. Such boards were a common feature of all four countries from the nineteenth century onwards. What unites all four is the influence of government and the accompanying straightjacket of regulation that has accompanied its hegemony. All four countries are currently emerging from periods where the government played a significant role in direct production of goods for domestic and international markets. This was carried out either by direct management of productive enterprises, or through the direct control of the outputs of private sector companies. With the onrush of rapid reforms and, in particular, the rigours of international competition, those organisations have had to undergo a massive systemic change in their outlooks and ways of doing things. In other words, the institutional systems have had to undergo a sea change in their behaviour and actions. The lack of organisational innovation is therefore accompanied by huge changes in internal management, which we will come to later, and in the institutional environment in which these organisations find themselves. These external constraints affecting the capacity of the organisations to adapt to these changes is the subject of the next section.

External factors affecting the capacity of support agencies

This section addresses the issue of capacity factors directly relating to the relative strengths and weaknesses of the respective private sectors in India, Sri Lanka, Ghana and Zimbabwe. The analysis specifically links the examination of the entrepreneurial environment at the micro level with the broader focus of the chapter, which lies within the capacity of agencies at the meso level of the industrial system.

In many ways the weakness or strength of the private sector is the final arbiter in the success or failure of the agencies which are promoting it. At the same time, the attitudes of the entrepreneurs and the relative economic condition of the firms will have a significant effect on the success or failure of the policies pursued and the range and types of services provided. In this way, *civil–public interaction*, particularly the interaction between public and private sectors, *private sector development*, and *political interference* may be seen as fundamental constraints on the capacity of agencies to perform their roles.

Civil–public sector interaction

As in most of SSA the governments of Ghana and Zimbabwe do not derive the bulk of their support from the private sector. The post-Independence government was committed to socialism and public-sector-driven industrialisation. As a result the private and public sectors regard each other with a considerable degree of suspicion. In Zimbabwe this is exacerbated by the racial issue, particularly with such a high proportion of businessmen being white with links to the previous regime.

Despite this both the government and the private sector have largely coexisted peacefully since Independence and most complaints from the private sector regarding the public sector usually involve slowness and attitude rather than direct hostility and opposition. In addition the President's office has remained above direct involvement in interference in business through favouritism, other than through directed credit programmes to encourage indigenous business. One of the main complaints has been the uncertainty about industrial policy and inconsistency in legislation (such as the early removal of export incentives).

In general, however, civil–public interaction is good in Zimbabwe largely because of the well-supported and effective business associations, CZI and ZNCC, both of which are well regarded by government and carry out their tasks effectively (particularly the dissemination of information). CZI in particular has a high profile and is capable of influencing policy decisions. Historically, CZI has been part of the formal sector/government alliance dating from the colonial era, which has largely continued throughout the 1980s (Skalnes, 1994). Informal sector firms do not have the same degree of representation but they are supported through agencies such as the IBDC and by the CZI and ZNCC, both of which have small business sections. In general, however, the conclusion would have to be that small business is underrepresented relative to large, formal business.

Many Ghanaian entrepreneurs are viewed with suspicion by government and frequently discriminated against because of their size, their ethnic group (Lebanese in Ghana), or simply because the government views them as a threat to its authority.[12]

Weakness in civil–public interaction initially prompted USAID to establish the PEF whose brief includes a role of liaison between the private sector and the government since the original associations designed to do this had begun to fail. It was felt that there was no working interface between public and private sectors for largely historical reasons (which will be examined in more detail in the sections below). Many entrepreneurs still voice doubts over confidence in the Rawlings regime and its commitment to the private sector (PEF, 1993). Many of the organisations, such as the Association of Ghana Industries, still have a lack of confidence in the government. In one interview we were told: 'Certain political utterances by the President against certain local businessmen who have sympathy for opposition parties do not help the private sector.' This was a comment heard in several different organisations, and certainly the PEF documents indicate that a more positive stance from the President would greatly restore confidence amongst the Ghanaian private sector (PEF, 1993).

Such problems, although present, are relatively small in India, where the private sector has played a significant role in the economic growth enjoyed by the country under reform. Although the public sector plays a significant role within the economy as a whole, the democratic nature of Indian politics assures the country of at least a relatively balanced view towards private sector managers and entrepreneurs. The Government of India's view has always been to curb the powers of certain parts of the private sector in order to favour others, and even though there has been widespread public ownership of some enterprises, the main means of control has been through regulation, rather than nationalisation. The reliance on protection of the domestic market and the heavy regulation of the industry has, however, created a different type of public–private sector interaction.

Protection from international competition and the lack of modern technology in the industry has created a group of firms that have become reliant on regulation to maintain their 'competitiveness'. Much of the mill sector, for example, needs modernisation, and has been reliant on guaranteed domestic markets. This, coupled with the fact that the history of direct government control has virtually always been to support sick industrial units, has produced a relatively unproductive publicly-owned sector.[13] Against this, India also has some of the most dynamic firms in the world, and her competitiveness is steadily increasing, particularly in the apparel sector. The Government of India further recognises the importance of this sector to the economy and, consequently, the interaction has undergone a marked improvement. The example of the Indian Chamber of Commerce (see below) is a tangible example of this improvement, and its representation on a number of advisory committees to both Central and State government is further evidence of the positive interaction.

We have already mentioned the role of the AEA and the CTMA in Sri Lanka, above, but their positive efforts in fostering private–public dialogue are of further interest here. The history of state intervention before 1977 provided a damaging background to the current reforms, in that the government was dominant in all aspects of industry. After 1977, the structure of the industry changed markedly and Sri Lanka embarked on a strident pro-market approach with regard to industry. Many firms within the country have little to do with the government, except in so far as they control the quota system. In fact, most firms within the country regard the government ministries as being extremely inflexible and worth avoiding. They are frequently cited as being used for firm registration, quotas, duty rebate (MFP) and some administrative support, but not support service provision. In particular, entrepreneurs within the Sri Lankan textiles industry feel that the government is inflexible with regard to duty rebate schemes and also in restructuring themselves.

Private sector development

The private sector in Zimbabwe is relatively well developed and the manufacturing sector in particular is relatively modern. ESAP has severely hit some firms with many of them going out of business, but the core still remains. The main problems currently facing them are the availability of capital to expand and the high interest rates making the servicing of their debts extremely high. Many companies interviewed reported that they were making profits before interest. In addition, there are shortages within the private sector regarding the capabilities necessary to respond to the incentives offered by ESAP, including a lack of middle-level management and marketing skills. Furthermore, the lack of consistency in government policy has led to many firms suffering from short business horizons.

The economy exhibits several areas of high transaction costs for carrying out business. A survey carried out by the World Bank identifies communications (especially telephones) as the main problem followed by electricity and workers' transport (RPED, 1993). Road networks are good and the government is planning an Export Processing Zone in conjunction with Malaysian capital.[14] The problem with water may be temporary since much power generation is hydroelectric and there was a severe drought in 1991–2.

The problems facing private enterprise in Zimbabwe act as a constraint upon the government's performance of the 'new roles' in that most of these new roles require increased participation of private sector actors in the decision-making and implementing process. For example, the private sector should realistically be involved in the formulation of a long-term industrial strategy otherwise they cannot be expected to have a commitment to that strategy. In addition, the withdrawal of government from certain areas relies either upon the ability of private sector firms to undertake those tasks or existing organisations to act as private sector firms, in some cases becoming private sector firms and providing services for profit. In this case the constraints facing the private sector as a whole will become relevant to those organisations. Agencies facing reductions in budgets from central government and are instructed to raise funding elsewhere, can raise it either by selling their services as a firm would, or by taking loans from the private sector. In such a way, problems in the development of the private sector may act as an external constraint on the operation of government or quasi-government agencies, particularly if there is lack of loan capital and/or the potential customers (i.e. private firms) are suffering financially.

Structural weaknesses of the private sector has severe implications for government capacity to fulfil the new roles identified. Lack of funding has already been established as a major problem in Ghana, and yet many of the new roles require additional funding both from public and private resources. If the private sector is financially weak then it will be unable to take advantage of new incentives offered to it, or to invest in long-term schemes which will eventually bring significant gains, such as research and development and developing relevant training programmes.

In addition to finance, the private sector suffers from a short business planning horizon because of the inconsistency of government policy (PEF, 1993). Private sector entrepreneurs are thus hindered in their long-term planning by lack of finance, low confidence in the government's commitment to the private sector and by uncertainty as to future policy. All of this greatly increases the risks and transaction costs associated with manufacturing.

The private sector operates within an economy characterised by high transaction costs (Herbst, 1993). Infrastructural services (ports, airports, roads, railways) in Ghana are often very weak; statistical services (as we have already mentioned) are inadequate, and communications, particularly telecommunications are poor. Most of the World Bank effort since 1983 has concentrated on rehabilitating the road network, which (despite this effort) will not regain the same state of repair as 1957 until the late 1990s. As Herbst (1993) points out, since the state bears much of the responsibility for this rehabilitation, there will be significant financial flows to the state for some years yet further decreasing the capital available within the economy. Deficiencies in the meta level are transferred through the system, affecting meso, macro and micro levels.

The chief problem within Sri Lanka is related to the foreign dominance of the textiles sector and the lack of backward linkages into the economy. Around 90 per cent of firms import all of their raw materials, and virtually all garment producers on the island concentrate primarily on export markets. Product marketing is usually undertaken by through known clients, buying agencies and buying visits. Most firms also rarely subcontract to other firms in the sector, in line with earlier findings on the lack of linkages within the Sri Lankan garments industry. Whilst the private sector on paper is strong, it is effectively divided into two groups: domestic producers and footloose international firms. The lack of backward linkages further exacerbates the degree of freedom of international capital, and the current concern amongst Sri Lankan policy makers must now be to maintain the economies of agglomeration gained by the concentration of textiles industries on the island. This will presumably entail building linkages with a competitive local industry in order to make the most of the MFA phase out.

The situation in India is far more complicated, due to the variation in production sectors (i.e. handlooms, powerlooms and mills). Historically, the handloom sector was carefully protected by government and it is undoubtedly uncompetitive in terms of straight cost competition. As a sector, therefore, it has an interest in the maintenance of the strict system of controls which have operated in its favour since independence. On the other hand, the mill sector has an interest in lifting the restrictions placed within the domestic market, so that it can compete against the handlooms and powerlooms, but not in the lifting of international restrictions since its lack of modern technology, skills and quality consistency means that it may not be able to compete with international firms. In addition, the powerloom sector is currently the most competitive sector of the textile pyramid, but has benefited from the restrictions placed on the mill sector. Its competitiveness rests on its ability to fill gaps in the domestic market, but a very small amount of material is actually exported. The powerloom sector therefore has a peculiar position with regard to government, since it has traditionally been treated with some degree of disdain as the handlooms were singled out for protection, but at the same time benefited from the restrictions placed on mills. The position of this sub-sector outside the handloom or mill sector, and its composition (mainly small producers), means that it is virtually unrepresented at national level.

The Government of India, at the same time, is receiving very mixed signals from the textile sector as a whole. The high number of associations representing every conceivable fabric at national and regional level, provides a very varied picture of the needs of firms. It is highly likely that the Indian textile industry will benefit from economic liberalisation, but, at the same time, it is also unlikely that the required transition can be achieved without significant pain for at least some of the textiles producers, hence the division of interests between the newer mills and public mills on the one hand and within the powerloom sector itself. It is also clear that the handloom sector that has enjoyed protection for so long is the sector most likely to lose out in terms of mass production, even if it can gain access to lucrative niche markets.

Political interference

Historically the Government of Zimbabwe has interfered extensively in the economy. This has significantly changed since the introduction of ESAP and there is little public sector interference in textiles (except equity involvement in three main textile companies and also the running of the Cotton Marketing Board, the monopoly supplier of domestic cotton). Most private-sector entrepreneurs still show disquiet over uncertain government policy and the delay in cutting public sector deficits which they see as driving up interest rates and thus exacerbating their own problems. On a positive point, however, the role of the President in marketing Zimbabwe abroad was seen as positive, particularly in terms of establishing links with the Far East (particularly Malaysia).

The political structure is very much of the traditional hierarchy model based upon centralised planning. The chief functions of the MIC have altered significantly under ESAP away from the traditional role of licensing and control and towards a more strategic role of framework setting and guidance. MIC itself has not undergone radical alteration in terms of staffing or training and interviews within the textiles department in particular showed that the main functions being carried out were to commission reports from private sector consultants which were then passed to a higher level. Certainly many businessmen interviewed during the research and during other firm-level surveys, and many officials in other organisations dismiss the MIC as being ineffectual in its new role. This is a constraint upon the other organisations dealing with industry such as Zimtrade and ZIC since the upstream functions of co-ordination and policy have not been clearly carried out.

The role of the PNDC government, and particularly the President, was mentioned above. The Ghanaian economy is dominated by SOEs, all of which are open to some kind of political interference and appointment. There is no guarantee that SOEs will be allowed to respond to price signals without political interference (Herbst, 1993). Many entrepreneurs interviewed voiced disquiet at what they claim is political interference gaining SOEs unfair advantage in the marketplace – through access to credit, for example. This was not so significant in the textiles sector, however, since the involvement of SOEs has been significantly reduced and virtually the entire sector is privately operated. In terms of the government agencies themselves, the procedure for appointment will be dealt with in the detailed sections below.

There is a significant body of anecdotal evidence that may point to piecemeal political interference. For example, all export rights at the airport are reputed to be controlled by one individual. According to new regulations, all exporters are to pay for storage at the airport, and the storage is all owned by one entrepreneur who, in effect levies a private tax on all produce shipped out of the airport. As always this type of evidence is difficult to verify, but its importance lies in the number of people in influential private sector positions who relate such stories.[15] This adversely affects confidence in the state and therefore adversely affects the state in carrying out the roles required to provide an enabling environment for that industry. It implies interference, which reduces an orientation to the most efficient approach and to the service of the industry.

This picture of political interference is not repeated to the same degree in either India or Sri Lanka. A number of organisations are structured in exactly the same way as the African institutions – for example, the Export Development Board of Sri Lanka is responsible directly to the President in the same way as the GIPC in Ghana – but the degree, or type of political interference is less parasitic. In Sri Lanka, the Board of Investment is one of the most powerful organisations on the island, and it remains directly responsible to the government. Created out of the Greater Colombo Economic Commission (GCEC), a body that had been open to some political interference, the BOI has successfully managed to co-ordinate investment across the island, overseeing an impressive economic performance. In addition, this has been managed with very little perception of political interference within the BOI. Even if it has taken place, the perception is critically important within the private sector, even more so, when it is considered that the BOI has also merged with the Secretariat for Infrastructure Development and Investment, making the BOI one of the key development organs of the government.

Undoubtedly, one of the factors reducing the effect of political interference within India and Sri Lanka is the strength of the private sector. It indicates not only the success of the public sector, but also the relatively favourable bargaining position enjoyed by business in Asia as opposed to Africa.

Conclusions

This chapter has outlined the external factors affecting the capacity of agencies delivering services to the private sector in the four countries. It began with a detailed analysis of the weaknesses within the private sectors in the countries and related them to the experience of reform shared by all four. In particular, it focussed on key weaknesses related to the strengths and weaknesses of the private sector vis à vis the public sector, and to this end I also examined the historical context and current institutional frameworks of each country. This analysis then led on to the construction of the external factors affecting capacity, which I divided into three main groups: public/private interaction; private sector development and political interference.

Despite significant differences across the four countries, they have all been defined in terms of deep divisions between public and private sectors at some time, and this has frequently been one of the chief causes of the reform process. At the same time, the differences in relative strengths and weaknesses in the private and public sectors do not seem to have had a significant influence over the organisational forms used by government to either regulate or support the private sector. Notable agencies involved in the support systems of the countries primarily comprise government ministries, departments and non-departmental public bodies (sometimes termed executive agencies).

The main difference seems to have been the mix employed in all four, and the modes of regulation. In this respect, India and Zimbabwe stand out as countries where widespread nationalisation happened, but to a limited degree. The private sector remained, but was effectively fenced in by webs of regulation and control. Sri Lanka and Ghana, on the other hand, both followed strategies of direct government control, and to a certain extent the reform processes of each has been partially defined by the divestiture process. In this, Sri Lanka has been markedly more successful than Ghana, and the difference in relative strengths of the private sector has been a key feature of the relative lack of external constraints on the government agencies expected to work with it.

5
Facilitation and Regulation

Introduction

So far we have concentrated primarily on the more general factors affecting all agencies within industry. Structural adjustment sets the context and, to a certain degree, sets the external agenda for any agency seeking to promote industry. This framework effectively governs the other external conditions in terms of the condition of the private sector, public–private sector relationships and the degree to which politicians may arbitrarily interfere with state-sponsored organisations. Making concrete judgements about the external factors affecting capacity of agencies is problematic, if only because the causal relationship between the work of a promotion agency and the actual performance of the industry is a relationship that is difficult to quantify.

One of the assumptions facing the business support sector under structural adjustment is that government will withdraw completely, leaving the capacities examined under this research to relate to the ability to enhance *someone else's* capacity to engage in productive activity. In the case of business, there are so many variables involved that there may not be a direct relationship between the activities of an agency and a clear outcome. One of the points I have tried to make repeatedly is the importance of agencies in relation to a system. It is the linkages within the system that produce competitiveness, not just individual, atomistic organisations, whether they are firms or ministries, consequently one of the most important features of agencies is their ability to network with their clientele and the government, and this is addressed below.

This chapter is the first of two that address the internal capacities of individual agencies within the four countries. Divided by activity into promotion, facilitation, regulation and representation, the agencies are not particularly diverse or innovative with regard to organisational arrangement, rather their relative performances provide the focus of the analysis, given similar formal structures. This chapter begins by looking at what I mean by internal capacity, providing a brief framework of analysis relating back to material in chapter 2. It then moves on, to look at those organisations engaged in facilitation and regulation. Chapter 6 continues the analysis to examine the further two groups of agency covered within the research: representation and promotion agencies.

Which agencies were looked at?

In all, the research took into account several agencies involved in the provision of support services, but took a base of fourteen agencies as a core group.[1] The agencies were spread across all four countries: Ghana, Sri Lanka, Zimbabwe and India. These agencies were: the EDB (Sri Lanka: Export Development Board); BOI (Sri Lanka: Board of Investment); TTSI (Sri Lanka: Textile Training and Services Institute); CITI (Sri Lanka: Clothing Industry Training Institute); AEPC (India: Apparel Export Promotion Council); ICC (India: Indian Chamber of Commerce); CSIR (India: Council of Scientific and Industrial Research); Zimtrade (Zimbabwe); IDC (Zimbabwe: Industrial Development Corporation); ZIC (Zimbabwe Investment Centre); PEF (Ghana: Private Enterprise Foundation); GIPC (Ghana: Ghana Investment Promotion Centre); SAZ (Zimbabwe: Standards Association of Zimbabwe) and MIC (Ghana: Ministry of Industry and Commerce).

This wide-ranging group may be sub-divided in several ways, but the simplest is by activity. They may be divided into:

- Those agencies undertaking some form of *promotional* activity, where the organisational will probably have a marketing- or information-oriented focus, but may of course have a wider role. Agencies such as the EDB and AEPC have explicit roles in terms of promoting exports.
- Those agencies engaged in *facilitation*. Closely related to the promotion role, but more in terms of helping firms meet the demands of the international market through improved working practices, better technology, and so on. Many of these agencies are training institutes or research and development organisations providing services to industry.

- Those agencies *regulating* the industry. In terms of structural adjustment, these organisations have tended to see a huge reduction in activity as deregulation has progressed, although in terms of some specific activities, where regulation of, for example, standards, is necessary to expand export markets, the agency could see a radical increase in activity.
- Those agencies fulfilling a *representative* role on behalf of the private sector. Whilst not necessarily part of the public sector, these agencies pay a crucial role in terms of engaging in policy dialogue and improving the external constraints on capacity facing the industry.

Given the history of the reform process and the plethora of new roles expected of these agencies, it is only expected that there may have been some significant reinvention of roles within the agencies themselves. Apart from subdivision by activity, the groups of organisations may be further subdivided by the success or otherwise of this reorientation process. Put simply, the three basic paths followed by the various institutions have been either stagnation, reorientation or innovation. The agencies in question can be placed in a matrix as shown in Table 5.1.

Of these, the GIPC and ZIC have explicitly moved from a regulation to a promotion role within the period of the reform programme. Both were initially formed from a number of departments previously located in several different ministries and both were formed as 'one-stop shops'. The group of innovating institutions within the promotion column is not particularly surprising. All of them are children of the reforms process in that they address the two main concerns of structural adjustment: investment and exports. There is a thin line between those agencies reorienting and those innovating. For example, part of Zimtrade was previously located in another ministry. The main

Table 5.1   Classification of agencies

	Promotion	Facilitation	Regulation	Representation
Stagnation			MIC	
Innovation	EDB BOI Zimtrade AEPC	TTSI CITI		PEF
Reorientation	GIPC ZIC	IDC CSIR	SAZ	ICC

difference is the fact that Zimtrade was formed for an explicit purpose, rather than as just a means to place dispersed departments together.

The facilitation organisations are, in some ways the most interesting, since they are divided into two clear groups. Those held to be innovating are both training and research institutions established to fulfil a specific role for the textiles industry. Perhaps the most interesting box in the matrix contains IDC in Zimbabwe and CSIR in India. Both of these institutions are long-established organisations set up by government to fulfil roles that have been subverted or at least partially curtailed by government action in the pre-reform period. With the onset of liberalisation, both have been able to reinvent themselves, by not only taking on their original roles, but expanding their own scope as service providers. Both have been able to use their expertise to effectively privatise themselves from the system and become even more arm's length from government, whilst at the same time enjoying certain privileges such as (in IDC's case) some tax dispensation.

In terms of regulation, the plight of most ministries of industry is well-documented (for example, see Alemayehu, 2000 and World Bank, 1997), but the research chose to look at one that had been subject to adjustment for some time. The MIC in Ghana has virtually stagnated under reform, losing all of its original roles. With declining budgets and influence, and only a limited role under liberalisation, the MIC is still looking for a clear role after twenty years of reform. On the other hand, the importance of regulation and the positive role that can be played by organisations encouraging compliance with international regulatory standards is outlined by the experience of SAZ in Zimbabwe.

Finally, having identified private–public interaction as an important external constraint on capacity and a critical element of any economic growth strategy, representative organisations become increasingly necessary. The ICC in India has been trying to reinvent itself as a more representative organisation than in the past, and as a conduit by which the concerns of the business community are articulated to the Indian state. This is a return to its original role, somewhat lost in the pre-reform period. The PEF in Ghana is an attempt to resurrect dialogue between the government and private sectors after the previous difficult history and the collapse of the previous organisation, the Association of Ghana Industries (AGI). The AGI became ineffectual as its members went out of business under liberalisation, and new members were not forthcoming, particularly from the smaller firms who felt that AGI had been compliant with the pre-reform state and represented only those who had benefited from import substitution. The

PEF is an external attempt to construct a membership organisation from the grass roots.

Interestingly, there does not appear to be a clear organisational pattern within or between the groups. MIC is, of course, a ministry directly responsible to government, Zimtrade is a government-owned agency established by an Act of Parliament and governed by a separate Board, AEPC is a private company established under the Companies Act, and IDC is a publicly owned private company (parastatal) with legal autonomy.

The innovation that has taken place has been largely to reinvent old organisational forms rather than to undertake new ones. In particular, the renovation of the agency idea, with an agency established by and Act of Parliament as a 'non-departmental public body' appears to be the main feature of many newer organisations. This may be a function of the fact that the private sector has always had such arrangements, and also that the *formal* arrangements may not matter if *actual* arrangements allow organisations to fulfil their roles, in other words institutions in the sense of 'ways of doing things' are more important than organisational arrangements.

A brief note on internal capacity

Some of this has been covered above, but before analysing the agencies in some detail, it is necessary to provide a note of what factors can be identified in affecting internal capacity of organisations. The internal capacity of organisations determine the level of technical efficiency in service provision and the orientation of organisations towards consumers. The dimensions affecting the internal capacity of organisations can be outlined as follows (following Batley, 1995):

- *the skills and professionalism of personnel and orientation to the consumer*: in other words maintaining and developing skilled and experienced personnel who are highly motivated (and rewarded), and are adept at dealing with donor organisations and international firms. In addition, within government a primary skill would be a medium- or long-term strategic approach, or an understanding of and commitment to 'where we are going'; culture of the organisation, transparency, 'boundaries' around workspaces, attitudes and motivations, and ability to reorganise skills;
- *organisational and administrative structures*: are performance, monitoring and evaluation systems in place?; clear objectives; customer

responsiveness; management and decision-making; fragmentation and information; changes in structure;

- *availability of capital and finance*: both of the above elements of internal capacity rely upon adequate funding. The external conditions in the above section indicate that all government agencies will be subject to severe cash budget constraint, which will impinge on the infrastructure of the organisation itself (such as the availability of computers).

In short, the analysis of the internal capacity of the organisations is three-dimensional, with the first dimension given by the type of activity undertaken, the second by the success or otherwise of the process and the third by the capacity grouping, as above.

Agencies engaged in facilitation

From the sample of 14, four of the agencies analysed were engaged in facilitation of one type or another. By this, I mean that the agency fulfils a general support function through technical support, expertise, research or training. The four agencies within this category include the TTSI and CITI in Sri Lanka, both training institutions, and the IDC in Zimbabwe and CSIR in India. The IDC is a publicly owned private company and CSIR an autonomous organisation registered as a Registered Society with the Prime Minister as an ex-officio President. The nature of the four institutions lends itself to separate analyses of the different types, with the first part dealing with the TTSI and CITI together, then moving on to the IDC and CSIR.

TTSI and CITI

In the late 1970s, the government of Sri Lanka identified the absence of institutionalised training for the textiles sector as a significant hindrance to the development of the industry. An early study carried out by the UNDP in 1981, showed that up to 90 per cent of middle- and lower-level managers in the sector had not received any formal training and, consequently, the technical problems in the industry were not addressed systematically. During the 1980s it also became obvious that the growth of the clothing industry required similar institutional support. Consequently, the TTSI and CITI were established by government to increase the human resource pool available to a growing industry.

The TTSI was established as an autonomous government statutory body by legislation. Its primary purpose was defined as training of personnel, and the provision of consultancy and advisory services to the textiles industry. The non-departmental form of organisation was intended precisely to provide TTSI with the operational autonomy in achieving the specific objectives. At the same time, TTSI receives some of its capital and operational funding directly from government, and is governed by a Board partly composed of government officials. Despite this, the TTSI has managed to construct a reputation for functional autonomy (Slater et al., 1997).

CITI is structured in a very similar manner, with a Board and direct responsibility to government, but with separate legal responsibility enshrined in legislation. Like TTSI, the bulk of funding (and all capital funding) comes directly from government. Both organisations, however, have significant scope for generating their own funding. In terms of services provided, CITI mirrors the functions of TTSI with provision of advisory services, consultancy, research and dissemination to the industry. In short, TTSI and CITI are two sides of the same coin, one concentrating on textiles and the other on apparel.

Skills and professionalism

CITI has had a relatively successful history. To date, it has trained over 12,000 people, most of whom returned to the clothing companies on the island. Currently, the 27 or so courses offered by the Institute are delivered to around 1000 students. The success of these courses has resulted in a positive relationship with the private sector and the consequent continuous increase in the generation of user fees for its services. By the mid-1990s, the Institute was earning around half of its recurrent income, allowing it to pay its own staff higher salaries than equivalent levels within the civil service. In fact, this has created friction in the past between government and CITI, where increasing income from user fees has been used for increasing salaries.

The performance of TTSI also shows an improvement since its inception. Like CITI, TTSI charges user fees on direct services to clients. The provision of client services, defined as training, testing and consultancy, generates around 40 per cent of funding for the institute. The division of the three types of service shows that training accounts for some 54 per cent of user fee income, testing 25 per cent and consultancy services 21 per cent.

TTSI may be seen as performing regulatory, promotional and developmental roles. The functional activities of the centre (training, testing and consultancy) regulates technical and quality standards, promotes efficiency and productivity, and contributes towards the development of the industry. Hence, inter-institutional co-ordination and industry linkages constitute and important dimension in its functioning.

The Board of Governors represents both government and private industry, but remain appointed by the Prime Minister. Other than this Board, there is no institutionalised way in which TTSI interacts with the private sector. The chief link is with alumni of the Institute, primarily on an informal basis, furthermore, there is no systematic way in which courses are designed around the actual needs of the industry since, apart from anything else, there is no means to determine those needs in any consistent sense. This is undoubtedly a weakness in the present operation of the institute, and a potential future source of development.

CITI also carries out the bulk of its interaction with the private sector through alumni or through the Ministries. The Board contains several representatives from government and from the private sector clothing interest groups. For CITI, co-ordination with the representative associations is crucial in terms of providing skills for a rapidly changing, highly international industry. The garment industry within Sri Lanka is also dominated by multinational companies who additionally have high standards with regards to skill requirements.

Whilst CITI does have agreements with the National Apprenticeship and Industrial Training Agency (NAITA) to train apprentices, there remains very little institutional contact between the institute and their clientele. For an organisation that purports to be serving a dynamic private sector industry, there seems to be very little interaction with that industry, and, consequently, a lack of knowledge about what the industry actually demands.

Organisational and administrative structures

There are three levels of management decision-making structure within CITI: the Board; the Director; and, the technical departments. The Board is the senior decision-making body of CITI, empowered to enact all of the powers within the legislation, and also carrying the responsibility for those decisions. The Director is effectively the chief executive of the organisation and is responsible for the day-to-day management of the agency. The main criteria for the Director include technical qualifications in textiles and good industry linkages, and certainly during the time of the research the Director was a particularly dynamic individual with extensive international experience of the industry.

For the purposes of most management, CITI is organised around four technical departments and separate offices of finance and administration.

The departments are not organised in the hierarchical style common across the rest of the public sector, being rather more loosely structured without any formal heads of department. This does mean that the organisation is flexible, but can also mean that there is a lack of direction, with assignments being taken on an individual basis, rather than on a team approach.

Staff within CITI fall into three broad categories: senior professionals who are designated technical training officers; junior staff designated as technical training assistants; and support staff. Professional staff must come from the industry, which, in itself, constitutes a problem for the institute as it cannot pay similar rates to the private sector.[2] In addition, CITI also has to comply with government public sector practices and associated conditions. To date, the institute has not experienced any government 'interference' in appointing staff.

TTSI is very similar to CITI in terms of the constraints it faces in recruiting and retaining staff. Having said this, the Institute has been able to free itself from many of the restrictions faced by CITI, particularly by developing the ability to pay its staff salaries as much as 30 per cent higher than in the civil service. Despite this, however, these salary levels still remain well below those possible within the private sector, making it difficult to retain qualified staff and turnover has been high in the past. Staff turnover, however, as pointed out by TTSI can actually be an asset when the turnover is between the TTSI and the industry. This serves to strengthen linkages between the institute and the private sector.

The centre is organised around eight functional departments, each one covering the different stages of the textile process, such as spinning, weaving, dyeing, and so on. Each department carries out the three main activities of training, testing and consultancy. The day-to-day running of the centre is handled by a Director, who is responsible to a Board, similar to CITI. There are around 80 staff divided in the same way as CITI into three levels.

Availability of capital and finance

The issue of generating revenue from user charging has been addressed above, and both organisations have been relatively successful in this endeavour. Both CITI and TTSI receive all of their capital funding from central government, and their budgets must be approved by government before they are enacted. For TTSI in particular, an examination of the audited accounts showed that the Auditor-General did not feel that the centre was complying with its budget and found significant variances.

CITI is funded from grants voted by Parliament annually through the government budget. These funds are channelled through the government that overseas its operation. CITI has its own 'fund', established by law and administered by the Board. Again, the reports of the Auditor-General show that CITI does not use its budget as a means of controlling activities. Internal financial control may not, therefore, be the highest priority of either organisation. This may be a function of an organisation operating in a framework determined by growth, rather then decline, in that money, although scarce, is still being generated.

TTSI and CITI have much in common in terms of legal status, organisational form, functional autonomy and operational context as well as management practices and procedures related to personnel and finances. In both cases, the rapidly changing environment, and the ability of larger firms to provide internal training, represent significant challenges.

The primary purpose of both institutions is to provide support to the textile and garment industries, necessitating the development of a close relationship with the private sector clientele. The non-departmental form is an inherently difficult organisational form to fit into this relationship, since it brings so many difficulties in terms of role definition and relationships. To the private sector, it may seem like government, and to government it may seem like the private sector. In a sense, however, this may be a distinct advantage in terms of giving it the flexibility and ability to interact with both.

The directors of both CITI and TTSI state that they operate on 'private sector principles' in terms of operational autonomy from officials in the Ministry. However, this functional autonomy is limited in terms of funding, since around 50 per cent of recurrent funding comes from government grants and all capital expenditure also has to come from the government. Even with regard to donor funding or raising capital on the market, both organisations require approval or mediation from the government.

In terms of organisational structures, CITI is less formally structured than TTSI. This may partly be a function of the lower levels of staff within CITI relative to TTSI and the smaller numbers. CITI was a relative latecomer on the training scene and consequently had a smaller pool of expertise to call on initially. In addition, many firms involved in the local garment industry do not require highly skilled personnel, rather they locate in Sri Lanka for the access to cheap labour and machinists who are trained in-house. Both organisations also have problems in recruiting and retaining qualified staff, given the success and higher wages of the private sector, their main competitor for human resources. Despite these problems, both organisations have been able to expand their range of services and generate increasing amounts of user fees to supplement government grants.

The IDC

The IDC of Zimbabwe is responsible for 'general policy issues' to the companies in which it has an interest, both private sector and parastatal, and its influence is exerted through the board of directors of each company. Areas of expertise would include technology, investment and human resources development. Monitoring of the companies receiving such guidance is through appraisal officers who maintain contact with companies on a regular basis. In turn the IDC keeps government informed about the progress of the companies and in some cases, if the government is aware of problems in parastatals, the IDC may be brought in on a 'rescue mission' such as Zimglass, a Gweru-based bottle and plastic container manufacturer.

The IDC was established in 1963 with government and private sector shareholding to spearhead industrial development, and it is now 100 per cent owned by government. Originally the IDC was a 'sanctions buster', venturing into greenfield, import substitution investments. The mission statement of the IDC is to:

- promote and facilitate rapid sustainable and employment-generating industrialisation through research and development on new products, inputs, markets and technologies;
- implement new technically feasible, financially viable and environmentally-friendly strategic projects;
- manage existing portfolio investment optimally in order to generate new investments;
- attract and develop skills for the operation and development of new projects, improve human resources and act as a 'responsible corporate citizen'.

Once projects were off the ground with the raw material supply stabilised and a market for the product developed, the firms were sold to the private sector. In this way the IDC was the main incubator for infant industries effectively removing the start up risks for private entrepreneurs. Sums realised from the sales of these firms were then reinvested into new projects. The IDC continues to work with many of the companies that were established, particularly in developing new products. Currently IDC is developing 12 new greenfield projects and has become involved in developing a Z$14 billion industrial park, including an EPZ partly funded by Malaysian cash.[3]

IDC is essentially a holding company with assets in the region of Z$1.5 billion covering companies in the motor industry, civil explosives, chemicals industry, quarrying and minerals, heavy engineering, wood processing, textiles and clothing, and packaging and financial services. Many of these companies are 100 per cent owned by the IDC but the majority are privately owned with the IDC as minority shareholder. The wide range of activities of the companies is mirrored by the employment profile of the IDC which includes engineers and chemists amongst managers and financial experts.

Periodically the government requests particular services from the IDC. These can vary from attempting to start up more indigenous businesses (a problem due to the lack of funding available to most of the indigenous businessmen) to taking over ailing industries (such as Cone Textiles recently, or Zimglass) largely to preserve employment in situations where management is perceived to have failed.[4]

The main criticism of IDC has been that many of the companies built up by the IDC have not been relinquished by it. In interviews we were told that appraisers' performance is measured on the grounds of how successful their companies are. There is therefore an incentive for appraisers to hang on to successful companies and not sell them to the private sector. This is exacerbated by the IDC's financial autonomy which also provides an incentive to keep successful companies that yield money.[5] In this way the IDC acts more like a private corporation than a holding company guiding infant industries for sale to the private sector.[6] The IDC has therefore pursued a direction driven by an incentive system which has lost sight of its original purpose – that is, developing greenfield sites as opposed to running companies. In a sense the IDC has enjoyed *too much* autonomy since it has been able to retain successful companies in its own interest rather than returning them to the private sector. Both government and the private sector in Zimbabwe have been unable to guide the activities of IDC in such a way as to benefit the industrial system as a whole. The complete independence of IDC has acted against the systemic approach to industry – *it is no longer embedded in the industrial system.*

Organisational and administrative structures

IDC has a clear remit but a wide range. Many of the companies controlled by the IDC have been referred to it by government with the specific objectives of stopping them going out of business. Once this has been achieved, however, IDC has had a tendency to carry on running the companies and not return them fully to the private sector. In this way the IDC has effectively become a self-financed holding company. The overall role of the IDC, to foster new industries, has undergone a change in emphasis under ESAP with the organisation resurrecting industries with histories of bad management and running them as successful companies. In addition, the role of the IDC in developing greenfield sites has received new impetus with the idea of developing an export processing zone in conjunction with Malaysian investment. IDC has therefore digressed considerably from its original role of developing greenfield sites for on-sale. In a sense, for the IDC, its main capacity constraint is its own success. It has been so successful at diversifying its operations and running companies (with the aim of retaining funding), that it is perhaps losing sight of its own purpose.[7]

There is a great deal of overlap or duplication of effort between the IDC and the ZDC. The ZDC was established by the Ministry of Finance both to extend its influence and to compete with the IDC for investment funding. In addition there was a political motive in that the IDC had been established under UDI largely for white businesses whereas the ZDC was seen as a parallel, indigenous version. This is a similar problem to the ZNCC and CZI overlap, and has been recognised as a problem by the authorities who have been holding discussions with both sides, the aim being to rationalise operations.[8]

Staff of the IDC have tended to be long term and have developed high morale within the organisation due to a history of success. Staff work on a portfolio basis with each specialist controlling a group of companies with which they develop a relationship over time. There is a degree of freedom of decision making for staff within these portfolios. The IDC as an entity has a wide degree of decision-making autonomy and is controlled by its own board of directors which it appoints itself.[9] Autonomy is enhanced by the fact that the organisation makes a profit, does not rely upon government subsidy and is free from political interference – in effect it is a state-owned private holding company.

Skills and professionalism of personnel

The IDC itself is essentially a holding company. As such it employs a relatively small staff of 45 (21 being support staff). Staff turnover is very low at only one or two each year and many staff members have been there for a number of years.[10] Salary scales are equivalent to the private sector.[11]

Most of the staff are able to develop long-standing relationships with the companies in their portfolios and generally enjoy good working relations and communication. IDC operates under private sector criteria – that is, if its staff do not perform then the companies they control go out of business; decisions are therefore taken on business criteria. The history of success coupled with the low staff turnover implies that there is a considerable body of expertise within the IDC.

As already stated above, the assessment of staff is on the performance of the companies within their portfolios. This produces a bias in the incentive system which leads to individual managers keeping the most successful companies and not floating them off back to the private sector. The staff incentive system is therefore at the root of the key finding of work on the IDC – that too much autonomy may lead to selfish behaviour which is detrimental to the industrial system as a whole. In a sense, the IDC has been 'captured' by an interest group in the sense identified by Messner as detrimental to the overall policy network (Messner, 1997). The organisation now pursues activities of benefit to itself (as a private company in this case) whereas its original purpose was as an enabling agency for other private companies.

Availability of capital and financial control

IDC does not receive any funding from government.[12] Since 1993 it has received nothing from the Public Sector Investment Programme (PSIP), and has effectively become financially autonomous.[13] At the same time the IDC has a good working relationship with government which draws on its expertise with regard to the private sector. It also controls assets of Z$1.5 m.

Funding is generated from the companies where IDC has intervened as a controller, advisor or minority shareholder. IDC essentially operates as a private company with private sector pay scales and budgets. The strong financial situation of IDC means that not only is the organisation able to maintain autonomy of decision-making from government but it is also to transfer money to the centre. One of the main worries voiced by managers within IDC was the potential for changes to the taxation system as it is applied to them – in other words, they fear the government demanding a higher return from IDC, thus potentially constraining their capacity to undertake the types of investment currently being so successful. In other words, IDC is being recognised as a successful company by government, who now wishes to tax it.

Conclusions

IDC is an interesting case for several reasons, the main one being that it has become so autonomous that it is a private company holding companies on behalf of government. The essence of this is that IDC is an arm's-length state-owned enterprise, but it is so arm's-length that the government control is, in practice, nominal. Certainly in terms of day-to-day management and even with regard to appointments to the Board the government has no say. The main criticism of IDC is that when it builds or resurrects a successful company it appears reluctant to let it revert to the private sector. The reason for the long-term historical success of the IDC largely rests with its financial success and the autonomy arising from this. There is no doubt that the IDC has a great deal of expertise in running companies and that it has a good track record in terms of turning companies going out of business into successful enterprises, but if that success arises out of holding on to successful companies is that not in contradiction to the overall aim of the IDC – that of shouldering some of the risk in developing green-field sites, rather than merely running a private company? In a sense then, IDC has something of an identity crisis, even though the organisation exhibits all of the characteristics of a body with a high degree of capacity and performance.[14]

The IDC may represent an example of too much autonomy being granted – it no longer acts in the interests of the macro or the micro level, but in its own interest. It is no longer embedded and has effectively become a private company. At the same time, the costs of this action must be weighed against the benefits of having a company, which does not draw heavily on the public purse but is able to keep state-owned enterprises with poor financial histories going.[15]

The CSIR

The CSIR of India was originally established in 1942 to co-ordinate and exercise administrative control over the existing Board of Scientific and Industrial Research. Since its inception, CSIR has been involved with the development of a wide range of scientific and industrial activity. The objectives of the organisation were initially non-commercial and primarily concerned with building up a national science and technology base including a cadre of highly qualified and trained R&D personnel. At the same time, CSIR was concerned with providing support for the industry in general. Officially, the main functions assigned to CSIR are: the promotion, guidance and co-ordination of scientific and industrial research; the establishment and development of institutions for the study of problems affecting particular industries; management of research studentships; and, the utilisation and dissemination of research materials.

CSIR has constructed a wide range of specialised R&D institutions as well as acting as a nursery for a large number of scientists and engineers. Currently, CSIR has a network of 40 laboratories and 80 field centres across India, and employs some 25 000 staff, of whom 6000 are qualified scientists, including 3000 PhDs.

Organisational performance

To date, CSIR has developed over 3600 new technologies and designs, of which 2000 have been licensed to more than 6000 clients. CSIR has bilateral collaboration with 25 different countries. The organisation has identified a set of key indicators of performance against which it can be measured. One of the main indicators relates to the effectiveness of International Property Rights (IPR) as a tool for improving competitiveness. The filing of patents in particular has been taken as an indicator of innovation within industry and over the last two decades, there has been a steady rise in the number of patents filed, with the exception of 1993–94. In the six-year period 1987/88 to 1992/93, for example, there was an average annual rise in the total number of patents filed around 14 per cent. This has increased to around 20 per cent currently.

A further important aspect of IPRs is the proportion of international patents filed in relation to domestic ones. This has been an impressive area for CSIR with an average annual growth of 65 per cent in the mid-1990s, and comprising around 25 per cent of all patents filed.

Despite the impressive performance in filing and owning patents, CSIR has not been so successful at generating earnings from them. This has been the subject of a recent patent literacy campaign amongst staff and an area targeted for a detailed policy review.

Another measure of its performance is the estimated value of industrial production based on CSIR know-how. The organisation has been carefully monitoring this aspect of its work. Once again, the rise has been impressive, with the estimated value of production based on CSIR R&D rising from Rs. 6.5 bn in 1987 to Rs. 36 bn in 1997. At the same time, there has been a decline in annual R&D expenditure in relation to the value of industrial production linked to CSIR activity, from 26 per cent in 1987 to 16 per cent in 1993. This demonstrates the increasing level of returns to CSIR investment and an improved value for money performance (Slater et al., 1997).

Finally, CSIR has been placing increasing importance on the generation of income through external cash inflow from contract R&D and consultancy. Cash inflow has increased from Rs. 800 m in 1992 to Rs. 2.25 bn in 1996.

Skills and professionalism of staff

There is no single explanation for the steadily improving performance of CSIR over such a long time. Rather, the explanation lies somewhere in the mix of different initiatives and changes within the organisation. CSIR is a knowledge-based organisation, and as such, human resource development has been instrumental in encouraging the changes. Above all, there has been a commitment to the concept of promoting and managing change within the organisation. This has produced a developing interest in strategic issues, formulation of mission statements and development of strategic plans.

The statements within the '2001 Vision and Strategy' outline a number of aims, including moves to increase self-financing and generation of funding from private industrial clients, generation of income from patents and improved development rates for patents. Linked to this, CSIR has enacted a strategy structured around re-engineering the organisation, linking research to the market, optimising resources, creating and enabling infrastructure and investing in high quality science.

With regard to the staff of CSIR, the organisation has cut costs by imposing ceilings on staff numbers for its sub-units and aiming to reduce administrative/scientific staff ratios from 5:1 to 1:1 by 2006. In support of this strategy, CSIR has been given a high degree of autonomy of staff recruitment for junior- and middle-level managers and scientists. In addition, success and improved performance has been fuelled by a clear reward structure for staff. Individual staff members now face no ceilings on their earnings, and have access to private sector earnings through consultancy, where staff members take a share of the fees in the form of an honorarium. The organisation has also made big efforts to attract good, young staff members and to actively encourage existing staff to improve their intellectual capacities through study leave, sabbaticals and placements in industry.

Organisational and administrative structures

CSIR is governed by a Governing Body acting under the Registration of Societies Act 1860. As such, it nominally enjoys a great deal of freedom. However, its history is one of gradually reducing autonomy since 1948 with enforced compliance in relation to civil service pay and conditions, hiring and firing, promotion and allowances. This has been significantly eroded with the onset of liberalisation, and the organisation is invoking the Act of 1860 in its new, more autonomous role. As a society under the 1860 Act, CSIR enjoys considerable financial autonomy, something that it has started to act upon in its scrapping of civil service pay rates and ceilings on earnings.

This has proved to be a positive background for the extensive organisational restructuring that has taken place since the start of the reform process. In particular, the composition of the various structural tiers of management has been broadened, helping to legitimate change as a function of increased stakeholder participation. At the same time, a deliberate attempt to include clients in the decision-making process brings a sharper focus to CSIR activities and their relevance to their client base.

Availability of capital and finance

One of the main areas of restructuring within the organisation has been financial management, particularly the introduction of a performance-related budget system. A financial management information system has been established that not only measures finance, but also qualitative targets. There has also been considerable work with regard to budgeting and costing. Operating units, for example, meet regularly to discuss performance against budgets. One interesting aspect of the new financial system is the devolution of control over externally generated finance to the operating units. This has encouraged units to start their own capital development programmes, whilst the centre will match funding on a 50:50 basis. This has allowed considerable updating of capital equipment.

Agencies engaged in regulation

From facilitating agencies, we can now turn to regulating agencies. The two regulating agencies discussed in this study are both in Africa and have had hugely contrasting experiences. SAZ has started to develop considerable facilities to help industry identify areas where its own expertise can help. It has also been financially successful – gaining, for example, a good credit rating with the private banking system. On the other hand, MIC is an old-fashioned ministry trying to search for a role. Many of the reforms involve stopping MIC activities, and the external situation regarding government cost-cutting means little cash available for enabling activities.

The MIC in Ghana

The MIC is the 'traditional' arm of industrial policy in Ghana. Currently, it is pursuing activities designed to 'meet the challenges posed by the changed domestic and international environment' by introducing 'market-oriented policies which will spur businesses to adopt efficient management and marketing practices' (Republic of Ghana, 1993). The policy framework for the industry was determined by the ERP and consisted of four major thrusts (after Republic of Ghana, 1993) to:

(a) shift relative prices in favour of production, particularly in the export sector;
(b) rehabilitate the production base and the social and economic infrastructure;
(c) move progressively away from direct controls and government intervention towards greater reliance on market forces; and
(d) build capacity in entrepreneurship and management (including research and development and finance).

The main activity of the MIC since the introduction of the ERP has been dismantling the complex system of import licensing which it used to administer, although it has become involved in some planning activities, such as the proposed EPZ at Tema. Several people we spoke to had been sent on government-sponsored missions abroad, particularly to East Asia, and the MIC has been involved in running several trade fairs and overseas trade missions. In addition, the MIC, with help from UNIDO, has been attempting to improve the collection of statistical data relating to its portfolio.

Organisational and administrative structures

The MIC has a significant problem in defining its new roles. Although its brief is relatively clear (to enable industry to thrive), it is also extremely broad. In addition, the Ministry is left with a significant staffing problem, with most of the staff having been carried over from their original functions of regulating industry rather than encouraging it. The new roles surrounding enabling involve a significantly different skill bundle to granting (or refusing) licences to import or export. There is, therefore, an urgent need for retraining and a reorientation towards the new roles expected of the Ministry. Currently this is problematic since the new roles remain vague and unrefined, an uncertainty which transfers itself through the industrial system through the lack of an industrial policy, which further undermines the confidence of the private sector in the government of Ghana's commitment to private sector led development.[16]

The problematic relationship with the private sector is exacerbated by the perceived lack of a consistent policy over time. Whilst most decisions at a high level have been clearly taken in line with the ERP's thrust towards liberalisation, entrepreneurs seem unwilling to express confidence in the government's commitment to the reform process, even after 15 years.[17] This is partly a macro problem, but it is exacerbated by the MIC's seeming inability to communicate with the private sector. As the main industrial policy-making body in the country, the MIC should be the main communicator of the government's strategic plans for industry – it should be providing the information and reassurance that entrepreneurs require.

Skills and professionalism of staff

Staff numbers are relatively small in the MIC with about 200 staff in a hierarchical structure (Republic of Ghana, 1993). Around half of the staff are classed as managers or 'executives'. There are various initiatives being carried out at present aimed at clarifying roles within MIC. For example, most staff do have relatively clear job descriptions, even if anecdotal evidence tends to downplay their use.[18] At the same time budgeting is tightly controlled and staff do not control their own budgets within their areas. Overall policy of the MIC is largely determined by the ERP and has consisted largely of reducing its traditional activities (that is, licensing). There is also a DFID[19] sponsored civil service reform programme which is having some influence in terms of procedural mechanisms such as job descriptions (Larbi, 1997). The MIC budget is centrally decided and controlled, so the Ministry has very little financial autonomy. In addition, severe financial constraints effectively mean that the MIC budget pays the wages of its staff and not much more. The scope for independent activities is therefore limited which in a sector that has a high degree of market orientation, severely limits efficiency in service provision. Organisational rigidity prevents the MIC successfully interacting with the private sector (their consumers of services) which is, by necessity, flexible in a market-oriented economy.[20]

Information within the Ministry does filter down but officers at the bottom complain that they never really know what is going on. It is difficult to disaggregate the effects of lack of hard information from a belief amongst officers that overall ministry policy is inconsistent. The MIC itself has arranged seminars and overseas visits to gain additional information. One officer interviewed had been to the Far East on a tour of EPZs. However, this particular officer was not involved in the drawing up of the new plans for the EPZ at Tema. The transfer of information within the industry remains unclear, but this in itself is indicative of the internal problems facing staff when their superiors do not communicate knowledge – they are then unable to fulfil their function of transferring that knowledge into the private sector.[21]

Some of the functions of the Ministry overlap with other organisations. The figures held by the textiles department, for example, are different from those held by the NBSSI, which are different again from those held by the Statistics Office. This illustrates both overlap and a complete lack of communication. It may also illustrate a degree of self-protection on the part of bureaucrats in fear of their positions.

Staff turnover is low in the MIC, even though salary levels are well below private sector rates.[22] This is probably more a function of the weakness of the private sector to provide alternative job opportunities (and possibly the opportunity for moonlighting) rather than a lack of motivation to leave.[23] Most of the staff are career bureaucrats but the MIC has just appointed a new minister[24] with private sector experience so it is expected that there will be more private–public linkages, an area where the MIC has been historically weak (this is a feeling reflected within the ministry and amongst the private sector). It is also hoped that the influence of the private sector will lead to a more participative approach in decision-making. Most staff members receive instructions (usually in line with the ERP), rather than being directly involved in the formulation of strategy. Many staff feel that they operate in an atmosphere of uncertainty (within an era of retrenchment) with a lack of transparency in decision making and a hierarchical structure.[25] There are also significant informal information networks. During one interview we were interrupted by a phone call from another section asking if the interviewee knew anything about a change in the caller's own department.

The seeming lack of any formal appraisal[26] or feedback systems within the Ministry further accentuated the feelings of isolation amongst members of staff interviewed. There was a feeling that decisions were made without consultation and the knowledge they had gained through working with the private sector day to day was therefore wasted.

Availability of capital and financial control

The lack of funding is a recurring theme throughout Ghana. The budget for the MIC comes directly from parliament and is influenced by the ERP. The MIC does have an industrial policy statement but there does not appear to be any evidence which would suggest that the budget is determined according to these requirements. In fact, specific policy packages such as the Business Assistance Fund (BAF) are funded centrally, not from within the MIC. In 1993, out of a total budget available of c753 949 000, 350 000 000 (46 per cent) was allocated to staff costs and 277 896 000 (37 per cent) to 'subvention', i.e. subsidy. This leaves only 17 per cent of the budget to repair buildings, carry out training programmes, fund travel costs to conventions, etc., fund specific programmes through its subsidiaries (such as the Export Promotion Council and the Ghana Standards Board), and fund important projects such as the Export Promotion Zone (EPZ) at Tema and the divestiture programme.[27] Clearly, the budget is a severe constraint. In particular the use of 37 per cent of the budget for subsidies to poorly performing state owned industries represents a significant drain on resources.[28]

In terms of capital, the MIC does have a building but it does not have access to a great many items of equipment. For example, the 1993 Annual Report of the MIC shows that there were three computers and three printers in the entire Ministry (another three were added in 1994 and UNIDO supplied two more for the statistics office).

The Ministry has been successful in reducing the number of trade restrictions affecting industry in Ghana, but is essentially still seeking its new roles in collecting and disseminating information, strategic planning and providing a regulatory/legislative framework within which private industry can flourish. Currently, the main preoccupation of much of the MIC is the administration of the BAF. This was originally established to provide financial assistance to 'ailing but viable' industries with working capital. The 10 billion cedi fund is administered by the MIC, but most decisions are taken by a private sector committee. The maximum loan granted is some 250 million cedis, and small-scale industries return the loans at 15 per cent interest, large firms paying 20 per cent.

There do not appear to be many reliable statistics on the disbursement of the fund, and opinion is sharply divided about it. Undoubtedly much of the money has gone to ailing industries, but whether an attempt has been made to establish the viability of the industries is unclear. Many entrepreneurs interviewed stated that they had applied to the BAF but had not received any kind of loan.[29] These included all of the relatively successful women entrepreneurs who were beginning to export. On the other hand, representatives (all men) from many of the larger textiles firms claimed that the BAF funds were inadequate and the interest rates were too high. This may indicate that the BAF was being used in ailing industries, but may actually be better employed as a venture capital fund for those businesses (frequently owned by women entrepreneurs) which cannot borrow money at any rate from the private sector but which are beginning to export.

Like most ministries the MIC suffers from severe external constraints. In particular, the economic situation within the ministry is deteriorating with severe budget cuts leading to a lack of equipment and declining real salaries – all of which combined with a sense of dislocation caused by the change in role – reduces the morale of staff. In addition, within the Ministry there are insufficient funds available for specific schemes, a case in point being the EPZ at Tema (which the MIC can plan but not fund). The mechanisms to bring in foreign capital to fund specific schemes such as this also appear to be undeveloped, or at least behind those of Zimbabwe, for example, where the government has been able to create lucrative links with Malaysia. Having said this, the GOG was instrumental in establishing the Ghana–China Chamber of Commerce, aimed at adding to the level of Chinese investment, but at the same time it is not clear how much additional investment has entered the country as a result of this organisation.[30]

Conclusions

The lack of money has influenced the MIC's interaction with the private sector. The MIC used to protect industry through a series of licences, but now these licenses have disappeared, introducing 'unfair' competition, and the MIC has no cash to help industry any more. This type of reasoning is commonplace amongst private-sector entrepreneurs, as is the demand for the MIC to reintroduce protection against foreign competition. At the lower levels of the Ministry, however, the officers who deal with the industries themselves, particularly in the textiles sector, appear to have an excellent relationship with frequent contact, good interchange of ideas and much empathy.[31] It is at this level that the MIC exhibits signs of knowing exactly what is happening in the private sector, but this kind of interaction does not appear to spread upwards, something which the appointment of more higher-ranking officials with experience in the private sector is designed to remedy. This may also represent a reduction in political interference in appointments at a high level.

The SAZ

SAZ is a non-government, non-profit-making body operating under the Zimbabwe Companies Act and was established in 1957. The governing body is the General Council, which consists of representatives from the government, local authorities, professional institutions, industry and commerce. The council determines the overall policy of the association. Funding is from monies collected under the Standards Development Levy Fund (which is levied on the wage bills of businesses), income from its mark certification scheme, registration under quality management standards, laboratory testing fees and sales of publications.

Before independence the import substitution strategy did not hold quality standards as being important. However, since the introduction of ESAP and the new emphasis on exports, quality issues have come more to the fore as one of the crucial elements of international competitiveness (particularly in textiles). Trade liberalisation has also led to an increase in the availability of imports which has in turn forced Zimbabwean companies to improve quality in order to compete on the domestic market. Again this was particularly important in textiles with the imports of fashionable clothing in western styles. As a result, many companies have begun to realise that SAZ is becoming increasingly important.

The objectives of SAZ are to promote standardisation and quality improvement, to provide information services on national and international standards and technical regulations and to provide technical facilities for quality testing manufactures and raw materials. In meeting these objectives SAZ undertakes the following activities:

- *standardisation:* mainly consisting of the writing and formulation of standards for local industries. Usually the standards are taken from international standards (about 75 per cent) since the priority areas are in exports. Each standard is prepared by a technical committee, of which there can be anything from 35 to 135 operating at any one time at various stages of completion. At the original offices SAZ could only allow one technical committee to meet at any one time therefore the process was slow, however, SAZ has just moved to bigger premises to cope with the increased demand;
- *product certification* allows Zimbabwean products to be certified according to the appropriate standard, providing protection for the consumer and an additional marketing tool for the producer. Demand for product certification has increased since ESAP. In 1994/95 22 licences were issued for 34 products involving over 300 visits to 81 companies;
- *registration of ISO 9000 quality management systems:* SAZ registers companies under the ISO 9000–9004 standards, now accepted world-wide. It provides an in-depth assessment of each firms quality management system and capability. SAZ undertook significant internal training in British audit techniques to be able of undertaking

this work. There was general agreement amongst companies and the government (and SAZ) that registration under the ISO standards would benefit Zimbabwean industry and although only 15 companies have so far been accepted, SAZ is considering 120 companies which were interested in the scheme;

- *technology transfer:* SAZ maintains an information centre holding copies of all Zimbabwean standards, International standards (ISOs), International Electrotechnical Commission standards (IEC), British standards (BS), South African standards (SABS) and many other potential trading partners standards. The centre also sells publications (ISOs which are now a best-seller) and maintains a computerised database on European standards, codes of practice and environmental standards;

- *technical services:* A technical committee has been appointed to look at ISO 14000 standards on the environment, another to oversee consumer affairs in conjunction with the Consumer Council, and another to liaise with the Drugs Control Council. Technical demands on SAZ have increased (and continue to do so) and in response SAZ has increased its technical staff. For example the laboratory originally employed one scientist and now employs six. Most of SAZ is currently undergoing full computerisation in order to link the various laboratories and offices in Harare, Bulawayo and Mutare. The main technical problem facing SAZ is keeping up with demand for services;

- *training:* SAZ runs comprehensive training programmes for its own staff in Zimbabwe and abroad in South Africa and the UK in order to keep them up to date with international trends. In addition SAZ staff run training programmes for industry personnel through a Training Department which specifically deals with the private sector and frequently works in conjunction with private companies from Zimbabwe and overseas (e.g. quality management training has been carried out with a Norwegian company called DNV).

SAZ has a staff complement of around 108 with the aim being to increase this to 150 to cope with the rapidly increasing demand for its services. Equipment is also being improved and is largely up to date, the problem being that there are insufficient computers and lab facilities to cope with the number of enquiries.

Information dissemination is through monthly newsletter mailed to all those on the database. This newsletter contains details of matters such as updated quality standards and forthcoming courses. In addition,

SAZ regularly publishes reports and books of standards and holds several lecture and seminar courses with CZI and ZNCC where it also receives valuable feedback on the services provided.[32]

The main elements of internal capacity may be divided into the three main areas outlined above: organisational and administrative structures; skills and professionalisation of personnel; and capital and financial control.

Organisational and administrative structures

One of the main advantages of SAZ is that it is subject to a clear set of objectives and has a clear purpose: to raise the quality of Zimbabwean products so that they match international standards. The role of SAZ is set out in statute and the international standards are set externally by the International Standards Committee. Such a purpose requires a fragmented structure in which experts in specific areas are able to make decisions regarding that purpose. However, SAZ does have 'traditional' hierarchical management structure, even though it may be less rigid than much of the central government bureaucracy, due to each member having his/her area of expertise.[33] The main features of the organisational structure of SAZ may be summarised as follows:

- most staff are clear about their roles since they relate to specific areas, there is therefore very little internal overlap in roles or responsibility, something which is reflected at the level of the organisation;
- the organisation as a whole has a clear objective and has functional autonomy from political interference since standards are set at an international level – it advises government rather than taking orders from it;[34]
- information is its business and the organisation has managed to publish a wide variety of standards information which is made available to firms through its library and publications. The high profile of SAZ has been increased through the courses run by the centre;[35]

The administration and organisation of SAZ appear to contribute positively towards the capacity of the organisation to carry out its role in maintaining standards. The nature of the work itself means that the information dealt with by SAZ is external (that is, it relates to international standards) and specialised, therefore it is more likely that constraints will come from a lack of expertise amongst staff and/or the finance to disseminate or gather the information required.

The senior management of SAZ tends to be of a technical rather than a political nature. Interviews indicated that the Board effectively selected itself. Managers interviewed were more concerned with changing standards than political interference. Because standards are externally regulated, SAZ is effectively insulated from political interference. The prevailing attitude of staff was of high morale brought about by a high external profile and a sense of 'being in demand'.

Skills and professionalism of staff

The organisation has salaries that conform to the public sector pay scales. Despite this, there is very little staff turnover and SAZ is currently recruiting staff as it expands its operations. The plan is to increase the number of staff from the current level of 108 to 150 to cope with the additional demand. The fact that the organisation is in demand, is expanding and has clarity of purpose has implications for the capacity of staff to fulfil that purpose:

- most of the staff are recruited for their expertise and are subject to internal training programmes (they also run some of their own). Many members of staff have been on secondment abroad;[36]
- standards and quality are relatively easy to measure.[37] SAZ officials are able to appraise firms compliance with standards such as ISO which are regulated internationally. The international regulatory authorities thus act as an external measure of performance;
- SAZ deals with specific programmes from external organisations such as ISO and has built up a cadre of staff experienced in dealing with international organisations;
- there is no real evidence of firing, although SAZ is hiring as mentioned above.[38]

The nature of the work carried out by SAZ has contributed to the prevailing culture of open and 'scientific' discussion. Senior managers are frequently less well informed about specific areas and standards than their juniors leading to a collegiate atmosphere.

Availability of capital and financial control

The main constraint facing SAZ is funding. The main source of funding is the government and this is becoming increasingly uncertain due to the budgetary stringency of ESAP. Although SAZ has been largely successful in developing alternative sources of funding to increase its income, the danger is that firms will demand expansion of the services provided whilst government cuts the available funding to SAZ.

SAZ has attempted to diversify its funding by selling services such as licensing and registration, published standards, product certification, information, technical services and training. All of these services have been subject to increasing demand, and if the current policy of increasing budgetary autonomy from government for agencies is continued there is the possibility that SAZ could overcome its major constraint, retaining suitably qualified staff by paying them more than the state salary. There is no evidence to suggest that the alternative sources of funding will be sufficient to cover the entire budget of SAZ in the future.

The raising of alternative funding has, however, allowed SAZ to re-equip its laboratories and update its computer and information systems.[39] The current situation of reductions in government funding has forced SAZ to review its budgetary and financial control systems and to tighten up expenditure. The organisation has been prudent in its financial controls. For example, the new laboratory was financed by a loan from CABS which has now been repaid in full (a stark contrast to the performance of many other government agencies across Africa).

Conclusions

If Zimbabwe is going to improve its export performance, SAZ has to play one of the leading roles. International markets demand certain minimum standards and if firms do not conform to these standards then they will fail to export. Central to the success of SAZ is the ability to attract and retain quality personnel who understand the nature of standards in their field. Currently, SAZ is managing to do this, although at least one manager stated that the recruitment drive could experience problems due to the inadequacy of the salaries being offered. Despite this, SAZ is still expanding. Certainly the main constraint facing SAZ is the ability to diversify its financial base away from government and towards cost recovery where it has been partially successful so far.

Conclusions

This chapter has analysed a number of different institutions involved in two groups of agencies examined in some detail within the research. In particular, we have examined those involved in facilitation of industry and those related to regulation. In terms of the experience of those institutions, they represent a range from those that have stagnated under reforms, through to those that have been created as part of the process, to those rediscovering some degree of economic and managerial freedom through increasing autonomy.

The following chapter continues with the second half of the analysis of the agencies. It moves on to look at those organisations involved with the representation of the private sector, and then, the largest group, those established to promote industrial development.

6
Promotion and Representation

Introduction

This chapter follows on directly from the previous section. We have already analysed those agencies engaged in facilitation and regulation, and now we move on to look at those established to represent the private sector's view and to engage in policy dialogue with the state.

The structure of the chapter is similar to chapter 5, with a first section looking at representation and a second examining those engaged in promotion. The two representative organisations are sufficiently different to merit a separate and individual analysis and comparison, but the promotion agency group is largest group of the entire analysis and, therefore, will be dealt with as a group under a series of themes.

Agencies engaged in representation

The research looked at two agencies that played a crucial role in the industrial system. The first of these, the ICC, is a long-established organisation that has gone through a significant amount of reorganisation and reorientation under structural adjustment as the demands and needs of its members have changed rapidly. The second, the PEF, has been deliberately established with external help, to replace the discredited previous organisation, the Association of Ghana Industries (AGI), which was considered to be out of touch with new businesses, compliant with the previous regime, and consisting of managers of businesses that had predominantly gone into liquidation under adjustment.

Whilst not strictly speaking government agencies, the roles played by these organisations are important within the government/private sector interface. Without a well-organised and very public representative voice, the private sector will be unable to engage fully in policy dialogue with the state. From the point of view of the state, functioning representatives of the private sector are valuable sources of information, opinion and perception and, as such, play a critical role in the success or otherwise of policy towards industry.

The Indian Chamber of Commerce

The ICC has a long history, dating back to the formation of the Bengal Chamber of Commerce in Calcutta in 1874. The ICC is currently registered under the Companies Act as a voluntary limited company, and has seen a huge shift from its original role as a protector of Indian industry to a promoter, addressing issues such as facilitating a healthy business environment, anticipating future needs, promoting global trade and ensuring consumer welfare.

ICC endeavours to provide its members with information on all aspects of economic policy. A meeting point for business, policy makers, the press, academics and intellectuals, the ICC considers itself to be a clearing house of information, an opinion builder and a catalyst for future economic development. The ICC also plays a leading role in bringing international expertise to India, with the aim of facilitating Indian industry in international competition. Since its inception, ICC has maintained a constant interaction with government at central and state levels, providing a valuable dialogue forum.

Other activities carried out by the ICC cover the organisation of conferences, international relations with other representative organisations, dialogue with international bankers, training and a comprehensive social responsibility programme. The social development activities range from providing encouragement to rural enterprise, citizen action forums, running a substance abuse cell, and organising a Ladies Study Group. The ICC, through addressing this wide range of issues, is trying to place itself at the centre of the socio-economic transition experienced under adjustment.

Skills and professionalism

There are approximately 70 staff working full time for ICC. Unlike many government departments, the organisation does not appear to be obviously overstaffed. In fact, within some departments there is a shortage of skilled clerical staff. Greater office automation and downsizing due to restructuring has led to a reduction in overall staff numbers.

There is a minimum requirement for staff recruitment of at least degree-level qualifications, and for more senior levels this increases to a

Masters degree or relevant professional qualification. Human resource management is the responsibility of the independent Executive Committee.

In terms of pay, the ICC offers rates significantly better than state-level employees, but lower than national civil service rates. The nature of the job and the opportunity to make numerous contacts, are seen as the main incentives for senior managers to join the ICC. There are also additional perks in terms of working on specific high profile projects and secondments.

Every member of staff is subject to annual staff appraisal, that then lead on to promotions and increments. The attitude of staff members within ICC is extremely positive about favouritism, and the continued motivation and ability to recruit high calibre staff should be seen as a clear indication that the promotion and increment system is perceived as fair. The appraisals take into account a whole range of activities, including the management of databases, running meetings, etc. and good information management. In general, the well-managed human resource system means that the ICC rarely needs to hire external skills, except for specific research such as drug use.

There is a cash incentive system with an annual bonus payable to all employees and annual increments to salary dependent on the annual appraisal. Employee turnover is low within the organisation, but this is partly related to limited alternative opportunities in West Bengal. However, for senior employees, there are significant opportunities for external and lucrative business consultancy, an opportunity that continues after retirement.

ICC prides itself on its open management culture. Senior members and officers are open and accessible and promotions and benefits are transparent. The culture of the ICC has changed rapidly with the onset of the reform process, and above all, these changes have been driven by the membership and are therefore demand-led.

Organisational and administrative structures

The head of the ICC is a President elected annually by the membership. Duties are shared by two vice-presidents, also chosen by the members. The Executive Committee consists of members elected from all members (plus a small number of co-opted members). This Committee is the central decision-making body, and is informed by a series of sub-committees addressing specific specialised subjects. ICC is represented on several industrial boards and advisory committees, usually by the President or one of the vice-presidents.

ICC also maintains a permanent secretariat, administering several functional departments and managing the comprehensive management information system. It also handles the day-to-day dealings with the numerous additional organisations either affiliated to or associated with the ICC.

The information system run by the ICC is comprehensive and is fully integrated into the decision-making bodies of the organisation. In addition, the ICC draws up regular five-year plans for achieving membership growth. As well as this planning, the Chamber has a good budgetary preparation system and control for its annual system. The effectiveness of such a system may be questioned in terms of performance, on the grounds that there is no incentive system for improving performance. This is, of course, included in the annual review, but remains only one part of the review process. At the same time, the Chamber does not formally measure the quality of services provided to membership, although members are not forced to use services provided. The benefits arising out of the ICC's activities are difficult to measure, primarily because many of them are carried out jointly with other chambers and institutions, and their benefits are frequently difficult to measure in any quantitative sense.

Capital and finance

The chief source of funding for the ICC is from membership fees. Currently there are three categories of members:

1. Corporate group members, who are entitled to enrol themselves in the Chamber. The corporation then receives all of the benefits of membership and, being a special category, they can nominate one of their representatives on the Executive Council.
2. Ordinary members are the bulk of ICC membership. Any firm is eligible for ICC membership.
3. Associate members consist of those firms with a turnover of less than Rs.25 lakhs.

One of the best measures of performance is the number of firms willing to become a member of the ICC. This shows that the types of membership services are considered a worthwhile investment. As a general indication, membership rose from 1500 firms in the mid-1980s to around 2000 by the mid-1990s. At the same time, several of the older companies have gone out of business and therefore ceased to be members, and their places have been taken by younger companies with aims similar to the current ICC in terms of dynamism and market liberalisation.

The ICC is also eligible to raise finance on the private market for capital development and has, historically, received some funding for specific projects from the public sector. The current healthy state of membership, however, effectively makes concern over cash flow relatively small.

The Private Enterprise Foundation

The PEF was set up in 1996 due to an initiative led by USAID which, along with UNDP, has also provided much of the funding. The organisation has four founding members, all of which are leading business associations: Association of Ghana Industries (AGI); Ghana National Chamber of Commerce (GNCC); the Ghana Employers' Association (GEA); and the Federation of Associations of Ghanaian Exporters (FAGE). The organisations' stated aim in forming the PEF is to 'exert greater influence on policy initiatives for the creation of an enabling environment in which private sector businesses can thrive as partners in the Economic Development of the Country' (PEF publicity leaflet).

The PEF was created as a non-political, non-profit-making, autonomous institution, and is incorporated as a company limited by guarantee. Any private business or trade association is eligible for membership of the organisation (the Ghana Association of Bankers is also included in this definition). The stated objectives of the PEF can be summarised as follows:

- to represent the interests of the business community and act as their representative in negotiations with the government;
- to fulfil an advocacy role with central government, influencing regulations and policies;
- to act as a focal point for the collective interests of the private sector in Ghana and provide technical, managerial, marketing and financial support;
- to operate the Accra Business Centre with the aim of providing services and facilities to business such as information, access to communication systems, and providing secretarial and conference facilities for business associations.

The PEF is therefore one of the institutions charged with enabling the private sector to respond to the changes in the incentive system produced by the ERP. Furthermore, it is an organisation squarely within the meso level of the industrial system. Since it is an independent, autonomous unit it is not susceptible to many of the external environmental factors, which could impair its capacity, except the very weakness of the private sector it represents. In particular, the representative organisations which originally formed the PEF have become discredited over time.[1] Many of them became associated with the historical record of corruption and then inability to deal with the government of the early 1980s. In addition, the AGI became associated with large-scale industry, precisely that which suffered most during the 1980s. Consequently, the firms of most of its members, including the director, have gone into liquidation.[2]

Organisational and administrative structures

The organisation itself is non-hierarchical, even though there is a director. The PEF operates more like a consultancy firm than a government department, with each officer having his/her own area of expertise. Decisions are autonomous of government since it is a representative organisation of the private sector (and therefore part of its brief is to represent views of the private sector), and decision-making autonomy is enhanced by the financial independence provided by USAID. The PEF is primarily funded by donors (leaving it open to represent donor views). The very nature of the organisation – as a representative group for the private sector – effectively means that it is permanently oriented towards its consumer group. In addition, the external funding and perceived political independence increase the capacity of the PEF to carry out its technical role in relation to its objectives.

Skills and professionalism of staff

Staff are paid higher rates than government employees and salaries are more in line with private sector levels in order to attract highly qualified staff (which has been successful).[3] There is very low staff turnover within the organisation and the internal policies have remained consistent over time.[4] Staff in the PEF do not face the same degree of uncertainty that exists, for example, in the MIC.

Staff are all fully aware of their positions and roles within the organisation. Most professional staff members have been hired for their expertise in particular areas, and are largely left to provide consultancy within those areas.[5] Most of the staff have come from other international organisations such as UNDP and the World Bank, so their overall understanding of Ghana and their professional skills are sound. The central problem of the PEF is in its association with USAID which plans to pull funding within five years. The financial sustainability of the organisation must therefore be thrown into doubt. In fact, the Board was established by USAID, but has been subject to USAID 'distancing itself' from the organisation. It was felt by USAID that it originally played a useful role of an 'honest broker', but that the organisation should now be made to stand on its own two feet.

Communication within the organisation and externally – both to its client groups and to the government – is very good. There are frequent meetings and discussion forums which are usually attended by government as well as the private sector. The formation of the Private Sector Roundtable Group in 1993 was significant in that it formed the only representative independent private sector group within Ghana which had not had a 'tainted' history.

Independence has been enhanced greatly by the organisation's roots within an external donor organisation, USAID, giving it credibility both within government and the private sector which does not associate it with past indiscretions. Although the organisation is relatively new, the large number of private sector firms and organisations which have joined the organisation serves to illustrate its growing influence (as does its mention in the government's Vision 2020 document). The PEF not only acts as a forum for discussion but also undertakes consultancy work for other private sector organisation – producing, for example, credit reports for the banking sector. In this way the organisation is capable of supplementing its income and enhancing its own expertise. The organisation has adequate capital to fulfil its functions and has access to a developed computer system, international information and communication systems.

Availability of capital and financial control

Finance is not a problem in the short term, since the PEF is funded by external donors.[6] In the medium to long term, however, the sources of funding are uncertain. The business centre is designed to complement the existing funding streams by providing technical reports (on the state of industries and credit risks for the banking sector for example). However, the structural weakness of the private sector leaves the future ability of the potential customers to pay in question. This has not been resolved.[7]

Conclusions

The PEF is the type of organisation that is required by business to represent and help them in the global market. Such organisations are necessary to cement the industrial system in place. An economy where there is a lack of dialogue between public and private sector is extremely damaging to both government and the private sector. The very existence of the PEF, which is essentially an international NGO, carrying out work which would usually be within the brief of, say, the MIC, suggests that USAID lacks faith in the capacity of the government to carry out these types of role. In effect they have sidestepped the issue of government capacity and have set up a unit which is affiliated to, and yet independent from, the state. The central question with regard to the PEF, however, remains its sustainability after USAID stops providing funding.

The PEF is at an early stage of its growth. ICC has been around for some time, and therefore has defined routes of access. The experience of ICC does show that representative organisations will grow not only if they address the needs of their members, but also if the membership reflects the structure of the industry represented. One of the chief criticisms of the ICC, for example, is that it does not clearly or adequately address the needs of smaller producers. In many ways this is unfair, since it is not clear whether any chamber could represent semi-formal, small firms, but it is true that the ICC's structure is biased in favour of corporate members who have direct access to the Board. This has been a criticism levelled at most business associations across the world (see, for example, the Confederation of Zimbabwe an Industry). The difference with the PEF is that this bias has been removed by the larger firms largely going out of business and it has a chance of building from the bottom up.

Agencies engaged in promotion

This is the largest group of agencies covered in the research, which is not entirely surprising since investment and exports remain integral elements of reform packages. The agencies studied cross all four of the core countries and are mainly innovative agencies in that they were specifically established to fulfil explicit roles within the process of economic liberalisation. The common consensus has been one of establishing 'one-stop shops' for both companies wishing to export and overseas investors. Two of the agencies have been categorised as reorientation rather than innovation in the initial matrix, because although they were new organisations, the core of the agencies existed beforehand, albeit in different places.

The agencies involved in promotion include the BOI and EDB in Sri Lanka, the AEPC in India, ZIC and Zimtrade in Zimbabwe and the

GIPC in Ghana. As such, all of the agencies engaged in these activities are concerned with either investment or exports.

Organisational structures

Typically, the agencies established under the reform process were established under the same principles and rules. All of the examples studied were established as separate legal entities controlled by Acts of Parliament. In some cases, as in the BOI in Sri Lanka, GIPC in Ghana and ZIC and Zimtrade in Zimbabwe, the organisations are responsible directly to the President, thus making them independent from the sluggish parliamentary process.

With similar modes of establishment come similar governance structures. Typically the highest governing body consists of a Board with varying mixes of private and public sector representatives.

The exception to the rule here is the AEPC of India, which was incorporated as a company under the Companies Act. It is owned by the Ministry of Commerce and acts as a non-profit-making service organisation for the promotion of apparel exports. In terms of management, decisions are taken jointly between the Ministry of Commerce and the exporters, and, as such, also exhibits the autonomous nature of decision making that characterises the other promotional agencies.

The range of services provided by promotional agencies are not unduly innovative, rather they provide fairly predictable and consistent ranges of services. Typically, they provide the following:

- Buyer/seller meetings, aiming at giving a wider market exposure to exporters and investors through the creation of business ties with foreign buyers.
- Participation at international trade fairs.
- Maintaining a presence at overseas missions and embassies – sometimes known as export or investment 'windows'.
- Inward buying missions, specifically to support inward buying missions by agents and multinational companies.
- Support for individual exporters marketing efforts through provision of funding to facilitate marketing ventures. In the case of Zimtrade this extends to provision of subsidised World Wide Web space for advertising.
- Schemes for helping small and medium-sized industries either to find investment partners, or undertake export marketing. This may also consist of undertaking separate promotional activities for these

groups (for example, small industry trade fairs), or by facilitating access to agents or export trading houses.

- Provision of information to investors and exporters. ZIC and Zimtrade were specifically formed to provide information and guidance through official procedures for both investors and exporters. This is also one of the rationales behind the formation of most promotional agencies. ZIC and Zimtrade also use a jointly developed database of Zimbabwean companies information, as does the EDB in Sri Lanka. Both have business libraries.

The issue of performance

Performance varies considerably across the agencies. In general, Sri Lanka and India have performed positively, Zimbabwe satisfactorily and Ghana fairly poorly, but there is a serious causal relationship problem in assessing the agencies through these criteria. With regard to investment, for example, there are so many variables involved in generating investment that it is difficult to put any specific increase down to, for example, the BOI in Sri Lanka.

India's garment exports have shown impressive growth since the launching of the economic reform process. In quantitative terms, exports increased from 705 million pieces in 1991 to 1098 million pieces in 1996. It is difficult, however, to attribute this success purely to the AEPC, and in fact the organisation itself does not maintain a record of its own performance. Similar problems extend to the BOI and EDB in Sri Lanka where the environment for exports and investment has been very favourable. However, the impact of the BOI has certainly been influential in accelerating the growth of inward investment in Sri Lanka, if only through the provision of extensive infrastructure. At the same time, the BOI has been influential in terms of advice given to the Government dealing with changes in investment incentive schemes.

Since the formation of the GIPC at the beginning of 1994, Ghana's investment performance has had a mixed performance. From a total level of investment of US$271.49 million in 1992, the total increased to US$448.23 million in 1994. This increase masked an overall downward trend in 1994 following an investment rush immediately after the formation of the GIPC and the acceleration of the divestiture programme. Over the four quarters of 1994, total investment increased to US$149.82 million in the second quarter from US$149.52 million in the first, then declined to US$148.89 million in the third quarter, but then investment went into free fall, declining to US$10.70 million by the last quarter, a low level of investment which continued into 1995, with US$27.00 million in the first quarter, and a partial recovery in the second quarter, to US$73.15 million. Overall, the formation of the GIPC coincided with a serious decline in overall investment throughout 1994 and only began a faltering recovery in mid-1995.

The overall figures for investment also hide numerous internal trends of interest to the manufacturing sector. In 1992, 55 per cent of investment was concentrated in manufacturing of some form, 13 per cent in agriculture, 22 per cent in services and 5 per cent each in tourism and building and construction. Within manufacturing, one-third of investment was in the wood industry and another fifth was in food processing. During 1994, the quarterly breakdown shows that manufacturing investment started at US$39.21 million (26 per cent of total investment), increasing to $57.46 million (38 per cent) in the second quarter and then declining to 19 m (13 per cent), then to 1m (1 per cent), a decline which partially recovered to 12 m (44 per cent) in the first quarter of 1995, and then 10 m (14 per cent) in the second quarter.

What is clear from these figures is that whilst the decline in overall investment was severe enough, manufacturing investment in particular entered a deeper trough. Again, this decline in manufacturing investment coincided with the formation and first 18 months of the GIPC's existence. There are some telling trends within the composition of investment capital. Although incomplete, the general trend of composition has been of a marked decline in Ghanaian investment and a slower decline in foreign ownership and joint ventures. It is by no means clear that this has anything to do with GIPC, however – rather the state of the Ghanaian economy has declined markedly.

Since Zimtrade has been in operation, exports have increased substantially. In 1991, total exports amounted to Z$5bn, by 1992 this had increased to Z$6.5bn, by 1993 to Z$9.5bn and in 1994 exports reached some Z$16bn (Annual Report 1994/5). The distribution of these exports was relatively even in 1994 between Southern Africa (32.9 per cent), Europe (35 per cent) and the rest of the world (32.1 per cent), although within an overall growth of 55 per cent between 1993 and 1994, 45 per cent of the growth was accounted for by increased exports to Southern Africa. This again illustrates a causality problem in that some export performance will have been influenced by Zimtrade, but much of this increase to Southern Africa will be due to the opening up of new markets in South Africa with the lifting of trade sanctions.

Skills and professionalism

The organisations vary considerably in size. Staff of the GIPC are paid according to public sector wage scales, but there is no evidence of high staff turnover – perhaps because of the fact there is nowhere to go or that the centre is relatively new. Most of the staff appeared to have some degree of expertise in an economics-related field and the general atmosphere of the centre was one of an 'elite' organisation. The staff are smarter than those found in most other governmental departments, the buildings are better, there are computers, staff are better qualified and there is a sense of purpose and a clear set of objectives. Staff did not seem to be as affected by the insecurity of many other government departments and therefore appeared to be more motivated. The centre does produce detailed statistics of investment in Ghana and provides analysis of the effects of various policies. They also maintain a link with previous investors by providing an information service for them.

Zimtrade employs around 50 people, with 30 of these being professional staff. Many of them originally came from the trade promotion department of the Ministry of Industry and Commerce, but many also came from the private sector, and the Director came from CZI.[8] Zimtrade uses private sector consultants' expertise, usually on a short-term basis, in order to facilitate flexibility in the programmes provided. Salaries are in line with the private sector but Zimtrade is aware that it cannot compete for highly qualified individuals in terms of salary; it therefore tries to compete in quality of work and also to develop in-house expertise so that any staff lost will not be greatly missed.

After one year of operation Zimtrade won additional support from the Zimtrade Support Programme (ZSP) funded by the European Union. Out of the 10.2m ECU programme with the European Union, over 7m was designated for foreign consultants' man hours. These consultants were fully integrated into the activities of Zimtrade and effectively provided free expertise.[9] Over the years 1994/95 the ZSP funded a six-man team providing expertise in market information, databases, trade research and analysis, assistance to foreign buyers, marketing of horticultural products, export market training and training to new exporters (Annual Report, 1994/5).

The involvement of many qualified staff has enhanced the ability of Zimtrade to deal with donors and to take on additional programmes – for example, the organisation is currently running two European programmes for small business development. In addition Zimtrade produces an impressive array of statistics and information relating to exports and business development. Most of these are available through the information centre.

ZIC has a staff complement of 35–40 people, of whom 67 per cent are professional staff and the remainder support staff. The professional staff are all university graduates or finance professionals. Many of them transferred from the various units of ministries dealing with investment. Salary scales are comparable with those in the parastatal sector and funding for the centre is through budgetary allocations by central government.

Internal training is being developed in conjunction with external donor agencies. The change in role towards promotion has led to a reassessment of staff roles, training programmes have been implemented in conjunction with private companies and donors (such as MIGA) and several staff have been placed on secondment to investment promotion agencies abroad. ZIC's funding situation may, however, slow this process down considerably and there is therefore a risk that the current high morale of ZIC staff will be adversely affected.

In contrast to the experience in Zimbabwe and Ghana, the EDB in Sri Lanka has had a mixed record with regard to staff. The vast majority of the 330 staff have been there for some time and, whilst staff numbers have remained virtually static, the workload has declined markedly. Staff are, therefore, underutilised. The lack of staff turnover has been partly a result of poor human resource management in the past and a lack of opportunities in the general economy for administrative staff.

In particular, EDB has been short of marketing and manpower development staff. Many staff members also lack technical, marketing and managerial skills, particularly at middle-management level. In addition, much of the work undertaken by staff involves project management, an area of expertise that is not really present amongst staff. In addition, there has been little the progress made by EDB in terms of human resource management. Many managers pointed to the fact that the organisation rarely sends staff overseas for training (a common technique in an export agency), and the low staff turnover puts off talented individuals who find themselves unable to gain promotion. Disillusionment at the lower levels is not mirrored at the senior levels of the organisation, where directors feel they have a major part to play in developing exports. However, the lack of a human resource skill base is likely to compromise that view in the long run.

The BOI in Sri Lanka also suffers from similar staffing problems. In particular, a lack of clear human resource strategy compromises the effective training and recruitment of staff. Whilst there are several well-qualified and capable staff within the organisation, the lack of flexibility of the organisation has been criticised (Slater et al., 1997).

The AEPC in India is a different scale to all of the other agencies. It employs some 600 staff, of whom 108 are designated as 'executive staff'. They are spread over the nine offices maintained by AEPC. The organisation does have something of a reputation for not being 'up to the minute' with regard to technology and modern manufacturing. This may be connected to the steadily ageing profile of its staff. Of the 108 executives, as many as 50 joined within one year of the establishment of the council in 1978, and 80 have been with the council for more than 15 years. This means that the vast majority of executive staff joined before the reform process began. In terms of age, the AEPC is staffed predominantly by men in their late 40s and early 50s.

Despite these problems, AEPC has been seen as a useful organisation by many exporters, if only to act as a 'one-stop shop' for information. Its proactive role is, however, limited, due to limitations in its staffing and lack of expertise. The static character of human resources within the organisation is also reflected in promotion policy and the lack of any real flexibility in structure.

Organisational and administrative structures

The AEPC is a hierarchically structured organisation, with a long command structure that does not lend itself to rapid decision-making. Apart from creating many files, this type of organisation distorts management communication and places a very large gap between the higher and lower sections of the organisation. Within an agency dealing with exports, where markets can change very rapidly, this could be a serious problem. In fact, the Director General of the AEPC is a civil servant, and the ambience of the organisation is very much one of a government department, with most communication happening through 'notings'.

In addition, there are severe constraints with regard to promotion, since the higher levels of the bureaucracy are characterised by low turnover. Limited opportunities for promotion was seen as a general grievance amongst staff at all levels, as well as the system of basing promotion on seniority, rather than ability or performance.

The structure of the EDB in Sri Lanka was deliberately established to insulate it from the civil service and from political interference. In general, political interference was distanced by the employment of professional or technical managers and executives. The statute that governs the EDB assumes that the Minister will handle policy, whilst leaving the day-to-day management of the organisation to the management. Importantly, the EDB was freed from government restrictions on finance, personnel, production and marketing. At the same time, this does not mean that EDB is completely free from government, and, in fact, government exercises controls on budgets, pricing and investment, and through planning ministries.

The organisation has a clear overall structure in keeping with its mission, but the distribution of tasks and duties between the different operating divisions of the agency appears to be unsatisfactory. In particular, there is some confusion between the divisions over roles, leading to considerable overlap. This in turn leads to great difficulties in monitoring performance of each division and, consequently, staff in general.

Management structure is reasonably flat, with only four tiers of management from the Chairman to the administrative assistants. Each staff member receives a job description, but it should be pointed out that these have not been revised since the formation of the organisation, despite the changes in circumstances and roles. Currently, there is a lack of direction within the agency and no setting of performance measures within the departments. This has spread to the promotions system, where promotion seems to be built to some degree on performance, but also on loyalty. Consequently, morale is suffering amongst staff, something that has deeper and more serious effects on overall performance.

The GIPC is wholly funded by the Ghanaian government, which does mean that there is some external financial constraint placed on the organisation. The role of the centre is no longer to control investment but to provide information, and to promote investment. Since it was established the GIPC has been running regular trade and investment missions, particularly to the UK and the Far East, usually headed by the President of the country. The greatest external constraint facing the GIPC is the weakness of the private sector and the overall lack of interest shown by foreign investors except in gold production and wood processing.[10]

The GIPC was established as a separate entity by Act of Parliament with one straightforward aim: to promote investment in Ghana.[11] The internal structure of the organisation reflects the fact that the GIPC is still a government agency with a hierarchical management structure. Since the GIPC was established relatively recently by statute its roles and responsibilities are very clearly set out. In addition staff at lower levels all have specific job descriptions. Information has become much clearer with the establishment of the new investment code which has been disseminated widely. It is hoped that this policy will remain constant over time and provide a stable environment for foreign investors (PEF, 1995).

The GIPC itself is controlled by a Board consisting of eight members, all appointed by the President of Ghana (Act 478). These are the Chairman, Vice-Chairman, Chief Executive of the Centre and five other members (at least three of whom must be from the private sector).[12] It is therefore clear that the President has a direct controlling influence in the GIPC, as well as undertaking a leading role in terms of conducting overseas visits. It is also clear that whilst the GIPC is aimed exclusively at private sector investment, the private sector itself is underrepresented on the Board. The lack of private sector input and the strong influence of the government of Ghana at the highest level must raise serious questions concerning the capacity of the GIPC to plan at a strategic level. The main issue affecting this potential lack of capacity is the role of the President. The essentially political interference of the President's Office may not necessarily reflect the strategic interests of the private sector, a problem that could be exacerbated by a lack of private sector presence on the Board of the GIPC.[13]

Presidential influence is also present in determining the budget of the centre which is disbursed by the Board.[14] Expenditure is clearly accounted for and the centre presents a set of yearly accounts directly to the President. Organisations such as the GIPC never have sufficient capital or finance to carry out as much promotion as they would like, but the GIPC does appear to be adequately funded – indeed, it is better funded than most other government departments. The standard of their building is higher and there is a working computer system.[15] Many of the staff came from other departments, which had historically dealt with investment.[16] The partial purpose of the centre, therefore, has been to reduce the number of overlaps between government departments, and to reduce the number of ministries a prospective investor will have to visit. This, in itself is a considerable improvement.

ZIC has its origins in August 1989 as a unit under the auspices of the Ministry of Finance. The ZIC Act, passed in November 1992, transformed it into an independent agency. Prior to the formation of ZIC any given investor would have to present their case to a great number of government ministries and departments. For example, industrial projects were submitted to the Industrial Projects Committee under the Ministry of Industry and Technology. If the project had foreign investment it was referred to the Foreign Investment Committee and if it had a loan component of at least Z$2.5 million it had to have the approval of the External Loans Co-ordinating Committee. Such a contrived and complex system of red tape led to the situation in the late 1980s where investment was declining. ZIC was established as an independent body to provide one investment window thus streamlining the investment approval process. Currently ZIC is changing its role away from investment approval and towards investment promotion.

The centre generally has good working relations with government and particularly its monitor, the Ministry of Finance, which also channels the funding. There is some confusion over exactly what constitutes success or failure for ZIC since investment tends to be a long-term phenomenon and ZIC has not been in existence for long enough to carry out meaningful assessment of impact.

The centre provides a 'single window' for investors where all formalities concerning investment can be dealt with. It helps investors go through all levels of bureaucracy until implementation of the project and also follows up investors to monitor progress and problems. In addition, the centre has the new role of investment promotion and provision of information for potential and existing investors, particularly given the relaxation of investment controls under ESAP.

ZIC also provides an array of information to the business sector, including the Investment Review detailing matters such as new investments, reviews of economic conditions and, changes in legislation. For overseas investors ZIC maintains lists of projects seeking joint venture funding or foreign participation. In addition, ZIC will have a business database linked to the Internet but this is currently only accessible by e-mail. ZIC has an investor tracking system which is designed to match investment enquiries to the relevant local companies. Zimtrade currently has a better information centre than ZIC but the two agencies are expanding their co-operation in this area.[17]

ZIC's role is relatively clear and it is hoped that the change in policy away from control and towards promotion will generate more investment, particularly from overseas. There is a degree of complementarity in activities between ZIC and Zimtrade and to this end the agencies appear to be co-operating effectively, building up computer databases of Zimbabwean companies and investment and export opportunities. This congruency is being seen as an opportunity for co-operation rather than competition between agencies.

The structure of ZIC represents an improvement in the previous haphazard structure of committees previously facing investors.[18] In effect it represents a serious attempt to come to terms with the need to attract foreign investment. The main constraint upon its capacity rests outside the organisation at the policy level.

One of the main constraints faced by ZIC is the minimal government support given to its activities. For example, the government has taken time over formulating a properly documented industrial policy which has held back ZIC's performance – for example, by not providing an incentive to invest due to uncertainty and not giving ZIC specific targets for areas to promote.[19] This is exacerbated by the lack of a clear policy on divestiture of parastatals where foreign investors are expected to play a major role, and also the delay in relaxing the previously strict investment code particularly as it relates to overseas investors.

Most members of staff have been transferred from the various departments across the ministries previously concerned with investment. There is therefore a comprehensive knowledge of the law relating to investment. Furthermore, the impression given by ZIC staff is that the move into a different organisation has allowed them to embrace their new role of encouraging rather than controlling investment.[20]

A serious internal area of dispute has been that many ZIC staff feel that senior management do not appreciate exactly what is required in the new role allocated to ZIC. For example, several of the people interviewed stated that there had been some resistance amongst government ministries to ZIC's computerisation programme, leading to delays in its application. In a sense ZIC is in a difficult position. Essentially it is part of the state, with its workers paid in line with state salaries, even though they are expected to do more and to be better qualified. ZIC's funding is also subject to the rivalries between ministries with regard to budgeting, and is in particular subject to the Ministry of Finance. There are therefore certain communication problems at the macro level relating to the Ministries of Industry and Finance which are effectively competing for 'ownership' of ZIC.

Zimtrade has a clear brief – to improve the export performance of Zimbabwe – but this necessarily encompasses a wide range of activities. One half of the Board of Directors of Zimtrade are appointed by the private sector, the other half and the chairman being appointed by the government. Currently none are civil servants and the Board is effectively free to appoint whom it wishes. Once a plan is developed for trade, Zimtrade has no responsibility to report to government, therefore its decision-making is virtually independent from government, thereby increasing Zimtrade's capacity to act in the best interests of its clients and exports, rather than for reasons of political expediency.[21] It also increases Zimtrade's credibility with the private sector, which remains distrustful of government.

Management is essentially non-hierarchical and is more one of 'first amongst equals' rather than of rigid structures. The extensive use of external consultants both from the Zimbabwean private sector and overseas adds to the flexibility of the organisation and the emphasis on knowledge-based management rather than managerial hierarchies.[22]

There is some overlap with other agencies, particularly ZIC, but Zimtrade has been proactive in developing links and strengthening the services provided to external agents. Part of the overlap is due to the fact that Zimtrade has been so successful at projecting itself and building a reputation that many foreign investors treat Zimtrade as the first point of contact in Zimbabwe rather than ZIC.

One potentially severe constraint facing Zimtrade was identified as a lack of information from central government.[23] This was a recurring theme within all of the organisations interviewed. Government, particularly the MIC, appears reluctant to disseminate information or communicate clear policy over time, something which could affect Zimbabwean firms ability to trade and Zimtrade's ability to help them. Zimtrade further felt that it was being restricted by a lack of a clear industrial strategy – in this way the lack of capacity at the macro level directly affects capacity at the meso level.

Availability of capital and finance

The basic constraint, or potential constraint, on the future operations of Zimtrade is sustainability, and issues such as how much the private sector should have to pay for the services provided when the aim is to reach as many companies as possible. Many small-scale industries, for example, cannot afford to pay export levies which Zimtrade relies on for its income. Having said this, Zimtrade's Director is confident that most companies which return to Zimtrade do so because they value its services. Successful programmes such as the European programme for small-scale industries are also reliant upon external donor funding. Sustainability of such schemes over the long term is therefore in question unless the funding issue can be decided.

The chief source of funds for Zimtrade is the 'Trade Development Surcharge', which is an export levy on all exports of companies registered with Zimtrade. In 1994 the surcharge amounted to Z\$11 612 881, increasing to Z\$16 538 974 in 1995.[24] This represented 81 per cent of income in 1993 and 89 per cent in 1995. Over the same time period, income from advertising declined from around Z$500 000 to Z$340 000 and the revenue grant from government also halved from 1 800 000 to 900 000, however, Zimtrade increased its revenue from interest by over 60 per cent to Z$730 000 (Annual Report and Accounts 1994/5).

At the same time, Zimtrade has managed to build up a significant capital base, particularly in terms of information systems. In 1995, its net assets were calculated at Z$2 344 356 (up from Z$1 936 641). The Trade Information Centre (TIC) expanded during 1996 and provides computer access, including Internet facilities, to firms which wish to use it. In addition, Zimtrade maintains a comprehensive Internet site on the World Wide Web providing information for potential foreign investors. Such a service may prove invaluable to exporters and firms looking for joint venture opportunities alike and the increasing usage of the recently expanded facility is testament to the high value placed upon the service by Zimbabwean firms. One overseas investor interviewed cited the information provided by Zimtrade as the main reason why he was going to invest in Zimbabwe rather than any of the other countries on his shortlist.[25]

The GIPC is fully funded from government, directly from the office of the President. This effectively means that the GIPC operates under a similar financial regime to the MIC – that is, lack of financial resources.[26] The association with the President has brought the initial benefits of availability of capital within the new building in terms of computers and new technology. There appears to be recognition that the provision of information to multinational investors requires a level of sophistication which has hitherto not been observable within other government departments. The long-term viability of the centre must to a certain degree rely on government, and in Ghana, this leads to financial uncertainty.

Threats over sustainability of finance also hangs over both of the Sri Lankan organisations. Both are primarily reliant upon government grant funding for their budgets, and the current environment of cost cutting and fiscal restraint has been a threat to all government departments. Funding follows the normal government pattern of defining a budget for the organisation and then negotiating with the financing authorities in the face of government spending priorities. Of the two organisations, the BOI has made some progress towards generating its own funding through the sales of services. It generates funding through:

- Ground rent.
- Registration fees and land premiums.

- Rent incomes.
- Water rates.
- Import/export service charges.

Currently, this income is difficult to estimate, but it amounts to less than half of the total budget.

The AEPC has an innovative financial structure, based around membership. Initially, the organisation received a marketing development grant from government, but by the early 1990s, this grant had been withdrawn and membership fees had become the chief source of funding for the AEPC. Currently there are around 32 000 apparel exporters registered with the AEPC. In effect there is a two-tier structure of 'members' and 'registered exporters'. In order to become a member, a registered exporter must have been registered for three years. Currently there are 6000 members. Every member pays an entrance fee and then an annual fee. Similarly, registered exporters pay an initial sum, followed by annual memberships.

The critical question here is whether or not this current source of funding is sufficient to run the organisation effectively. This is virtually impossible to answer in a meaningful way, except to state that there does not appear to be a current significant financial constraint on the activities of the AEPC.

Conclusions

There is significant variation in the performance of the various agencies across the promotion sector. One of the most interesting features is that the organisations within the most successful economies do not seem to be as effective as those within the weaker economies. The AEPC is effectively a membership organisation providing services to exporters, but it is structured and operates as a government department. The vertical, hierarchical structure is inflexible, there is no speed of decision-making, an ageing staff profile, and little staff turnover. Having said that, its finances are stable and members continue to join.

The EDB has a similarly poor record of human resource management. Slow staff turnover and as lack of technical and professional expertise within the organisation represent severe constraints on the future operations of the EDB. What is interesting about these developments is the fact that the EDB has presided over a period of rapid growth in exports. This may indicate that in the case of a booming economy the actions of such agencies become irrelevant, or at least superfluous, to industry. The growth of the export industry of Sri

Lanka has been driven by investment by international companies, many of which provide similar services to those provided by the EDB. The failure of the organisation may finally manifest itself, in the lack of development of indigenous companies capable of taking on these international networks.

At the same time, the operations of the BOI in Sri Lanka have been regarded as generally successful, with the general role of providing incentives and infrastructure for investors. The success of the island has certainly been linked to the position of the BOI and its services, but whether this is down to the organisation itself, or to the general situation of providing generous investment incentives, is not clear.

The two African economies in question have both been in some degree of decline. GIPC in Ghana was formed from a series of departments previously controlling investment, as was ZIC in Zimbabwe. The difference between the two is, on a simple level, that ZIC has been relatively successful in changing attitudes and providing a service to investors, whereas GIPC has been seen as remaining quite obstructive to overseas monies. Officials at ZIC are well-trained and knowledgeable and the organisation is linked into other promoting agencies such as Zimtrade. One of the main problems remaining within both of these organisations is reliance on government funding for finance, and the constraints therein.

Zimtrade has a different funding structure designed to get around this. The export levy, taken on all exports, serves as a performance incentive as well as a source of income, i.e. more exports means more funding for Zimtrade. This gives a significant degree of autonomy to Zimtrade, and a powerful reason for it to be interested in the export companies' performance. Better and more consistent funding for Zimtrade is not, however, universally approved of. The services provided by the agency are in demand and usually over-subscribed. This leaves the firms who do not get to benefit from those services in the unenviable position of still having to pay for them if they export.

The incentives provided for Zimtrade may also be questioned, since they may provide services to those companies who are most likely to export – that is, large, established firms. Whilst there is nothing wrong with this in principle, in the long run, the viability of Zimbabwean exports will rely on small firms growing into larger ones, and helping these firms is far more risky for Zimtrade than boosting exports through established companies. To date, this risk-taking has been shouldered by external funding from the EU, amongst others, who sponsor Zimtrade activities in the small business sector.

7
Conclusions: What Role Should Meso-Level Agencies Play in Industrial Development?

Introduction

African manufacturing industry, in general, has had a poor record since the 1960s. Manufacturing exports – a key indicator of industrial success – have made only a minor contribution to total output. With very few exceptions (Botswana and Cameroon) manufacturing exports have declined steadily since the early 1960s (Riddell, 1990). The drive to establish manufacturing enterprises, with the aim of saving foreign exchange through import substitution, tended to lead to the isolation of African industry from the dynamics of efficient production taking place elsewhere in the world economy. These deficiencies included: technical adaptation; management techniques; ancillary services; computers; and marketing developments. As Riddell stated in 1990:

> it would appear that efforts to alter the structure of manufacturing and, in particular, to raise the share of exports in total output, are highly unlikely to succeed by tinkering with tariff levels and rapidly opening up manufacturing to internationally competitive forces unless and until changes are made to address the problems of comparative inefficiency at the enterprise level. (Riddell, 1990: 38)

The story was similar in both India and Sri Lanka before the reform process. The experience of many parts of Asia has shown that the textiles and garments industry is one of the most likely sectors to become competitive in international markets at an early stage. In India, the textiles industry has a long history and a complex structure. Since independence, the government had strictly controlled the sector, aiming to protect the handloom sector from the more developed mill sector. Consequently, the mills were subject to restrictions on output and the handlooms gained access to subsidy. The net effect of all of this was that, over a period of 30 years, the mill sector became less competitive due to lack of investment and new technologies, the hand-loom sector remained non-competitive, but the real beneficiaries of the regulation were the powerlooms, who filled the gap in the market left by the mills. By the time of the reforms in the late 1980s, the power-loom sector was highly competitive in terms of price, but its history of domestic competition meant that the quality of product was very poor. The challenge facing the government and the sector therefore became to improve quality, consistency and marketing internationally and therefore to boost exports.

The Sri Lankan story is, in many ways, stranger still. The textile sec-tor barely existed before the reform process began in 1977, but was seen as the way to develop industry on the island. Taking advantage of MFA quotas and the development of an EPZ on the island, the Sri Lankan government created a series of agencies, notably the BOI to provide significant incentives for foreign investors to locate on the island. The current challenge facing the industry after the spectacular success of garment exports is to develop backward linkages into the rest of the Sri Lankan economy and to stop relying on the overseas investors on the island.

Manufacturing policy throughout the 1980s across the world was dominated by structural adjustment and conditionality. Firms were to be set free from the shackles of government and allowed to participate in market exchange. Entrepreneurs would respond to the new incen-tives offered by the market and Africa would experience an economic resurgence as industries aligned themselves with comparative advan-tage on world markets. The 1980s, however, were characterised by large reductions in manufacturing value added and large numbers of firm exits, particularly in Africa. The decline in agricultural and primary commodity prices adversely affected demand for manufactures and induced fiscal crisis. As a result many governments, prompted by the IMF, introduced deflationary policies with the aim of reducing fiscal deficits and inflation. This further hit demand, and also the ability of firms to obtain imported inputs. Manufacturing companies, unable to obtain imported inputs (such as dye in many textile factories), were forced to reduce capacity utilisation.

Industry across the developing world is characterised by a series of adverse factors: lack of interlinkages within the manufacturing sector; weak forward linkages to other productive industries; shallow, consumer-goods-dominated manufacturing; patchy and inconsistent import substitution; declining export markets; poor marketing networks; and absolute shortage of human resources; low investment; lack of information; and, low technology levels. The disappointing adverse affects of market-oriented reforms during the 1980s point to a more deep-seated source of problems built into the institutional structure of manufacturing. In most cases the supporting infrastructure for entrepreneurs is absent, leaving them unable to overcome the inadequacies of many firms.

Governance and systemic competitiveness

It is clear from the above analysis that there is a role for the state in terms of providing this long-term institutional framework providing incentives for entrepreneurs to switch activities into manufacturing. There is a significant difference, however, between forcing change inappropriately and providing incentives for manufacturing development. Such selective intervention requires a specific type of institution with specific capabilities. These institutional agents must be capable of delivering services to the private sector, which are relevant, and in demand. At the same time the agencies themselves must be capable of carrying out selective intervention without casual political interference which detracts from their economic objectives.

I have shown in the previous chapters how the state can provide incentives for industrial development, and also how agencies must relate to entrepreneurs and firms in order to maximise the value of the services provided. This analysis took as its starting point a model of entrepreneurship based upon how entrepreneurs view the context within which they operate and the capabilities required to allow them to engage in productive activity.[1] Once it is recognised that the likelihood of productive enterprise being undertaken is influenced by a number of variables facing the entrepreneur, then the relative importance of capabilities of agencies may be assessed. The model of the entrepreneurial environment presented above emphasises the interdependence of the contextual and the dynamic factors in enhancing entrepreneurial capabilities. Having established that entrepreneurs in Africa and Asia lack some capabilities, and that the state is the only realistic provider of certain services, it is crucial that the capabilities within those agencies relate to their relative position within the institutional environment facing entrepreneurs, i.e. how they relate to the industrial system and the complex network of institutions therein.

The argument places at its centre the concept of systemic competitiveness. This may be said to be based on the following four assertions (after Meyer-Stamer, 1995):

- A firm will not become competitive in isolation – that is, without the environmental support of service providers and suppliers;
- An environment that sustains competitiveness is rooted in the way in which society organises itself – its institutions. In other words, externalities are often created within governance structures;
- The state is an important actor within these governance networks;
- There are strong interrelationships between four basic levels of the economy: the meta, macro, meso and micro levels.

The analysis has therefore added two levels to conventional analyses of industrial economics: the meta level and the meso level. Most adjustment programmes concentrate upon the reform of the macro in order to stimulate the micro. The concept of systemic competitiveness, however, holds that the basic governance structure of society and its ability to build a basic consensus (the meta level) is important, as is the series of organisations and institutions serving specific geographical or sectoral groups within the industrial structure (the meso level). This requires the state to fulfil a new role as a co-ordinator, moderator and communicator within industrial policy networks, rather than providing top down, high level interventions (Porter, 1990; Meyer-Stamer, 1995).

Agencies attempting to insert themselves into the entrepreneurial environment require a largely new set of capabilities which differ considerably from the roles carried out by state organs since independence in many cases. The experience of Africa in the 1980s shows that the failure of many programmes designed to stimulate industrial development has been caused by internal management failures of the implementing institutions (Edgcomb and Cawley, 1991). The identification and analysis of the factors which affect the performance of agencies attempting to enhance the entrepreneurial environment is therefore crucial to the success or otherwise of state involvement in the stimulation of industrial development.

Any business support agency must have the capacity for productive efficiency, allocative efficiency and adaptive efficiency. Productive efficiency optimises the resources available for the task, allocative efficiency refers to the ability of the agency to respond to its 'customers' i.e. firms, and adaptive efficiency which governs the ability of agencies to respond and react to the market over time. In practical terms, using analyses from Batley (1995), Hildebrand and Grindle (1994), Farbman and Steel (1992) and Hogan, Keesing and Singer (1994), a basic division between internal and external factors can be made. External factors include: financial and economic conditions; private–public sector interaction; political structures and practices; and, legal and administrative structures. Internal factors include: vision and leadership; human resources; financing and financial systems; and internal policies and practices.

Internal capacities and agencies

There are significant internal factors affecting the operation of support agencies. Historically, the internal capacities of the implementing agencies have been largely ignored within programmes designed to enhance the capabilities of the entrepreneur, and these internal weaknesses have led to the failure of many of these programmes. At first glance it appears as if those agencies which are furthest away from government are the most effective. This would be a highly simplistic conclusion, however, and many other factors affect the capacities of the agencies to carry out their respective roles. The agencies were evaluated using a checklist of factors which forms the basis for this section. The three central categories held to be central to the analysis were: organisational and administrative structures; skills and professionalism of personnel; and, availability of capital and financial control.

It is clear from the detailed analysis of the agencies concerned, that the factors affecting internal capacity are heavily interrelated. Agencies such as GIPC may have a clear purpose, but if they lack the quality staff, or the finance to carry out this task then that is clearly important. Many of the agencies exhibit several of the internal indicators of capacity, and yet their ability is threatened either by external factors, such as lack of central government support, or poor financial support and organisation, compromising the ability of the agencies to retain competent staff.

In analysing the agencies covered by this study as a whole there has emerged a scale of effectiveness ranging from the most effective being, perhaps Zimtrade, ICC and SAZ, through to the least effective, being MIC in Ghana and, possibly, EDB in Sri Lanka. The temptation is merely to put this relative effectiveness level down to the distance between the agency and the government. Whilst this is partially true, it does not reflect the complete picture.

Distance from government does allow agencies to relate more closely with the private sector, which is crucial for an agency which is attempting to enhance private sector development. In many countries previously dominated by government there is a deep-seated mistrust between public and private sectors. This may manifest itself in a grudging coexistence, as in Zimbabwe, or, alternatively, as outward hostility as in Ghana. This effectively isolates the private sector from policy-making, a fatal flaw within an environment of adjustment, which relies almost solely on the private sector to generate industrial growth. Agencies which are in some way distant from government can incorporate private sector views, and in many cases act upon them. However, there is a danger that the agency will get so far from government that there is no feedback from the private sector into the overall policy process. In addition, agencies such as Zimtrade and ZIC report problems with the higher government levels, particularly the Ministry of Commerce and Industry. Most of these problems stem from the inability or unwillingness of the ministries to provide the required information, and, in some cases, the necessary long-term frameworks. This, in itself, may be symptomatic of the relative success of some of the agencies in carrying out new roles, whilst the ministries themselves are still seeking for their place in the post-import licensing world.

Even in countries where private sector development has been relatively successful, such as Sri Lanka, the relationship between government and agencies may be difficult. It is perhaps in the nature of the legislation used to establish such agencies that the boundaries are sometimes not clear. The Sri Lankan government, for example, is frequently changing the purpose of the BOI in terms of adding extra roles to its initial remit. In addition, the absence of clear frameworks and strategies has been identified as a problem in both Sri Lanka and India. In fact the Indian case is interesting for slightly different reasons. The nature of the Indian bureaucracy and the length of the decision-making hierarchies means that agencies and firms may be further away from decision-making than is helpful.

IDC in Zimbabwe has, in many ways, turned itself into a private sector holding company. While on the one hand it still carries out some of its role of taking over ailing companies and turning them around, and developing greenfield sites, IDC has a reputation for hanging on to those companies which have been successful and keeping the profits for the holding company (thus strengthening its own self-financing position). Whilst on the one hand this is perfectly rational for a self-financing agency, this is not the original role for which IDC was created. It is supposed to enhance the private sector, not become a subsidised private sector agent itself. This is the path followed by CSIR in India, with a greater reliance on consultancy and external financial generation, coupled with a knowledge-based culture and independence from government.

In Ghana, the MIC is still an arm of government, and yet the lack of arm's-length agencies means that as an organisation it is still required to carry out many of the new roles itself. For example, the role of managing an EPZ is carried out by the MIC in Ghana but by the IDC in Zimbabwe. Given the historical problems between the public and private sectors in Ghana, there are several problems with this arrangement, notably a healthy scepticism amongst entrepreneurs that the EPZ will ever be built. Chief amongst the problems faced by the MIC in Ghana is that of having to adjust its own roles further than most specific agencies, but having less capital and staffing resources with which to do it. Its close association with the government severely hinders policy dialogue between the government and the private sector, except at a relatively low level where there has been a history of personal contact. For example, on attending a meeting between several textile manufacturers and the MIC I was surprised that the entrepreneurs were willing to talk to the official I was accompanying, but as soon as her manager entered the room, they fell silent and were extremely reticent about discussing major policy issues. Dialogue is therefore present, but severely hindered.

A degree of distance from government is also perceived as important for escaping casual political interference. The GIPC in Ghana has a board and senior managers directly appointed by the President. Whilst there was no specific instance of wrongdoing observed, the perception amongst the business community was that it was going on. Thus, the GIPC has been hampered from the start. In contrast, Zimtrade has a board, which it appoints itself. It is therefore in a position to appoint managers who have direct experience of private sector management, which in turn enhances confidence in the organisation amongst the business community.

A feature of the more successful agencies – Zimtrade, ICC, CSIR and the PEF – is their internal administrative structures. All have relatively flat structures, avoiding the traditional hierarchical structures of government. There is a number of factors contributing to the effectiveness of this structure, amongst which is that certainly Zimtrade and the PEF have strong and clear leadership from donors. Zimtrade has a lead from the European Union, largely manifested in the provision of long-term consultancy inputs. PEF, on the other hand, has been established by USAID for a specific purpose. Many of the staff had been attracted to these organisations because of the pay and conditions associated with working for a donor organisation. There are thus several competent people within both agencies, allowing a much more relaxed managerial structure which encourages skill-based working techniques. The staff are also insulated from the depression and demoralisation which afflicts much of the public sector. The ability to pay staff improved salaries has also been a feature of the success of CSIR, and the opportunity to earn cash outside the normal scope of government budgets has been a feature of the ICC and CSIR.

The PEF, CSIR, AEPC and Zimtrade have developed alternative sources of funding. Zimtrade in particular has a relatively developed funding stream from the export levy and has also managed to build up a formidable domestic reputation amongst entrepreneurs. The indications are, therefore, that Zimtrade will have a pool of regular customers with which to retain its income stream. This is by no means clear for the PEF in Ghana. The weakness of the private sector means that there is very little cash available to buy services. In addition, the success of the PEF relies partially on the goodwill of the government in terms of dialogue, and as soon as this begins to break down firms will lose confidence in the PEF. In fact, the PEF can learn a great deal from the ICC, the closest to it in terms of structure and mission. The ICC has been successful for years and has successfully reinvented itself within the reform process, now representing a constituency more concerned with reform and liberalisation than in previous years.

It is a paradox that where the services are most required, the weakness of the private sector severely hampers the effectiveness of the service providers through limiting the availability of funding and therefore the employment of high quality staff. In the case of AEPC, the membership fees are sufficient to cover the operations of the organisation, despite the fact that the organisation itself may be lacking in the capacity to fulfil a full role.

The difference in funding was reflected not only by the relative skills of the personnel between Zimtrade and the PEF and MIC, but also by the equipment available to carry out their tasks. MIC has very limited access to computers, and information-gathering in general is weak in Ghana. The MIC, the Department of Statistics and the National Board for Small Scale Industry all have different statistics dealing with the same group of textile and garment firms. Reinforcing the lack of equipment and skills to handle information, there is a lack of communication between departments dealing with the same group of companies. Lack of communication between government departments is not only a feature of Ghana, Zimbabwe has its own set of problems. Many of the agencies, particularly Zimtrade and ZIC, complained of a lack of co-operation from the Ministry of Industry and Commerce with regard to the overall industrial framework, legislation and general information. The fact that many of the agencies were able to continue providing services successfully is partly a result of the historical development of these agencies. Many of the successful agencies such as IDC have been associated with white Zimbabwean industry and have built an existence almost independent of the government. Others, such as ZIC and Zimtrade, have external linkages – Zimtrade to the European Community and ZIC to the Ministry of Finance – which effectively take them outside the brief of the Ministry of Industry and Commerce.

This pattern of independence from government is followed in Asia by the ICC, CSIR and AEPC in India, but not by any of the organisations analysed in Sri Lanka (with the partial exception of the BOI). This may be because the nature of organisations such as the BOI has become so broad, but may also be a result of the strength of the bureaucratic tradition in India and Sri Lanka.

External factors affecting the capacity of agencies

There are a number of similarities and differences between the external factors affecting capacity.

Financial and economic conditions

The overall lack of resources is a significant constraint within all of these economies. The ERP in Ghana, ESAP in Zimbabwe and the reform programmes in Sri Lanka and India all have elements of financial repression aimed at reducing inflation and the public sector deficit. In Ghana, this shortage of finance has been exacerbated by external shocks and instability. As a result, donors have a high profile in policy making since the shortfall in domestic resources is partially met from donor funding.

Public sector employees have seen their remuneration packages significantly eroded, with consequent effects on morale. A similar situation is present in Zimbabwe and India, although the governments of India and Zimbabwe have successfully mediated the problem through reducing the pace of reform.

Ghana experienced an extremely deep economic slump in the late 1970s, from which she is still emerging. As a result donors have a high profile, and have been able to introduce programmes which have been extremely deep and all-embracing. Ghana has been very good at introducing reforms associated with structural adjustment programmes, but less good at enacting enabling legislation. In other words, the market has been 'unshackled' without the introduction of a complementary institutional framework.

This has not been the case in Zimbabwe, which, in any case, was a late adjuster. Although the economy was subject to a drought-induced slump during the early 1990s there has been no great economic crisis on the scale of Ghana's. The state has been a coherent, well-organised and relatively well-funded (in some areas) organisation within Zimbabwe, consequently the government of Zimbabwe has been in a stronger bargaining position than the government of Ghana with regard to donors. The reform programme has therefore not been so deep and financial repression therefore not so damaging to manufacturing.

The financial problems of Zimbabwe have also been mitigated by a relatively developed financial sector, despite the volatility of the capital market. The government has a good credit rating, which has allowed its agencies, such as SAZ, to borrow money for the development of capital resources. The private firms in the formal sector also have established credit histories, which allow the mitigation of the financial repression of adjustment, something which is certainly not the case in Ghana, where both formal and informal sector firms have great difficulty raising credit of any type. In addition, the financial sector in Ghana is extremely shallow, with very little development of financial institutions and recently privatised banks, which are more concerned with short-term speculation on government-issued bonds than with investing in longer-term returns from manufacturing. From the point of view of the agencies, there is relatively little chance of raising funding from sources other than donors or the government directly, whereas in Zimbabwe there is the possibility of alternative funding from the private sector.

The strength of the government in India and the size and quality of its domestic market have meant that India has been able to come to reform in a far more even-paced manner than weaker countries such as Ghana. The process of reform has been one of bargaining rather than instruction, giving the financial sector time to adjust to the new conditions. This is not to say that the Indian reform process has been without pain, but the existence of significant domestic markets for Indian goods and the positive history of the Indian private sector, has made the process a far more positive one for India.

Sri Lanka also has been an obvious beneficiary of reform. The rapid growth of the textiles industry and, more specifically, the garment export industry is evidence that the success of the reform process started as early as 1977, has benefited the industrial sector.

In conclusion, we can sum this section up in three short points:

- Lack of finance is an obvious constraint on the activities of the business sector as well as the activities of the agencies providing support services. Financial repression affects the ability of organisations to provide services through restricting budgets.
- The availability of finance under fiscal austerity programmes is a critical factor affecting the capacity of publicly funded organisations. Financial autonomy and the ability to diversify funding, in particular achieving some degree of financial autonomy, is an essential element in success.
- There is a paradox with regard to publicly funded organisations. During an economic downturn the business sector may require more support services (credit, information, export incentives, and so on.), but private sector financial support may become less viable and public budgets are likely to be squeezed. There is therefore less funding available for more demands.

Civil–public sector interaction

Across Africa and, to a lesser degree, Asia, governments tend to derive their political power from the public, not the private sectors. In the past this frequently relegated public–private sector interaction to a secondary concern, which in turn led to the alienation of private sector interests and their exclusion from the policy process.

In Ghana, there has been a history of explicit hostility on the part of the government towards the private sector, something which is still fresh in the minds of several entrepreneurs. In addition, the prominent position of ethnic Lebanese within the Ghanaian private sector has led to tension and in some cases discrimination against firms. The Ghanaian economy is characterised by a weak private sector and a strong public sector with a plethora of nationalised industries.

Zimbabwe, in contrast, has a highly coherent private sector dominated by a white Zimbabwean business class. Many of these firms originated during the UDI period and have continued their economic dominance. Well organised and represented through the CZI, these large-scale, formal industries exercise some degree of influence over economic policy which has tried to concentrate, since independence, on building up indigenous business interests. Despite initial distrust of the white business sector, the government has succeeded in pursuing a policy of 'peaceful coexistence' which has contributed to the breadth of manufacturing industry currently operating within the country. In contrast to Ghana, the Zimbabwean formal sector (less so the informal sector) is well represented by the CZI which forms an influential voice in economic policy. The Ghanaian equivalent has been largely under-mined by a series of factors, not least of which have been the collapse of many of its members, and also the lack of trust in the organisation to prevent repetition of past indiscretions.

The private sector in Sri Lanka had experienced similar problems with the public sector up until the reforms of 1977. The seemingly ran-dom policy of nationalisation and political control over industry effec-tively destroyed confidence within the private sector. Fortunately for Sri Lanka, the government embarked on a confidence-building exercise in developing EPZs and providing incentives for the private sector. Although initially benefiting foreign footloose capital through tax breaks, the policy of private sector incentives has progressively spread across almost the whole economy and the island has been able to build up a formidable private sector.

Direct conflict between the public and private sectors has not been an obvious feature of Indian economics, except in so far as hostile regula-tion from the public sector has affected private enterprise. There was, of course, widespread public involvement in industry, but at the same time, the private sector continued to expand, even in the face of hostile regulation (such as that affecting the powerloom sector) and often against the intent of the regulation. Undoubtedly, Indian industry has been fortunate in having access to a huge domestic market, but also a large pool of highly skilled workers and technicians to recruit from.

The private sector in all economies suffer from varying degrees from an inconsistency of policy reform and implementation which could potentially damage production through reducing business horizons. The government of Ghana, for example, has proved excellent at 'stroke of the pen' reforms but less competent at the complementary enabling legislation, whereas in Zimbabwe, whilst there was more confidence in the progress of the reforms, there have been disagreements, such as the early removal of export incentives for manufactures after an initial period of success. The success of the Sri Lankan policy has seen the growth of a private sector that would have been unheard of in the 1970s, despite an ongoing civil war, which has certainly reduced the amount of investment that would have come to the island.

Overall, Zimbabwe and India exhibit signs of positive public–private sector interaction and the ability of both to work together. There is considerable dialogue, and the existence of a developed financial mediation sector and also a wide range of meso-level agencies, facilitates discussion at a practical level. There are problems higher up the government chain, however, particularly with the Ministry of Industry in Zimbabwe, which is still seeking a role and appears unable or unwilling to carry out its primary remaining role of providing an overall, detailed framework for industrial development. Without this overarching policy role the uncertainty persists and the positive work carried out by ZIC and Zimtrade amongst others, is compromised. Even in India, the private sector is continually frustrated by the sheer amount of bureaucracy encountered in production and export.

One interesting example here is that of Sri Lanka. Despite the success of the private sector and the economy, the agencies analysed were not actively engaged with much partnership with the private sector. Much of the investment coming into the island was avoiding the agencies and moving in purely for the incentives and tax breaks. Building an economy on footloose industry is fine in the short term, but the lack of agency development and dialogue with the Sri Lankan industry outside the EPZs may produce problems later in Sri Lanka's development.

The situation in Ghana is somewhat different. There is no financial mediation sector, or a wide range of agencies able to engage in dialogue at the meso level. Communication between the macro levels of government and the micro level of firms has been strained, with the main representative agent of the private sector, AGI, being discredited and dissolving. The lack of public–private interaction in Ghana thus represents a serious obstacle to further industrial development. Again, India's ICC provides a very positive picture of what can be achieved through reforming management within organisations. Its responsiveness and the fact that it has been able to reflect changes in the structures of the industry through changes in the structure of its management has been a great advantage and gained it an enviable reputation in terms of influence and policy formulation roles.

Again, there are a potentially infinite number of issues that could be raised here, but in summary, the following five points should be emphasised:

- There is frequently a history of tension between public and private sectors, which in practice translates into mistrust and a lack of understanding. Particularly in Africa, this mistrust may develop into open hostility with associated disincentives.

- Given this background, *autonomy from government* is crucial for credibility with regard to the private sector.
- Relevance of support services and credibility of organisations may be enhanced by the involvement of the private sector in the running of organisations – for example, by being represented on the Board.
- Sales of services is not always the best barometer of the need for those services since working capital is frequently the most compelling constraint facing the private sector. Given this, many firms priorities will be to match immediate costs rather than to pay for additional services even though they may be required.
- Credible representative organisations (for the private sector) are important in developing an overall enabling environment. Dialogue forums which are associated with previous discredited regimes (as far as the private sector is concerned) and/or consist primarily of established, usually exclusively large-scale, interests benefiting from the status quo, may be counter–productive in terms of creating the conditions for an enabling environment.

Private sector development

Whilst the private sector has thrived in both India and Sri Lanka, as outlined above, the weakness of the private sector in the two African countries considered here acts as an additional constraint on support agencies, where, ironically, they are more needed.

The Ghanaian private sector has been in decline since the mid-1970s, with the low point hitting during the early 1980s. Since then a series of measures designed to encourage the market have led to further firm exits, although, overall, manufacturing has made a slight recovery since 1983. The textile and garment sector has been particularly hard hit, with formal sector firms losing markets to imported second-hand clothing and overseas competition, and smaller firms gaining export markets but being unable to exploit them due to the fragile financial sector. The manufacturing base in Ghana is also relatively narrow, with few inter-firm linkages and poor technology levels making it inflexible. Most firms in Ghana suffer from a common set of problems: lack of capital, staff and technology; poor skill levels; lack of supporting and complementary services; high transaction costs; and low confidence in manufacturing. These all contribute to the decision of many Ghanaian entrepreneurs to quit manufacturing and take up employment in work which has shorter-term benefits, usually trading.

Most of these problems are endemic across Africa, not just in Ghana. Zimbabwean industry suffers from many of the same problems, particularly small-scale manufacturing enterprises. Most formal sector firms in Zimbabwe have access to the wide range of support services available. The banking sector in Zimbabwe, for example, is very conservative and prefers to invest in those businesses with a long track record, or the government. This effectively means that there is credit available to those borrowers, but not those outside this elite grouping. There are organisations in Zimbabwe which deliberately attempt to fill this gap, notably the VCCZ and the IBDC. In fact there is an impressive array of agencies within the economy, providing a comprehensive set of support services for firms.

Zimbabwe has an unusually diverse manufacturing sector for SSA. Whilst not being immune from the rigours of structural adjustment, many firms have fared reasonably well. They are attempting to cope with the new demands placed upon them. Undoubtedly the international contacts and business expertise of the formal sector firms has played a major role in this, but the role of support services such as Zimtrade and SAZ should not be underestimated since demand for their services is increasing.

Political structures and practices

Historically, the governments of Sri Lanka, India, Zimbabwe and Ghana have intervened extensively in their respective economies. All controlled a wide range of nationalised industries, or regulated extensively, dominating their economies. Since the introduction of the reform processes all four countries have embarked on privatisation programmes with varying results.

The Zimbabwean private sector has been somewhat isolated from the government, largely for historical reasons. However, the largely white-owned formal sector firms have peacefully coexisted with the government enterprises, consequently the effects of structural adjustment have been largely to free this sector from bureaucratic red tape. A major effect of this is that several of the agencies closely connected with industry are relatively free from political interference and are dominated by technical factors. This is similar to the experience of the Indian private sector, surrounded by a complex of regulation and bureaucracy and now becoming less constrained by rules. Of course, in the Indian case several private companies benefited from the import substitution regulations and, therefore, have an interest in preventing or slowing reform. The success of organisations such as the ICC in changing its position to one of liberalisation, from one of entrenched interests had been a major feature of the reform process.

A major problem of the industrial sector in Zimbabwe results from this dichotomy within the industrial sector. Whilst at a technical level, several agencies are able to interact with firms, they are hampered by the lack of an industrial framework and meaningful communication with the higher-level ministries, who are uncertain of their new roles. At the same time, the lack of planning in Sri Lanka in terms of detailed industrial strategy and relative impotence in terms of retaining quality staff in the face of multinational companies, has prevented more rapid development of the industrial sector.

The structure of the Ghanaian manufacturing sector does not exhibit the same signs of dichotomy as are found in Zimbabwe, nor the strength of the Indian private sector or the international features of the Sri Lankan sector. The Ghanaian economy has been dominated by public sector firms. The divestiture programme initiated in 1983 has been somewhat disappointing and there is a lack of investors, both domestic and overseas, who are willing to invest in Ghana's rundown industries. There has been significant political manipulation of appointments within the state-owned enterprises and a lack of private sector representation at the policy level. The role of the private sector is publicly acknowledged but most businessmen treat this enthusiasm with cynicism, citing historical precedent and casual political interference. In a sense it does not matter that many of the stories told about political interference on behalf of certain figures close to the President are provable or not. What does matter is that wide sections of the business community believe them, thus further undermining confidence in the government's commitment to reform.

In Sri Lanka, India, Ghana and Zimbabwe the external environment is characterised by fractures between the government and the private sector. Firms are conscious of the need to enhance their abilities in order to respond effectively to the new incentives offered by economic reform. The central difference between them is that the private sector in Zimbabwe has remained a relatively coherent body incorporating its own support agencies, the Indian private sector has been able to reinvent itself and the Sri Lankan industry has gained strength from international competitiveness. In Ghana the private sector has been actively been discriminated against for both ideological and ethnic reasons. The bridges that need to be built in Ghana are therefore much longer than they need to be in Zimbabwe, India or Sri Lanka.

In summary, political practices can affect the capacity of agencies in numerous ways, but particularly as follows:

- Closely linked to the public–private relationship, political involvement in business decisions creates distrust and a poor working environment. Furthermore, the promotion of senior politicians to decision-making levels within agencies may have detrimental effects on the credibility and effectiveness of that agency.
- There is a widespread mistrust of public sector motives in getting involved in business activities. This has been reinforced by widespread corruption in terms of licensing and regulation and a belief that many public enterprises are simply money making schemes for senior politicians or that many organisations merely generate overseas trips for other politicians.
- Commitment to the private sector is not always clear. The more vague the commitment, the more likely the private sector is to stay away from divestiture programmes and investment, and the shorter the business horizon.
- Prompt and planned reform in consultation with the private sector is pivotal in developing an enabling environment. Without this, the private sector loses confidence.
- Ministries need to be more active in defining and acting upon new roles. *Leadership* is vital in developing business confidence, as is the development of policy frameworks through clearly defined and transparent industrial policies. The absence of an integrated industrial framework is a constraint on the capacity of both firms and support agencies developing their own strategies.
- Provision of information on government policies and reforms in areas such as tariff reforms and environmental regulation appears to be important in fostering business confidence.
- Transparency and transfer of information increases confidence within the business sector and allows lengthening of the business horizon.

What are the critical constraints affecting the capacity of agencies?

Whilst all of the capacity factors identified above impact to varying degrees on the capacity of the agencies examined, it became apparent during the research that some were more important than others. Two factors in particular had to be present for any successful operation – indeed, in one case, these factors were virtually the only capacity factors present. These were: *financial and economic conditions*; and *ability of staff* (human resources) employed.

Financial and economic conditions represents the most critical external constraint. Essentially this factor determines the amount of finance available for the agency to carry out its role, a critical constraint in situations of financial instability and repression under structural adjustment programmes. The most successful agencies in each country, Zimtrade in Zimbabwe, the PEF in Ghana, BOI in Sri Lanka and the CSIR in India, had all achieved some form of external financial stability. Zimtrade derives the bulk of its income from the export levy, which whilst on the one hand forming a type of performance-related income, on the other hand represented independence from government and a steady, reliable income stream. The PEF also had access to external funding, initially from an external donor, USAID, but more latterly from membership subscriptions. In a sense this is also a performance-related income stream since if the PEF fails to deliver a service the membership will decline. ICC also has a steady financial base built on membership fees and BOI has been able to develop alternative sources of funding away from government.

Those agencies which perform less well, such as the MIC in Ghana, EDB in Sri Lanka and to some extent ZIC in Zimbabwe, were both subject to stringent financial controls. In addition, they were subject to centralised public budgets, which were driven by a desire to reduce public expenditure rather than directly relating budgets to activities. As a result, the MIC in particular suffered from a severe financial shortage which seriously compromised its capacity to carry out any new roles of industrial support. In the case of MIC the cash shortage had impeded its ability to determine a set of new roles for itself. In a sense, the MIC had the most need to reinvent itself in the face of adjustment, but the least resources with which to do it.

Financial reforms mean that all four countries face financial constraints with regard to raising funding from the private sector to supplement dwindling public sector funding. The constraints in this respect are significantly less stringent in elsewhere than in Ghana. The relatively well developed financial sectors in Zimbabwe and in India have been able to provide supplementary income to the public sector agencies for specific projects. An example of this has been the new buildings and laboratory built by SAZ, which was able to raise a loan (and repay it).

The situation is not similar in Ghana where the financial sector has not been able to provide long-term funding for such projects in either the public or private sectors. Financial deregulation in Ghana, coupled with the uncertainty of policy and the high interest rates, have led to the banks investing in short-term returns in government bonds rather than longer-term projects. The inhospitable financial climate in Ghana and the lack of opportunities to raise private sector funding, is a major factor in explaining why, in general, Zimbabwean agencies outperform Ghanaian agencies.

The other major factor in determining the ability of agencies to carry out their roles is the ability of staff to carry out their own individual roles. In a sense this factor is intimately related to the ability of the agency to raise funding. In a situation of absolute shortage of skilled personnel it is essential that any organisation has the ability to recruit and retain qualified and competent staff. In order to do this, an organisation must have access to a guaranteed and sufficient income stream.

In situations where other external factors affecting capacity may be absent, the presence of these two factors together may be able to overcome the other external constraints. The PEF in Ghana faces a hostile external environment where public–private sector interaction is characterised by mistrust and a poor history, there is a history of anti-private sector political behaviour, and a weak and demoralised private sector. The PEF has been able to circumvent the extremely hostile financial and economic conditions by receiving external funding from USAID which, in turn, has allowed it to employ capable staff who have been able to build up a reputation within the private sector. In turn this has led to increasing membership of the association and increased income from membership subscriptions. The PEF is a case where the initial vicious circle was broken by external funding, and was then built into a virtuous circle by competent staff and an improving track record.

In Zimbabwe, Zimtrade similarly targeted these two factors as crucial in building up a successful organisation. Initially Zimtrade was established as part of a European Community (EC) initiative. The EC did not, however, merely plough cash into the fledgling organisation. Aid was directly related to the problem of recruiting and retaining quality staff by providing aid in the form of 'man hours' for suitably qualified consultants. This has meant that Zimtrade has been able to retain a core of quality staff whilst training up several Zimbabwean staff members. A significant part of any organisation's budget is staffing costs, and Zimtrade has directly linked the financial and quality elements of this in their financial structure, allowing them to build upon this and develop the services they provide.

Both of these examples show one element very clearly: it is the fact that *both* of the constraints – of external financing and internal staffing – have been overcome that is the significant factor. It is by no means clear that one element without the other will make for a successful agency, what is clear is that both elements together will have a good chance of overcoming other constraints on capacity.

Qualified and well-motivated staff are instrumental in overcoming the additional constraints on capacity. The primacy of the financial and economic conditions and the ability of staff should not be taken to imply that the other constraints on capacity can be any less damaging on the operations of an agency. The presence of these two elements merely makes it more likely that the other elements may be overcome. A competent staff will, for example, be able to clarify their individual roles within an organisation as well as clarifying the overall vision of the agency. If there is no clear aim, then competent staff are more likely to seek clarification.

In the same way with external constraints, a well-performing staff will usually be operating in a situation in which there is a weak private sector, since if it wasn't weak there would be less need for an industrial support agency.[2] This weakness may be partially overcome by the performance of the agency itself. In the same way, given the history of all of the countries, the lack of meaningful dialogue between public and private sectors, for whatever reasons, may be overcome by an agency which is seen to be autonomous but not independent. In order to achieve this, the agency must have a method of circumventing the external constraints upon finance and be able to recruit staff who are technically competent and seen to be politically independent of government.

Embedded autonomy

The capacity of agencies does not, however, merely come down to the availability of cash and the resulting ability to recruit competent staff. Significant though these issues are, in themselves they are insufficient to increase the performance of agencies. I have continually emphasised the importance of entrepreneurial environments in facilitating industrial development and the important role played by meso level agencies within that environment. The crucial point is that agencies must be *embedded* into the system, but not be captured by either the macro or the micro level – they must be *autonomous*. Autonomy allows the meso institutions to pursue policies which are beneficial to the system as a whole rather than to one specific social grouping within the industrial network (Messner, 1997). Evans (1992) identifies the potential problem of capture by specific social groups within the system. He identifies the core of the problem as the formulation of cartel behaviour of the agency and social network leading on to the maintenance and protection of the status quo typical of much cartel behaviour. In an organisation which needs to evolve and to act within the framework of a continually changing market, adherence to the status quo may be a dangerous policy leading to the loss of competitiveness for the system as a whole.

In addition, autonomy is not synonymous with independence. Independence implies detachment from the industrial system, autonomy implies the freedom to make decisions which do not benefit specific groups, but the system as a whole. The distinction is simple: independence is outside the industrial system; autonomy is within the framework of the industrial system.

The best-performing agencies all have decision-making autonomy. They can pursue policies which benefit their clients, themselves and the government. Zimtrade has a clear mandate to increase exports – this benefits the government through increased taxes, trade and prestige; the firms through increasing revenue; and Zimtrade through increasing the export levy therefore their income. Decision-making autonomy allows Zimtrade to pursue policies that benefit all exporters, not those who are close to the government, or those who are members of a particular association. Autonomy is therefore crucial to the ability of agencies to pursue policies that benefit their clients and the industrial system as a whole.

Embeddedness, by contrast, is the other side of the same coin. Industry operates in a complex web of networks constituting an industrial system. For an agency to operate effectively and to provide services, which are relevant and required, it must be embedded within these networks, not be independent of them. The example of the IDC in Zimbabwe provides an example of an agency that has become too autonomous. Although the agency does still carry out some specific tasks on behalf of the government,[3] the vast majority of the IDC's work consists of running companies much in the way of most private sector holding companies. The IDC has a reputation for keeping control of those companies that become successful. This is a direct result of the internal assessment system that is based on the performance of the firms within the portfolios of each individual manager. The IDC has therefore managed to become detached from its original role within the industrial system and this, in itself may be a capacity failure.

Overall conclusions

The overall conclusions of the study are that agencies are constrained within three main areas:

Autonomous, but not independent

Agencies occupying the meso level between the government and entrepreneurs must be autonomous, but not independent. Autonomy is crucial to establishing credibility amongst entrepreneurs and is necessary to undertake technical support services, which are not subject to casual political interference. Independence is not desirable since in the same way that agencies need to relate clearly to entrepreneurs, they need to relate to government. A successful information conduit may only carry out a dialogue if it is deeply rooted in both sides of the discussion. Agencies also provide a series of services, such as information provision, which are only obtainable from government. This is not to say that many of these services cannot be provided by the private sector, but in the short term most private sector firms which are capable of doing this are either not present, have insufficient access to information or are prohibitively expensive for most entrepreneurs. The optimum short-term solution is therefore the establishment of autonomous agencies capable of acting as a 'go-between' for government and the private sector.

In addition, the source of value for meso-level agencies derives from their role within the networks, which constitute the industrial system. Independence leads agencies away from their roles within that system – agencies are not private firms, they exist to fulfil a purpose deriving from the unwillingness of private firms to provide services.[4] The discharge of these roles requires autonomy of decision-making in order to carry out those roles, but an embeddedness within industrial networks in order to shape and adapt those roles in line with market changes and the demands of those industrial networks.

Primary capacity constraints

Other than the degree of autonomy, agencies are subject to several constraints, both external and internal. The critical constraints which affect the capacity of agencies to carry out their roles effectively are:

- financial and economic conditions; and
- the ability of staff.

These two closely related factors provide the framework within which the agency operates. Although both of these are clear a priori, their interrelationship and their interplay with the other capacity factors is less so.

It is perhaps self-evident that the ability of an agency to circumvent adverse financial and economic conditions is crucial. Particularly given the harsh economic conditions of structural adjustment in both Zimbabwe and Ghana, the ability of agencies to break the vicious circle of funding and gain external, reliable sources of income may prove crucial. All of the successful agencies, such as the PEF and Zimtrade, were able to break this circle, receive funding, and then build upon their success in order to develop funding sources – the PEF through increasing membership subscriptions, and Zimtrade through the export levy.

Closely linked with the circumvention of financial and economic conditions is the recruitment and retention of quality staff. In a situation characterised by an absolute shortage of quality personnel, the ability to attract suitably qualified staff is critical, and the ability to fund such personnel is critical. The relationship between staff and income is a reciprocal one. The mere ability to get hold of funding does not mean that agencies will suddenly be able to carry out all of their roles with great success. The ability of staff to employ that funding effectively is a major constraint in its own right.

In this way, the two critical constraints are interdependent. When both elements are present there is a good chance that the agency will be able to overcome some or all of the other external and internal constraints affecting the capacity of that agency.

Secondary constraints

The existence of the two primary constraints does not mean that the other constraints are insignificant, merely that the ability to overcome any of the secondary constraints will be severely compromised if the two primary constraints remain in place. All of the external and internal constraints represent a threat to the capacity of the organisation. A weak private sector with little or no dialogue with the public sector and a system accustomed to casual political interference in everyday affairs will seriously affect the capacity of agencies to carry out their roles. Unfortunately, this is the very situation which faces most industrial support agencies across Africa as a whole.[5] It is clear that, given these circumstances, the need for industrial agencies to enable entrepreneurs to respond to the new set of incentives offered by liberalisation is greater than in a less hostile environment. The relative success of the PEF in Ghana, BOI in Sri Lanka, ICC and CSIR in India, and Zimtrade, ZIC and SAZ in Zimbabwe, illustrates that when the two primary constraints can be overcome, the agency is in a better position to address these additional external constraints.

Internally, agencies have historically been handicapped by inadequate management systems, as identified by Keesing and Singer (1991). Confusion of purpose, neglect of commercial services, inflexibility of government procedures and the unsuitability of government staff for provision of commercial services, are all identified as constraints upon the capacity of government agencies. Whilst each of these represents a significant capacity constraint, none of them is insurmountable with access to funding and professional staff. ZIC in Zimbabwe is partially successful in that the agency does centralise many services for investors, which were previously spread around several departments, but the agency does suffer from two main defects impeding performance. Firstly, many of the staff of ZIC came from existing government departments: they were bureaucrats. As a consequence, many businessmen, whilst recognising the improvement, still dismiss ZIC as another government department. This is exacerbated by the second constraint, which is the uncertainty over funding. Funding comes directly from government and is frequently inadequate – that is, that there is an end of year shortfall. This represents a capacity constraint. So while ZIC has access to internal capital (such as computers or a new building), has an amount of goodwill from several members of the private sector, has a clarity of purpose and has clear personnel rules, all of these are undermined by the inability of ZIC to overcome its two basic problems of external funding and the retention and recruitment of qualified staff.

One of the more interesting elements of the analysis is that there does not appear to be a relationship between relative success and the legal status or organisational arrangement. Rather, the level of actual autonomy in day-to-day decision-making is far more important. For example, AEPC is a private company, but its head is a member of the Indian Administrative Service, and its culture is similar to that of a government department. In general, the closer to government the steeper the hierarchy.

There has been no real innovation with regard to organisational structures within industrial support. The most successful agencies seem to have been renovated forms of organisation dating back to the colonial era. Most common organisational arrangements include independent companies incorporated under Companies Acts through to charitable bodies, quasi-government agencies established under their own legislation and conventional government departments.

Models for the development of agencies?

Whilst it would be difficult to generalise the lessons learnt from this study across the whole of the developing world, the general conclusions regarding the position of agencies and the importance of the duality of the two central capacity factors remain crucial. The minimum requirements of a means to circumvent the constriction of financial repression, and the ability to recruit and retain professional staff, are crucial for any agency in any economy. The proviso that any of the other capacity factors may be overcome given the presence of these two allows a degree of replicability in the model. As long as these two are present, then any economic circumstance within the meso level may be overcome.

The fact that many entrepreneurs in different circumstances identify similar constraints to their economic development, in a sense, means that there is a common need for similar agencies carrying out similar roles. It may therefore be too strong a statement to say that the more successful agencies, such as Zimtrade, form a replicable model, but it is not too strong a statement to assert that there are important lessons from the performance of these agencies for other such organisations across the developing world.

The importance of the meso level in the overall environment of entrepreneurs cannot be overstated. Whilst several analysts have recognised that markets do not operate along textbook principles and have developed analytical frameworks to deal with this, these frameworks are incomplete. Given the model of the entrepreneurial environment laid out above, Northian institutional analysis only covers the contextual factors affecting the overall environment. Entrepreneurs depend upon a far wider economic system to support their activities and to encourage them to take up productive, as opposed to unproductive activity. These 'ability factors' are predominantly found at the interface between the macro and micro levels of the economy – the meso level. The fact that across much of Africa in particular, the relationship between the macro and micro elements of the economy has also broken down places increased emphasis on this meso level to perform, and gives meso-level agencies additional responsibility in terms of being independent from historic policy problems. The formation of agencies at this level, with autonomy from government, may also give industry a new opportunity in terms of building up systemic competitiveness without relying purely on government goodwill or political interference.

Crucially, the existence of an enabling environment in terms of enhancing entrepreneurial abilities allows industry to compete internationally with multinational companies which internalise many of these functions. Without access to complementary services most small African firms will not be able to grow into larger firms, particularly with domestic markets being no longer protected and external competition undercutting most domestic production.

Future policies

Finally, one element underpins much of this analysis and that is credibility. Most of the dealings between agencies and firms rely crucially on some degree of trust. This may be enhanced by a history of success from a particular agency, but in most of the cases examined the private sector has been, at best, mistrustful of the public sector. Trust and confidence is difficult to build and impossible to measure. Perceptions are critical.

The biggest doubt over the future of the more successful agencies is the continuation of the funding for those organisations. In particular, the PEF in Ghana needs to secure a reliable source of income, which is independent of external funding from USAID. A start has been made in terms of building up a consultancy capability and a fee-paying membership, but it is by no means clear whether this will be sufficient when external funding is withdrawn. In particular, there is a danger of a downward spiral in that once funding becomes questionable, it becomes difficult to retain the staff who have built up a reputation. Membership will therefore decline, followed by funding, followed by reduced staff, and so on. In the same way, there is a danger with Zimtrade, for example, that export earnings, and so the export levy, will decrease through no fault of Zimtrade. This could seriously compromise the ability of Zimtrade by reducing funding and therefore the numbers and quality of staff which can be retained by the organisation.

Having said this, there is a degree of desirability in directly linking performance to funding. If this becomes feasible, then there is the possibility of opening service provision to the private sector. As mentioned above, the private sector does not tend to become involved in supplying services to African industry for a variety of reasons, including an inability of most African firms (other than multinational companies) to pay relatively high prices, and the absence of private sector companies in many cases. Once private sector businesses are growing and becoming more successful, they may require information that government agencies cannot supply, or they may require it in a format which cannot be provided. Once they are able to pay, firms may switch to private sector providers. Since this is not the current status of most African business, it is to be expected that direct, large-scale, private sector competition with the public sector will not be seen for some time, leaving the crucial role of service provision to the agencies. Ironically, in India and Sri Lanka, where the need for services may be less urgent, the ability of the private sector to pay for them makes them more available, bringing us back to the paradox of services being least available where they are most needed.

Notes

Chapter 1

1. For example, in the last 15 years there has been only one World Bank publication addressing the meso level.
2. This has developed into a debate in itself relating to deindustrialisation. See, for example, Stein (1992).
3. I use the label 'Northian' to denote those institutions that are, in effect, the 'ways of doing things' identified by Douglas North.
4. Wilson does point out that organisations such as the police, whom he categorises as a craft organisation, are rarely content to measure only outcomes and procedures do matter. Most craft organisations rely on the goodwill of their staff to uphold good practice but this may not be the case. In the police, for example, procedures must be in place to prevent corruption, excessive force or engaging in political favouritism. Wilson concludes that the bulk of control in these situations is still down to the individuals sense of duty (Wilson, 1989).
5. As an example, in Bulawayo, I spoke to several entrepreneurs and organisations who all stated that I should ask Zimtrade for further advice since they 'really knew what they were doing'.
6. In practice, most African countries are subject to the second set of problems rather than the first. Most African countries are not currently subject to MFA quotas, they are primarily concerned with saving, or building up basic industries, or higher value added niche markets.
7. It is not entirely clear why Edward regulated wool imports, but it is doubtful he regarded textiles as a 'take-off' industry. What he did realise was that textiles made money, therefore generated tax.

Chapter 2

1. There are varying degrees of each of these in different countries. In India and Sri Lanka, for example, it would be difficult to argue for the decline of the state, but market distortions are widespread, whereas in many parts of Africa the state has virtually collapsed and markets may be at best, embryonic.
2. In this way, the concept of autonomy is similar to concerns expressed over regulatory authority and 'regulatory capture'.
3. It could be argued that in Africa, the state expanded but did not begin to exhibit the characteristics of a complex system. Rather the traditional hierarchy was merely expanded without the accompanying internal changes. The result is that most African bureaucracies are now facing this problem the 'wrong' way around, i.e. they are becoming more complex and losing their hierarchical structures whilst *contracting*, not expanding.

4. See for example, Messner (1997), Schmitz and Musyck (1993).
5. This may not be good, grammatical English, but these labels do convey the meaning of the authors.
6. The term 'agency' is here used to equate to 'institution'.
7. For Messner, this belief arises out of a view of the global economy consisting of competition based upon industrial clusters or regions, rather than firms, similar to the analysis of industrial geographers such as Michael Storper (1992) and A.J. Scott (1992).
8. For example, Whites in Zimbabwe and Kenya and Lebanese in Ghana.
9. Messner (1997) claims that developing countries in general suffer from inadequacies at all four levels.
10. See for example Zaaijer's (1997) study of the Municipality of Bulawayo. This shows that several skilled groups, particularly engineers, leave after their bonded period.
11. For example, just for textiles in India, there is a ministry with seven divisions. Within this there are three Commissioners with separate office structures, three technology institutes, five public corporations, four boards and five advisory councils. In addition, there are seven export associations for textiles and garments, and around ten large representative organisations. This is for textiles alone and does not include the more general export and investment promotion agencies, for example.
12. These factors may be said to be similar to North's institutional factors, or the contextual elements of the entrepreneurial model laid out in Figures 2.1 and 2.2 i.e. the 'big picture'. With regard to industry, a crucial factor amongst this group would be the ability to enforce contracts which is lacking in many African contexts (Herbst, 1993).
13. However, India is notably competitive in some areas, particularly the growing software industry.
14. NTC Mills reported accelerating negative growth rates for sales, exports, capacity and growth, coupled with declining profitability since 1992.
15. For example, technology is usually taken as constant within neoclassical comparative statics. A dynamic view of market failures recognises the importance of constantly changing markets including those institutional elements which neoclassical economics fails to recognise or assumes out of the model.

Chapter 3

1. One of my Ghanaian colleagues insists that the government decision to make schoolchildren wear uniforms is almost single-handedly responsible for keeping the industry alive.
2. This includes tie-dying, batik, *kente* cloth, etc. production and is sometimes referred to collectively as Afrocentric production.
3. Unilateral Declaration of Independence – see the following chapter on the evolution of government support.
4. This seems like a very unlikely percentage breakdown. One explanation could be that it represents firms registered to pay tax, in which case several private sector firms would be excluded. In addition, if multinational companies were taken out of the equation, this could refer to solely Ghanaian firms. Herbst

provides no detailed back-up, but the essential point remains valid: the public sector remains dominant.
5. It could also be argued that at least they have access to employment, even if it is white-owned.
6. The name change was aimed to reflect an appeal to popular capitalism, similar to Mrs Thatcher's approach in the UK, and the desire to avoid a narrow corporate base.
7. The CD was previously the secretariat to the Commission on Peopleisation.

Chapter 4

1. Though punitive in the sense that very few can afford them, they may actually be real. This would lead to the conclusion that real interest rates could price out domestic industry, i.e. that it should not be there in the first place.
2. This was usually the very first point raised in interviews.
3. Interview with the BAF manager, MIC.
4. Many entrepreneurs recognise this and claim that the main reason for it is the uncertainty over government policy and lack of confidence in a commitment to the private sector.
5. Zimbabwean firms are invariably family-owned and managed. One manager stated that marketing was something you gave the least competent child to do!
6. World Bank representative, Accra.
7. A major problem of the AGI is that most of its members have gone out of business.
8. The Department for International Development, UK.
9. This is enhanced by the appointment of several private sector personnel to agency staff, particularly to higher management positions, something that does not happen with the same frequency in Ghana.
10. For example, textiles firms were just as likely to use any of the services and it did not matter if they were in Bulawayo, Harare or Gweru.
11. These include the Ahmedabad Textile Industry Research Association (ATIRA) and sister institutions in Bombay, Southern India and Northern India, the latter extending their activities into Eastern and Central India.
12. This subject was raised within several interviews with Ghanaian as well as Lebanese entrepreneurs.
13. The progressive losses within NTC Mills and their inability to meet statutory social obligations of factories are the best known example of this.
14. Currently at the level of a plan awaiting approval from the President's office.
15. This is typical of a number of statements made by staff at numerous levels. The importance of these statements lie in their preponderance and the fact that several people seem to believe them, however unlikely. This severely affects trust between public and private sectors and has a detrimental effect on the overall attitudes to business.

Chapter 5

1. Several additional agencies were looked at, but in less detail than this fourteen.

2. The private sector currently pays around twice the amounts of CITI for similar qualifications.

3. At the time of writing this was still in the negotiation phase, but was receiving considerable publicity in the press.

4. This was confirmed in an interview with Eric Bloch, an economic analyst and another of the 'troubleshooters' employed by government and banks to turn around unsuccessful businesses.

5. Financial information was difficult to obtain within IDC since the government was considering taxing IDC at the time of the study. Managers were therefore unwilling to release sensitive information.

6. This was something mentioned frequently by entrepreneurs, government officers and donors, including the ILO. They tended to feel as though IDC was acting in its own interest and was no longer trying to enable them.

7. This view was confirmed by several entrepreneurs and Jason Moyo, director of the ILO office in Harare.

8. This has also been a theme in the Zimbabwean press.

9. Nominally, the Board is appointed by the government, but they have not made a direct appointment for several years.

10. In one interview I was told that only three members of staff had left in the last fifteen years and that they had retired.

11. In interviews, questions about relative salaries were greeted with broad smiles. One interviewee just said: 'Let's just say I earn more than many people in government'.

12. This in turn adds to the incentive to keep successful companies.

13. This clear within the annual reports and financial statements.

14. It should be pointed out, however, that IDC does still develop greenfield sites and is currently doing so in a joint venture with a Malaysian company – a deal set up by the President on his recent trip to Malaysia.

15. Of course, if the IDC did not run these successfully reconstituted companies then the financial benefits from taxation and the effective running of the companies would go back to the government.

16. Interviews with entrepreneurs and the PEF.

17. This was repeated in virtually every interview we held with entrepreneurs and again in the workshops held in the country.

18. Interviews within the MIC.

19. Known as ODA at the time of the research.

20. One of the chief complaints of the private sector is that the Ministry does not include any private sector officers, only bureaucrats who have historically granted licences without understanding business (PEF, 1995). The appointment of private sector ministers is an attempt to ameliorate this.

21. The information officer, originally employed by UNIDO, was initially unwilling to give us any information even though this was his sole reason for being employed in the Ministry. This did not only happen to us. When we replied with a report (a non-sensitive report relating to the number of textile firms in Ghana), the other officers in the textiles department asked for a copy because they had been unable to prise it from the information officer!

22. For example, the Annual Report for 1993 identifies three resignations, one retirement and three officers redeployed into the MIC – a total staff turnover for the year of one.
23. When asked if they would like to work in the private sector, most staff shrugged their shoulders and asked 'Where?'
24. Mrs Emma Mitchell, appointed 1 March 1993. She was accompanied into office by two Deputy Ministers and a new Chief Director who replaced all of the previous leadership cadre.
25. Interviews with various staff members of MIC.
26. This is despite their mention within the Annual Reports for 1994 and 1995.
27. The actual categories given in the budget are: 'Travelling and transport' c37 091 000; 'General Expenditure' c56 124 000; 'Maintenance, repairs and renewals' c6 162 000; and, 'Other current expenditure' 26 679 000.
28. I was informed in an interview with one of the Directors of MIC that the percentage figures for 1995 expenditure would be 'roughly the same'. The drain from the state-owned sector is still extremely great due to the poor performance of the divestiture programme. Many of the companies which have been sold, e.g. Ashanti Goldfields, were in profit. The MIC has therefore been left with the unprofitable ones which require increased subvention as they become increasingly uncompetitive under liberalisation and increased competition.
29. This is also mentioned in the PEF documentation (PEF, 1995).
30. The Chinese in general, both businessmen and the Chamber, were unwilling to be interviewed (with one exception – Volta Garments).
31. The textile development officer, Ms Julia Anokye, accompanied me on several visits and was clearly warmly, rather than politely, received. On the other hand, most of the entrepreneurs who attended the workshops with the MIC stated that this was the only time they had spoken to anyone remotely senior.
32. Interviews within CZI and ZNCC. SAZ also uses the British Council conference facilities in Harare to run several courses for which there are brochures.
33. In practice this means that a senior manager cannot overrule a more junior colleague who is an expert in his/her particular field if that senior manager is not also an expert.
34. Interviews with Ministry officials, also echoed by CZI and ZNCC.
35. Most businessmen involved with exports in particular had consulted SAZ either directly or indirectly. Demand for the services offered is clearly increasing, for example in terms of enrolments for courses which are invariably oversubscribed.
36. Several members of staff interviewed had attended conferences overseas ranging from South Africa to Malaysia.
37. Relative to the success of investment promotion, or the provision of information.
38. Annual reports and interviews with staff.
39. This has been funded through income other than government, which told the director that there was no money for capital expenditure for SAZ in the near future. Interview with the director.

Chapter 6

1. Interviews with entrepreneurs and government. The AGI has managed to become discredited with both its members and the government, much to the despair of its director.
2. Interview with the current Chairman of AGI, who himself had just gone into liquidation.
3. Staff are notoriously coy in relation to their salaries, but I was informed that they are paid at a higher rate than government staff. This was confirmed by the USAID representative who stated that staff were paid according to 'international rates'. In fact several staff had worked abroad for international agencies and had returned at similar salary levels.
4. This may be a function of the fact that the PEF was only established in 1996.
5. According to interviews with the Chief Economist, the most lucrative market for them is carrying out credit history studies for banks, since they are amongst the few who can afford to pay.
6. The PEF is primarily funded by USAID.
7. Accounts were not available for the PEF at the time of the fieldwork. The Chief Economist did state that the income form consultancy work at the time amounted to around 20 per cent of their income. This could not be confirmed by published accounts, but if true, it would suggest that the PEF has a long way to go in building up a sustainable income, thus this issue remains uncertain.
8. He was the chief economist at CZI's Harare office.
9. It is not clear how this expertise gap will be filled after the termination of the project.
10. There is a causality problem here: how far can the GIPC be responsible in the lack of investment in Ghana when there is a general lack of interest?
11. The GIPC was established under Act 478, 'The Ghana Investment Promotion Centre Act, 1994'.
12. Note that at the time of writing (1999), only the minimum of three private sector representatives sat on the Board, reflecting a general lack of private sector representation.
13. Interviews with entrepreneurs reflected a lack of confidence already developing. The rather cynical attitude adopted was that the President had invented the GIPC to pay for his overseas trips. Even if this is not true, the fact that many businessmen *believed* it to be true is itself an indication of the lack of trust between public and private sector.
14. Act 478 states that the Government will provide money subject to the approval of parliament.
15. The most obvious improvement over several other public buildings in Accra is that it is air-conditioned.
16. The number of departments vary from interviewee to interviewee. Numbers vary from five to around ten separate departments. Given this, a system where a potential investor only has to visit one central office instead of five, must be beneficial.

17. For example, the director of Zimtrade was positive about developing joint information sources. The two agencies are currently working on a joint database.
18. Previously, investors had to visit anything between three and ten different departments in different ministries depending on the type of activity and the size of the investment.
19. The draft industrial policy drawn up by the Ministry does not provide a satisfactory industrial framework. It reads more like a 'wish list' than a policy.
20. One additional piece of fieldwork I was allowed to do was to accompany an Australian businessman through a series of meetings to see exactly what happened. He certainly felt that staff went out of their way to be helpful and constructive.
21. This is further enhanced by the involvement of donors, particularly the European Union.
22. Most of the external donor involvement is in 'man hours' of consultancy time for overseas trade experts.
23. According to Zimtrade's director, the government appears to be uninterested in Zimtrade as long as it does not demand cash – this could be a blessing or a handicap.
24. The 1995 figure was unpublished at the time of the study, but estimates from the Director were around Z$20 000 000.
25. This was the same investor who I had traced through the corridors of ZIC.
26. This may be inferred from the fact that all of the government offices are under financial restrictions under the ERP.

Chapter 7

1. That is, I recognised the presence of entrepreneurs, but also the possibility of non-productive entrepreneurial behaviour. The aim of enabling is therefore to alter the entrepreneurial environment in order to switch activities from non-productive and into productive entrepreneurship.
2. Having said this, the case of Ghana shows that where these organizations are most needed there may not be the financial and human resources available to run a successful agency.
3. For example, the government has asked the IDC to turn the Zimglass company around (this is a state-owned company) and to negotiate the EPZ contract with the Malaysian consortium providing the finances.
4. In other words, market failures.
5. This is certainly the case in Ghana and Zimbabwe where relations between the public and private sectors have been extremely tense and there has been a long history of political interference. This is a pattern also identified by Riddell (1990) across most of Black Africa, and also by the World Bank in *Adjustment in Africa* (1994).

Bibliography

Ahiakpor, J.C.W. (1986) 'The Capital Intensity of Foreign, Private Local and State-Owned Firms in a Less Developed Country: Ghana', *Journal of Development Economics*, vol. 20, pp. 145–62.

Akerlof, G. (1970) 'The Market for Lemons: Quality, Uncertainty and the Market Mechanism', *Quarterly Journal of Economics*, vol. 84, no. 3, August, pp. 488–500.

Alemayehu, M. (2000) *Industrializing Africa: Development Options and Challenges for the 21st Century*. Asmara: Africa World Press.

Amin, A. (1994) *Post-Fordism: A Reader*. Oxford: Blackwell.

Annual Report of the Textile Sub-Sector (various years) *Internal Report for the Ministry of Trade and Industry*.

Aryeetey, E., Baah-Nuakoh, A., Duggleby, T., Hettige, H., and Steel, W. (1994) 'Supply and Demand for Finance of Small Enterprises in Ghana', *World Bank Discussion Papers, Africa Technical Department Series 251*.

Athukorala, P. (1995) 'Direct Foreign Investment and Manufacturing for Export in a New Exporting Country: The Case of Sri Lanka', *World Development*, vol. 19, pp. 543–64.

Atkinson, M.M. and Coleman, W.D. (1989) 'Strong States and Weak States: Sectoral Policy Networks in Advanced Capitalist Countries', *British Journal of Political Science*, vol. 19, pp. 47–67.

Bahrani, H. (1992) 'The Emerging Flexible Organisation: Perspectives from Silicon Valley', *Californian Management Review*, vol. 34, no. 4, pp. 33–52.

Bardhan, P. (1990) 'Symposium on the state and economic development', *Journal of Economic Perspectives*, vol. 4, pp. 3–8.

Barwa, S.D. (1995) 'Structural Adjustment Programmes and the Urban Informal Sector in Ghana', *ILO Discussion Paper No. 3*.

Bates, R.H. (1983) *Markets and States in Tropical Africa*. Berkeley, CA: University of California Press.

Bates, T. (1993) 'Theories of Entrepreneurship', in R. Bingham and R. Meir (eds), *Theories of Local Economic Development*, Princeton, NJ: Princeton University Press.

Batley, R. (1995) 'The assessment of capacity', Unpublished Paper, Development Administration Group, University of Birmingham.

Batley, R. (1997) 'A Research Framework for Analysing Capacity to Undertake the new Roles of Government', *The Role of Government in Adjusting Economies, Working Paper No. 23*, University of Birmingham.

Baumol, W.J. (1968) 'Entrepreneurship in Economic Theory', *American Economic Review*, vol. 58, May, pp. 64–71.

Baumol, W.J. (1990) 'Entrepreneurship: Productive, Unproductive and Destructive', *Journal of Political Economy*, vol. 98, no. 5, pp. 100–31.

Bennell, P. (1994) British Manufacturing Investment in Sub-Saharan Africa: Corporate Responses During Structural Adjustment, *IDS Working Paper No. 13*.

Bennell, P. (1996) 'Privatisation in Sub-Saharan Africa: Progress and Prospects During the 1990s', *IDS Working Paper No. 41*.

Best, M. (1990) *The New Competition: Institutions of Industrial Restructuring*. Cambridge: Polity Press.

Biggs, T., Moody, G., van Leeuwen, J-H., and White, E.D. (1994) 'Africa Can Compete! Export Opportunities and Challenges for Garments and Home Products in the US Market', *World Bank Discussion Papers, Africa Technical Department Series 242*.

Bloch, E. and Robertson, J. (1996) *Zimbabwe: Facing the Facts*. Harare: Thomson Publications.

Boulding, K.E. (1987) *Evolutionary Economics*. Beverly Hills: Sage.

Bria, C. and Yaghmarian, B. (1991) 'Post-war Global Acumulation and the Transnationalisation of Capital', *Capital and Class 43*, Spring, pp. 234–42.

Burton, J. (1994) 'Collaboration versus Competition', Inaugural Lecture, Birmingham University Business School, 16 March.

Campbell, T. and Fiszbein, A. (1994) *Local Government Capacity: Beyond Technical Assistance*. Washington, DC: World Bank.

Chang, H.-J. (1996) *The Political Economy of Industrial Policy*. London: Macmillan.

Choi, C.J. (1992) 'Marketing Barriers Facing Developing Country Manufacturing Exporters: a Comment', *Journal of Development Studies*, vol. 29, no. 1, October, pp. 166–72.

Chowdhury, A. and Islam, I. (1993) *The Newly Industrialising Economics of East Asia*. London: Routledge.

Cooke, P. and Morgan, K. (1993) 'The Network Paradigm: New Departures in Corporate and Regional Development', *Environment and Planning*, vol. 11, no. 5 pp. 543–64.

Dawson, J. (1990) 'The Wider Context: The Importance of the Macroenvironment for Small Enterprise Development', *Small Enterprise Development*, vol. 1, no. 3, pp. 39–46.

de Valk, P. (1994) 'A Review of Research Literature on Industry in Sub-Saharan Africa under Structural Adjustment' in Van Der Hoeven and Van Der Kraaij, *Structural Adjustment and Beyond in Sub-Saharan Africa*, London: James Currey.

De Vries, B.A. and Brakel, W. (1983) Restructuring of Manufacturing Industry: the experience of the textile industry in Pakistan, Philippines, Portugal and Turkey, *World Bank Staff Working Papers, No. 558*.

Development Researchers Network (EC)(1994) 'Evaluation of EC Support to Structural Adjustment in Ghana', unpublished Report in collaboration with the Institute of Economic Affairs, Accra. Rome: DRN.

Dia, M. (1996) *Africa's Management in the 1990s and Beyond: Reconciling Indigenous and Transplanted Institutions*. Washington: The World Bank.

Dijkstra, A.G. (1996) 'The Impact of Structural Adjustment Programs on Manufacturing: Lessons for Nicaragua', *World Development*, vol. 21, no. 10, pp. 535–48.

Dore, R. (1993) 'Goodwill and the Spirit of Market Capitalism', *British Journal of Sociology*, vol. 34.

Drainville, A.C. (1994) 'International Political Economy in the Age of Open Marxism', *Review of International Political Economy*, vol. 1, no.1, Spring, pp. 105–32.

Edwards, S. and S. van Wijnbergen (1989) 'Disequilibrium and Structural Adjustment' in H. Chenery and T.N. Srinivasan (eds), *Handbook of Development Economics*, vol. II, London: Elsevier Science Publishers.

Elleithy, A. (1992) 'Economies of Scale and Small Firms in Developing Countries: Theoretical and Empirical Issues', *Journal of International Development*, vol. 4, no. 4, pp. 463–6.

Evans, David S. (1987) 'Tests of Alternative Theories of Firm Growth', *Journal of Political Economy*, vol. 95, no. 4, pp. 657–73.

Evans, P. (1989) 'Predatory, Developmental, and Other Apparatuses: a Comparative Political Economy Perspective on the Third World State', *Sociological Forum*, vol. 4, no. 4, pp. 561–87.

Evans, P. (1992) 'The State as Problem and Solution: Predation, Embedded Autonomy and Structural Change', in Haggard and Kaufman (eds) *The Politics of Economic Adjustment*. Princeton, NJ: Princeton University Press.

Export Development Board (Sri Lanka), *Annual Report*, various years.

Faber, M. (1996) 'What Role for Stock Exchanges, Venture Capital and Leasing Companies in Developing the Private Sector in Africa?', in Harvey (ed.) *Constraints on the Success of Structural Adjustment Programmes in Africa*. London: Macmillan.

Fafchamps, M. (1996) 'The Enforcement of Commercial Contracts in Ghana', *World Development*, vol. 24, no. 3, pp. 147–74.

Farbman, M. and Steel, W. (1992) 'Research Issues for Small Enterprise Development', *Small Enterprise Development*, vol. 3, no. 2, June, pp. 26–34.

Fisher, D., Hoselitz, B. and Shinohara, M. (1968) *The Role of Small Industry in the Process of Economic Growth*. Paris: Monton.

Foray, D. and Freeman, C. (1993) *Technology and the Wealth of Nations: the Dynamics of Constructed Advantage*. London: OECD.

Gerschenkron, A. (1962) *Economic Backwardness in Historical Perspective*. Cambridge, MA: Harvard University Press.

Ghana Statistical Service (1987) *Ghana National Industrial Census 1987: Phase I Report, Background and Results*. Accra: Statistical Service.

Gnyawali, D. and Fogel, D. (1994) 'Environments for Entrepreneurship Development: Key Dimensions and Research Implications', *Entrepreneurship Theory and Practice*, vol. 18, no. 4, Summer, pp. 43–62.

Government of Zimbabwe (1996) 'The future for industry in Zimbabwe: Assessment, Policies and Strategies', Unpublished draft industrial strategy, Ministry of Industry and Commerce, Harare.

Granovetter, M. (1992) 'Economic Action and Social Structure: the problem of embeddedness', in M. Granovetter and R. Swedburg (eds), *The Sociology of Modern Life*. Boulder, Co: Westview Press.

Greenaway, D. (1993) 'Liberalising Foreign Trade through Rose-tinted glasses', *Economic Journal*, vol. 103, pp. 208–22.

Grindle, M.S. and Hildebrand, M.E. (1995) 'Building Sustainable Capacity in the Public Sector: What Can be Done?', *Public Administration and Development*, vol. 15, no. 5, pp. 441–63.

Grossman, G.M. and Helpman, E. (1991) *Innovation and Growth*. Cambridge, MA: MIT Press.

Gunning, J.W. (1994) 'The Manufacturing Sector in Zimbabwe: Dynamics and Constraints', unpublished Paper, Economisch en Sociaal Instituut, Vrije Universiteit, Amsterdam.

Haggard, S. and Kaufman, R. (eds) (1992) *The Politics of Adjustment*. Princeton, NJ: Princeton UP.

Haggard, S. and Webb, S. (1993) 'What do We Know about the Political Economy of Economic Policy Reform?', *World Bank Research Observer*, vol. 8, pp. 143–68.

Haggblade, S. (1992) 'A Proposal for Monitoring Small Enterprise Promotion', *Small Enterprise Development*, vol. 3, no. 4, December, 15 pp.

Hailey, J. (1992) 'The Politics of Entrepreneurship – Affirmative Action Policies for Indigenous Entrepreneurs', *Small Enterprise Development*, vol. 3, no. 1, March.

Harper, M. (1991) 'Enterprise Development in Poorer Nations', *Entrepreneurship Theory and Practice*, vol. 15, no. 4, pp. 7–12.

Harriss, J., Hunter, J. and Lewis, C.M. (1997) *The New Institutional Economics and Third World Development*. London: Routledge.

Harvey, C. (ed.) (1996) *Constraints on the Success of Structural Adjustment Programmes in Africa*. London: Macmillan.

Healey, J. and Robinson, M. (1994) *Democracy, Governance and Economic Policy*. London: ODI.

Helleiner, G.K. (ed.) (1993) *Trade Policy, Industrialisation and Development: New Perspectives*. Princeton, NJ: Princeton UP.

Herbst, J (1990) *State Politics in Zimbabwe*. Harare: University of Zimbabwe.

Herbst, J. (1993) *The Politics of Reform in Ghana, 1982–1991*. Berkeley, CA: University of California Press.

Herrigel, G. (1993) 'Large Firms, Small Firms and the Governance of Flexible Specialisation: the case of Baden-Wurttemberg and Socialised Risk', in B. Kogut. *Country Competitiveness: Technology and the Organising of Work*. London: OUP.

Hildebrand, M.E. and Grindle, M.S. (1994) *Building Sustainable Capacity: Challenges for the Public Sector*. Cambridge, MA: HIID.

Hirschman, A.O. (1988) *The Strategy of Economic Development*, Boulder, Colorado, Westview Press.

Hogan, P., Keesing, D. and Singer, A. (eds) (1994) *The Role of Support Services in Expanding Manufactured Exports in Developing Countries*, EDI Seminar Series. Washington DC: World Bank.

Holden, P. and Rajapatirana, S. (1995) *Unshackling the Private Sector: a Latin American Story*. Washington DC: The World Bank.

Hope, K.R. Sr (1996) *Development Policy in the Third World: From Policy Failure to Policy Reform*. New York: M.E. Sharpe.

Humphrey, J. and Schmitz, H. (1996) 'Trust and Economic Development', IDS Discussion Paper No. 355.

Husain, I. and Faruqee, R. (eds) (1994) *Adjustment in Africa: Lessons from Country Case Studies*, World Bank Regional and Sectoral Studies. Washington DC: World Bank.

Institute of Statistical, Social and Economic Research (ISSER) (1993) *The Ghanaian Economy*. Legon: University of Ghana.

Jackson, P. and Slater, R. (1995) *The State and Economic Management: A Policy Framework for Industrial Development*, Role of Government in Adjusting Economies Working Paper No. 8, University of Birmingham.

Jackson, P. (1995) *The Role of the State in Business Development in Ghana: the Case of Textiles and Garments Sector*, Role of Government in Adjusting Economies Working Paper No. 9, University of Birmingham.

Jackson, P. (1996) *The Role of the State in Business Development in Zimbabwe: the Case of the Textiles and Garments Sector*, Role of Government in Adjusting Economies Working Paper No. 13, University of Birmingham.

Jackson, P. (1999) 'The Role of Government in Business Promotion: the Case of Textiles and Garments', *Journal of International Development*, vol. 11, pp. 791–6.

Jackson, P. (1999) 'The Capacity of Government Agencies to Support Manufacturing in Ghana and Zimbabwe', *Public Administration and Development*, vol. 19, pp. 281–98.

Jeffries, R. (1992) 'Urban Popular Attitudes Towards the Economic Recovery Programme and the PNDC Government in Ghana', *African Affairs*, vol. 91, no. 363, pp. 207–26.

Jeffries, R and Thomas, C. (1993) 'The Ghanaian Elections of 1992', *African Affairs*, vol. 92, no. 368, pp. 331–66.

Kapur, I. (1991) 'Ghana: Adjustment and Growth 1983–91', *IMF Occasional Paper no. 86*. Washington DC: IMF.

Kelegama, S. (1986) 'Review of Economic Policies and Progress 1977–84', *Sri Lanka Economic Journal*, vol. 10, no. 1, pp. 239–47.

Kennedy, P. (1988) *African Capitalism*, Cambridge: Cambridge University Press.

Kilby, P. (1988) 'Breaking the Entrepreneurial Bottleneck in Late Developing Countries: Is There a Useful Role for Government?', *Journal of Development Planning*, vol. 18, pp. 221–50.

Killick, T. (1994) 'East Asian Miracles and Development Ideology', *Development Policy Review*, vol. 12, no. 1, pp. 69–80.

Killick, T. (ed.) (1995) *The Flexible Economy: Causes and Consequences of the Adaptability of National Economies*. London: Overseas Development Institute.

Kim, L.J. (1995) 'The Korean Economy 50 Years After Liberation', *Korea Focus*, vol. 3, no. 4, pp. 41–54.

Kirchenheimer, D.W. (1989) 'Public Entrepreneurship and Subnational Government', *Polity*, vol. 18, no. 1, pp. 293–301.

Klitgaard, R. (1991) *Adjusting to Reality: Beyond State versus Market in Economic Development*. San Francisco: ICS Press.

Klitgaard, R. (1995) 'Institutional Adjustment and Adjusting to Institutions', World Bank Discussion papers 303. Washington DC: The World Bank.

Kurt Salmon Associates (KSA) (1996) 'Consulting service for the Zimbabwe garment and textile PHRD initiative.' Unpublished report for the World Bank.

Lakshman, W.D. (1979) *Public Enterprises in the Economic Development of Sri Lanka*. Colombo: NIBM.

Lal, D. (1995) 'Structural Adjustment and African Industry', *World Development*, vol. 23, no. 12, pp. 2019–31.

Lall, S. (1994) 'The East Asian Miracle – Does the Bell Toll for Industrial Strategy?', *World Development*, vol. 22, no. 4, pp. 645–54.

Lall, S., Rao, K., Wignaraja, G., Addario, S.D. and Akinci, G. (1996) 'Building Sri Lanka's Competitiveness', unpublished document.

Larbi, G. (1997) *Implications and Impact of Structural Adjustment on the Civil Service: The Case of Ghana*, The Role of Government in Adjusting Economies, University of Birmingham.

Lazerson, M. (1988) *Subcontracting as an Alternative Organizational Form to Vertically Integrated Production*, Discussion Paper No. 20. Geneva: ILO.

Leys, C. (1996) *The Rise and Fall of Development Theory*. London: James Currey.

Levitsky, J. (1992) 'Private membership associations and support for SMEs'', *Small Enterprise Development*, vol. 3, no. 1, March.

Levy, B. (1993) 'An Institutional Analysis of the Design and Sequence of Trade and Investment Policy Reform', *World Bank Economic Review*, vol. 7, pp. 247–62.

Liebenstein, H. and Ray, D. (eds) (1988) 'Entrepreneurship and Economic Development', *Journal of Development Planning 18*.

Liedholm, C. and Mead, D. (1987) Small Scale Industries in Developing Countries: empirical evidence and policy implications, *International Development Paper No. 9*, Michigan State University.

Little, I.M.D., Mazumdar, D. and Page, J. (1988) *Small Manufacturing Enterprises*. Oxford: OUP.

Marsden, K. (1992) 'African Entrepreneurs – Pioneers of Development', *Small Enterprise Development*, vol. 3, no. 2, June, pp. 86–91.

McPherson, M.A. (1991) Micro and Small-Scale Enterprises in Zimbabwe: Results of a Country-Wide Survey, *GEMINI Technical Report 25*, Maryland State University, Michigan.

McMullan, W.E. (1988) 'Entrepreneurial support systems: an emerging scientific frontier', *Journal of Development Planning*, vol. 18, pp. 53–62.

Meier, G.M., and Steel, W. (1989) *Industrial Adjustment in Sub-Saharan Africa*. New York: OUP.

Messner, D. (1997) *The Network Society: Economic Development and International Competitiveness as Problems of Social Governance*, GDI Book Series No. 10, Berlin: GDI.

Metcalfe, J.S. (1995) Technology Systems and Technology Policy in an Evolutionary Framework, *Cambridge Journal of Economics*, vol. 19, no. 3–4, pp. 243–68.

Meyanathan, S.D. (1994) 'Managing Restructuring in the Textile and Garment Subsector', *EDI Seminar Series*, Economic Development Institute of the World Bank.

Meyer-Stamer, J. (1995) Governance in the Post-Import Substitution Era: Perspectives for new Approaches to Create Systemic Competitiveness in Brazil, *IDS Discussion Paper, No. 349*.

Misra, S. (1993) *India's Textile Sector*. New Delhi: Sage Publications.

Mkandawire, T. (1988) 'The Road to Crisis, Adjustment and De-Industrialization: The African Case', *Africa Development*, vol. 8, no. 1, pp. 5–31.

Moore, M. (1994) 'How Difficult is it to Construct Market Relations? a Commentary on Platteau', *Journal of Development Studies*, vol. 30, no. 4, pp. 753–830.

Mosley, P. and Weeks, J. (1993) 'Has Recovery Begun? Africa's Adjustment in the 1980s Revisited', *World Development*, vol. 21, no. 10, pp. 1583–606.

Mutahaba, G., Baguma, R. and Halfani, M. (1993) *Vitalizing African Public Administration for Recovery and Development*. West Hartford, CT: Kumarian Press.

Muzulu, J. (1996) 'The Structural Adjustment Implications of Real Exchange Rate Depreciation on the Manufacturing Sector in Zimbabwe', in Harvey (ed.) *Constraints on the Success of Structural Adjustment Programmes in Africa*. London: Macmillan.

North, D. (1979) 'A Framework for Analyzing the State in Economic History', *Explorations in Economic History*, vol. 16, no. 2, pp. 347–52.

North, D. (1990) 'A Transactions Cost Theory of Politics', *Journal of Theoretical Politics*, vol. 2, no. 4, pp. 355–67.

North, D. (1990) *Institutions, Institutional Change and Economic Performance*. Cambridge: Cambridge UP.

Ntim, S., Boateng, M., Asante, E., Appiah, N., and Dotse, F. (1991) 'The Impact of Ghana's Structural Adjustment Program on the Food Processing and Textile Subsectors'. Background paper for the EDI/GIMPA Senior Policy Seminar on the Impact of Industrial Policy Reforms: Public and Private Enterprise Experiences, Accra.

OECD (1997) 'Integrating developing countries in a globalising world economy: key points emerging from the DAC informal experts meeting on capacity development for trade, 11 March 1997'. Unpublished OECD Documentation.

Ofori-Amoah, B. (1988) 'Improving Existing Indigenous Technologies as a Strategy for the Appropriate Technology Concept in Ghana', *Industry and Development*, vol. 23, pp. 57–79.

Parker, R., Riopelle, R., and Steel, W. (1995) 'Small Enterprises Adjusting to Liberalization in Five African Countries', *World Bank Discussion Papers, Africa Technical Department Series 271*.

Picciotto, R. (1995) 'Putting Institutional Economics to Work: From Participation to Governance', *World Bank Discussion Papers 304*. Washington DC: The World Bank.

Platteau, J.-P. (1994a) 'Behind the Market Stage Where Real Societies Exist – Part I: the Role of Public and Private Order Institutions', *Journal of Development Studies*, vol. 30, no. 4, pp. 753–830.

Platteau, J-P, (1994b) 'Behind the Market Stage Where Real Societies Exist – Part II: the Role of Moral Norms', *Journal of Development Studies*, vol. 30, no. 4, pp. 533–77.

Polanyi, K. (1944) *The Great Transformation*. New York: Rinehart.

Porter, M. (1990) *The Competitive Advantage of Nations*. New York: The Free Press.

Private Enterprise Foundation (PEF) (1995) 'Promoting Private Sector Economic Activities: Problems and some Suggested Solutions'. Study commissioned by the Private Enterprise Foundation, Accra.

Private Sector Roundtable Group (1993) Unpublished report on 'Private Sector Development in Ghana', Accra.

Prochnik, V. (1992) 'Spurious Flexibility: Technical Modernisation and Social Inequalities in the Brazilian Footwear Industry', *Working Paper 2-22/WP.222*. Geneva: ILO.

Quarterly Bulletin of Statistics (various) Accra, Ghana: Central Statistical Bureau.

Rasmussen, J. (1992) 'The Small Enterprise Environment in Zimbabwe: Growing in the Shadow of Large Enterprises', *IDS Bulletin*, vol. 23, no. 3. Brighton: IDS.

Ray, D. (1988) 'Introductory Essay: the Role of Entrepreneurship in Economic Development', *Journal of Development Planning*, vol. 18, pp. 3–18.

Regional Programme on Enterprise Development (RPED) (1993) 'Zimbabwe Country Background Paper.' Unpublished report, World Bank.

Republic of Ghana (1993) 'Industrial Policy Statement: A Strategy for Industrial Regeneration', unpublished policy report for the Ministry of Industries, Accra.

RPED (1993) 'First Report on the Zimbabwe Survey'. Unpublished report, World Bank.

Republic of Ghana (1992) 'Industrial Policy Statement: A strategy for industrial regeneration', policy report for the Ministry of Industries, Science and Technology.

Republic of Ghana (1994) *Act 478: Ghana Investment Promotion Centre Act, 1994*, Accra: Ghanaian Parliament.

Republic of Ghana (1995) 'Ghana – Vision 2020', Presidential report to Parliament on the co-ordinated programme of economic and social development.

Republic of Ghana (1995) 'Report on the survey of medium and large scale manufacturing'. Unpublished report for the Ministry of Trade and Industry, prepared in collaboration with UNIDO.

Riddell, R. (1990) *Manufacturing Africa*, ODI Publication. London: James Currey.

Rock, M.T. (1992) 'Public Sector Marketing and Production Assistance to South Korea's Manufacturing Exports: Did it Make a Difference?', *Development Policy Review*, vol. 10, pp. 339–57.

Rothchild, D. and Chazan, N. (eds) (1988) *The Precarious Balance: State and Society in Africa*. Boulder, Co: Westview Press.

Rothchild, D. (ed.) (1991) *Ghana: the Political Economy of Recovery*, SAIS African Studies Library, Boulder: Lynne Rienner, US.

Rueschmeyer, D. and Evans, P.B. (1985) 'The State and Economic Transformation: Toward an Analysis of the Conditions Underlying Effective Intervention', in P.B. Evans et al. (eds), *Bringing the State Back In*. Cambridge: Cambridge University Press.

Ryner, M. (1994) 'Assessing SAPs: Economic Policy in the 1980s, the Third Way, the Swedish Model and the transition from Fordism to Post-Fordism', *Economic and Social Democracy*, vol. 15, no. 3, pp. 385–428.

Sahley, C. (1995) *Strengthening the Capacity of NGOs: Cases of Small Enterprise Development Agencies in Africa*, Oxford, INTRAC.

Sally, R. (1994) 'Multinational Enterprises, Political Economy and Institutional Theory', *Review of International Political Economy*, vol. 1, no. 1, Spring, pp. 161–92.

Schaalden, E. (1991) 'Manufacturing Exports from Sub-Saharan Africa: Performance, Constraints and Prospects', *Economic Research Papers No. 14*, African Development Bank.

Schmitz, H. (1995) 'Collective Efficiency: Growth Path for Small-scale Industry', *Journal of Development Studies*, vol. 31, no. 4, pp. 529–66.

Schmitz, H. and Musyck, B. (1993) Industrial Districts in Europe: Policy Lessons for Developing Countries, *IDS Paper No. 324*.

Schmitz, H. and Nadvi, K. (1994) 'Industrial Clusters in Less Developed Countries: Review of Experience and Research Agenda', *IDS Discussion Paper No. 339*.

Schumpeter, J. (1939) *Business Cycles: A Theoretical, Historical and Statistical Analysis of the Capitalist Process*, 2 vols. New York: Macmillan.

Scott, A.J. (1992) 'The Collective Order of Flexible Production Agglomerations: Lessons for Local Economic Development Policy and Strategic Choice', *Economic Geography*, vol. 68, pp. 219–33.

Scully, G.W. (1988) 'The Institutional Framework and Economic Development', *Journal of Political Economy*, vol. 96, no. 3, June, pp. 652–62.

Sen, K. and Vaidya, R. (1992) 'Move Towards a Market Economy: Modern Austrian and Post Keynesian Perspectives', *Economic and Political Weekly*, 25 July.

Seringhaus, F.H. and Rosson, P.J. (1991) *Export Development and Promotion: the Role of Public Organisations*. London: Kluwer Academic Publishers.

Shapiro, S. (1987) 'The Social Control of Impersonal Trust', *American Journal of Sociology*, vol. 93, no. 3, pp. 623–58.

Sieber, S.D. (1973) 'The Integration of Fieldwork and Survey Methods', *American Journal of Sociology*, vol. 78, pp. 18–41.

Singer, H.W. (1988) 'The WDR 1987 on the blessings of outward orientation: a necessary correction', *Journal of Development Studies*, vol. 24, no. 2, pp. 232–6.

Skalnes, T. (1993) 'The State, Interest Groups and Structural Adjustment in Zimbabwe', *Journal of Development Studies*, vol. 29, no. 3, April, pp. 401–28.

Slater, R., Chandrasiri, S., Gunawardena, A. and Parajasingham, P. (1997) *The Role of the State in Business Development: the Case of the Textiles and Garments Sector in Sri Lanka*, The Role of Government in Adjusting Economies, Working Paper No. 15, The University of Birmingham.

Slater, R., Ram Khanna, Bhaumik, T.K. and Bhasu, R. (1998) *The Role of the State in Business Development: the Case of the Textiles and Garments Sector in India*, The Role of Government in Adjusting Economies, Working Paper No. 27, The University of Birmingham.

Sowa, Nii K., Baah-Nuakoh, A., Tutu, K.A., and Osei, B. (1992) *Small Enterprises and Adjustment: the Impact of Ghana's Economic Recovery Programme*. London: Overseas Development Institute and Legon: University of Ghana.

Spath, B. (1992) 'The Instutional Environment and Communities of Small Firms, *IDS Bulletin*, vol. 23, no. 3, pp. 8–11.

Steel, W. (1994) 'Changing the Institutional and Policy Environment for Small Enterprise Development in Africa', *Small Enterprise Development*, vol. 5, no. 2, June, pp. 4–10.

Stein, H. (1992) 'Deindustrialisation, Adjustment and the World Bank and IMF in Africa', *World Development*, vol. 20, no. 1, pp. 83–95.

Stein, H. (1994) 'Theories of Institutions and Economic Reform in Africa', *World Development*, vol. 22, no. 12 pp. 1833–49.

Stewart, F., Lall, S. and Wangwe, S. (eds) (1992) *Alternative Development Strategies in Sub-Saharan Africa*. Basingstoke: Macmillan.

Stiglitz, J.E. (1989) 'Markets, Market Failures and Development', *American Economic Review Papers and Proceedings 79*, No. 2, May, pp. 197–203.

Stoneman, C. and Cliffe, L. (1989) *Zimbabwe: Politics, Economics and Society*. London: Pinter Publishers.

Storper, M. (1989) 'The Transition to Flexible Specialisation in Industry', *Cambridge Journal of Economics*, vol. 13, June, pp. 273–305.

Storper, M. (1990) 'Industrialisation and the Regional Question in the Third World', *International Journal of Urban and Regional Research*, vol. 14, no. 3, pp. 1659–65.

Storper, M. (1992) 'The Limits to Globalisation: Technology Districts and International Trade', *Economic Geography*, vol. 68, pp. 60–93.

Sweeney, P. (1987) *Innovation, Entrepreneurs and Regional Development*, Pinter, London.

Taylor, E.O. (1994) 'The Effect on the Trade Liberalisation Policy on the Textile Industry', unpublished thesis, UST, Kumasi.

Teitel, S. and Thoumi, F. (1994) 'From Autarkic Import Substitution to Exports: Technology and Skills in Zimbabwe's Manufacturing', unpublished RPED Report, World Bank.

Tiffin, S. and Osotimehin, S. (1988) 'Technical Entrepreneurship and Technological Innovation in Nigeria', *Journal of Development Planning*, vol. 18, pp. 195–220.

Toye, J. (1987) *Dilemmas of Development*. Oxford: Oxford University Press.

UNIDO (1989) *New Technologies and Global Industrialisation*. Vienna: UNIDO.

Van Dijk, M.P. and Marcussen, H.S. (1990) *Industrialisation in the Third World: the Need For Alternative Strategies*. London: Frank Cass.

Van Liemt, T. (ed.) (1992) *Industry on the Move: Causes and Consequences of International Relocation in the Manufacturing Industry*. Geneva: ILO.

Vesper, D. (1990) 'Government responsibilities in times of social and economic change – experiences and prospects', *Vierteljahrsliefte zur Wirtschaftsforschung*, vol. 1, pp. 15–27.

Wade, R. (1990) *Governing the Market*. Princeton, NJ: Princeton UP.

Waterbury, J. (1992) 'The Heart of the Matter? Public Enterprise and the Adjustment Process', in Haggard and Kaufman (eds), *The Politics of Economic Adjustment*.

Williams, G. (1994) 'Why Structural Adjustment is Necessary and Why it Doesn't Work', *Review of African Political Economy*, No. 60, pp. 214–25.

Williamson, O.E. (1995) 'The Institutions and Governance of Economic Development and Reform', *Proceedings of the World Bank Annual Conference on Development Economics 1994*. Washington DC: The World Bank.

Willig, R.D. (1993) 'Public Versus Private Regulated Enterprise', *Proceedings of the World Bank Annual Conference on Development Economics*. Washington, DC: World Bank.

Wilson, J.Q. (1989) *Bureaucracy: What Government Agencies Do and Why They Do It*. New York: Basic Books.

Witt, U. (1993) *Evolutionary Economics*. Brookfield, VT: Elgar Reference Collection.

Wolf, C. Jr (1988) *Markets or Governments: Choosing Between Imperfect Alternatives*. Cambridge, MA: MIT Press.

Wood, A. and Berge, K. (1994) 'Exporting Manufactures: Trade Policy or Human Resources?', *IDS Working Paper No. 4*.

World Bank (1990) 'Progress Performance Audit Report: Zimbabwe Manufacturing Export Promotion Project', *Proceedings of the World Bank Annual Conference on Development Economics 1994*. Washington DC: World Bank.

World Bank (1993) 'Economic Reform and the Manufacturing Sector in Ghana.' Unpublished report for the Africa Regional Program on Enterprise Development.

World Bank (1993) *Ghana 2000 and Beyond: Setting the Stage for Accelerated Growth and Poverty Reduction*, Africa Regional Office, West Africa Department.

World Bank (1994) 'Ghana Financial Sector Review: Bringing Savers and Investors Together'. *Country Operations Division West-Central Africa Department. Report no. 13423-GH.*

World Bank (1994) *Adjustment in Africa: Reform, Results and the Road Ahead.* World Bank Policy Research Report, Oxford UP.

World Bank (1995) 'Zimbabwe: Achieving Shared Growth', Country Economic Memorandum, Harare.

World Bank (1997) *World Development Report 1997: the State in a Changing World.* Washington DC: World Bank.

Wunsch, E. (ed.) (1990) *The Failure of the Centralized African State: Institutions and Self-Governance in Africa.* Boulder, Co: Westview Press.

Yang, Y. (1994) 'The Impact of MFA Phasing Out on World Clothing and Textile Markets', *Journal of Development Studies*, vol. 30, no. 3, April. pp. 892–915.

Zaaijer, M. (1997) Urban Economic Restructuring and Local Institutional Response: the Case of Bulawayo, Zimbabwe, *Project Paper No. UM1*, Institute of Housing Studies, Rotterdam.

Zattler, J. (1993) 'Adjusting Adjustment: Supply Response and the Sequencing of Reform Policies', *Intereconomics*, Nov/Dec, pp. 293–301.

Zelditch, M (1962) 'Some methodological problems of using field studies', *American Journal of Sociology*, vol. 67, no. 5, pp. 566–76.

Zimconsult (1995) 'Cotton Industry Study', unpublished report for the Ministry of Industry and Commerce and the Central African Textile Manufacturers Association.

Zimtrade (1992–5) *Annual Reports*, Harare: Zimtrade.

Index

210